Broken Crayons Still Color:
Life After

i

Broken Crayons Still Color: Life After

Presented by Coach Stacy Bryant

Broken Crayons Still Color: Life After
Copyright © 2021 Stacy Bryant

ISBN: 978-1-7357666-1-4

Unless noted, all scriptures are from King James Version of the Bible.

This is a collection of authorized biographies. Names, locales, places, events, and people contained herein are purely from the authors' memory, and/or from public record. This story is not intended to defame, intimidate, or ridicule any persons, living or dead.

Author: Stacy Bryant
Email: stacy@stacybryant.com
www.stacybryant.com
Published by Pen 2 Pen Publishing
www.pen2penpublishing.com

Email: info@pen2penpublishing.com
Cover Design: Kasper Harris for Gifft Grafix
Editor: Vickie Tenwalde

Printed in the United States of America

Table of Contents

Many times, what we see as our biggest regrets, failures and mistakes become what God uses the most in our lives. Our brokenness can be transformed into something more beautiful than we can even imagine.

Chapter 1

Catalyst

BY STACY BRYANT

First let me say, this is the hardest thing I have ever written. Writing is healing for me. Emotional healing is comparable to healing a physical wound; to heal yourself properly, sometimes there are layers that you must pull back, removing the diseased, affected areas that prevent your health and wholeness. A catalyst is a person or thing that precipitates an event or change. Sharing my latest catalyst season, is just that--hard but healing, yet someone needs to hear this. Someone needs to know that you can still color after being broken. Someone needs to know that you can embrace your catalyst period and shine bright and vibrant. Your catalyst pushes you to greatness if you allow it. Some say that there are negative catalysts, some say that there are positive. For me it was neither. It was just that--a catalyst. Now I know many may say what does that have to do with being a broken crayon. Well, let's be clear. A catalyst is something that pushes you in to greatness, right? I was completely broken before and during my catalyst period. While broken, I was still coloring. Because I still colored, I was pushed into further greatness.

I was only in the room because I was being honored for some of my great work. Having just experienced a six-week round of chemotherapy and a breakup, I really did not want to be in public, but duty called.

I was sitting in the VIP section waiting for my time to shine, envisioning my swift escape afterward, when the finest man in the room passed by me. I had to know who he was. I asked my hostess if she knew him. She didn't know him, but she knew his friend, and would introduce us. I suddenly got excited, thinking maybe the night would not turn out so bad after all. As she made the introductions the gentleman kept eyeing me. I was eyeing him too. I gave my number to his friend, but it was that fine gentleman who called me after the event, although I had not given my number to him. We went out and I was flying high. I could not believe we had so much in common. I could not believe that he was so loving and caring. I could not believe he wanted to be with me.

Have you ever heard the saying, "when a man pours into a woman, she multiplies whatever she touches? It was like that for a while with us. As I mentioned right before meeting him, I had just completed a round of chemo but was still experiencing an extremely high rate of cancer markers. He poured so much love into me, I felt like I could conquer the world. I started picking up a little weight, and amazing things were happening for my business. At that point, I had a glow like no other.

It had become a habit for him to stay the night at my house, but one night, he did not. I went to his house the next morning. I had a strange feeling in my stomach something was not right, but I pushed it away. When I arrived, we were sitting there watching TV and he said, "let's go to the store."

As I was walking towards the door, there was a used condom wrapper in the trashcan. Once we got in the car, I asked him about it. He said that it belonged to his uncle. I remember thinking to myself, "Why is he lying to me like this?" I believe that was the day the trajectory of our relationship changed.

Although I didn't believe him, I could not prove it was a lie, so I dropped it. Before that day, I can absolutely say that I was not insecure in the relationship that we were building. Seeing that condom wrapper changed all of that. Maybe I was insecure, and the condom wrapper triggered it. Whatever I was feeling caused me to go on a social media hunt to see if I could find anything out of place. I did not believe it was her, but I did take a peek at his children's mothers' social media. I could not find anything out of place, so I dropped the whole ordeal, never to bring it up again.

A month later, the tables turned. We were lying in bed, laughing, and talking and he grabbed my phone to look at something. I did not mind, I trusted him, and hoped that he trusted me as well. I had forgotten all about the social media scrolling I had done. He saw it and took that as insecurity. I lied about it because I did not want to get in a confrontation about it. That one white lie made every issue we ever experienced in our relationship thereafter my fault.

I apologized for fibbing and he said he forgave me, but things were different. It went downhill from there.

He deleted me from all social media. He did not give me attention like he had before. He did come home every night, but his attitude was different. I spent the next year, losing myself, trying to get back the person I knew was in love with me. I endured an excruciating amount of mistreatment from him. Whenever we had issues, he was quick to point out I was the one in the wrong, when I knew I did nothing wrong. I was so attached, I lost myself and accepted the pain.

How sad. I was so broken, but I still served the masses, and brought it like no other. On the inside though, I was broken. I lost my focus, clients, and my will to live. I was killing myself trying to find any way possible to make this man I was so in love with, see me the way he saw me the day he met me. I spent our remaining time together trying to repair what I once thought was wonderful, all the while, I was breaking my own heart in the process. It turned out, he was just as broken. He was using me and not treating me the way that I deserved to be treated and sleeping with other women. It got ugly and it hurt like hell to let go of that relationship.

People develop attachment issues because they have poor self-confidence, low self-esteem, and/or a big desire for a romantic relationship. They often attach quickly to others because they find their self-worth in others and fear abandonment. If you feel that you are a likable person, you have a higher sense of self-worth. If you feel unlikable, your self-esteem and self-worth are damaged.

This means you tied your self-image into how they feel about you, so you are desperate to make sure they like you so you become attached and anxious, afraid you will lose them and your worth with them. Fighting cancer left me vulnerable. I was already weak. I thought I had found someone to support me in the fight, which gave me strength in the beginning, but eventually it all faded.

You may become attached because you feel you are not likeable. You may think you are not worth being liked, so the fact that they like you is a fluke, and you feel an obsessive attachment is necessary to try and keep them liking you so that they do not leave you. People often attach too quickly because they really want an extreme relationship. You may really want a best friend, or a life partner who loves you to the grave. I just really fell in love with the success of the honeymoon phase. It felt good to feel someone wanted to stand by my side while I fought the hardest fight of my life.

The best thing to do is to work on yourself. Be happier with who you are and be more confident with yourself. If your worth is not tied to another person, or you are not constantly in fear of their leaving you, or you realize what you are chasing is a goal or feeling, you will not be seen as "clingy" or "over attached." Working on improving your own confidence and self-image is often the best way to fix this issue. Once you have more confidence in how awesome you are as a person, those compulsive feelings for attachment often go with them.

That is why this was my catalyst. I was not losing a boyfriend; I was being pushed into my greatness. Seeing the brokenness in us both, was a reflection to us both. I could sit here and point out every narcissistic tendency he portrayed like most people would. Is he a narcissist? Probably. But accountability works both ways. We were two people who have both had traumatic experiences in the past and who were reminding each other of those traumas. That is why we both overreacted to each other's triggers. Although this man was a narcissist, I learned so many lessons about myself. I was able to understand that I had low self-esteem for many years. No matter how successful I had become, I had hit a ceiling that I was unable to shatter until I was able to heal the things that he reflected to me.

I cannot share his story; I do not have permission to do that, but I can say he is broken. While he is broken, he still colors, he just does not see it. I remember his blistering words, "You are too flawed. Do you think you are the only person that loves me? I do not value you. If you cannot help me with my struggles you are no use to me."

Every word was like a stab wound. I remember begging him to just please understand, I have cancer and I am growing. Grow with me. I remember his response being, "you're just not worth it Stacy." Many days

I would beg him to help me understand what I had done so bad to make him treat me this way. He never had an answer.

I would tell him how I had not done anything, his response was, "in my eyes you have." Hearing that I was too flawed, led me to believe I should just be thrown away, like we do with broken crayons. We throw them in the trash, as if they are not worth anything. Every time he told me I was too flawed, or I didn't deserve him, I'd cry inside and wonder why I had to be such a flawed person. Why? Self-esteem shattered. Self-worth next to nil. Self-value, none. I was broken, looking for my worth in another individual who was just as broken as I was.

I was determined to see myself color again. So, I fought that inner war to find myself, my esteem, my worth, so that I could color. So that I could impact the world. So that I could show someone else, that no matter the hurt, no matter the pain, no matter the words spoke against me, just because I am broken, I STILL COLOR.

My heart hurts for the relationship I really wish would have flourished. But it was my catalyst. It was designed to teach me, that I hold value. It was designed to teach me that I am worth it. It was designed to teach me that I am a beautiful flower. It was designed to teach me that I am beautiful. It was designed to teach me that my flaws are beautiful. It was designed to teach me I am GREATNESS. My catalyst.

Catalyst. He was my catalyst of change. Through many arguments and fights, he made me feel as if I were too flawed to be loved. He was never there to support me in the long run with anything, and I made excuses for his awful behavior. I admitted to things I had not done for the sake of keeping the peace. I was so broken. I just wanted him to love me. I wanted him to love me the way that I loved him. I wanted the look he had for me in the beginning to return. I wanted him to hold me like he used too. I wanted to hear him say, "you are my everything". I wanted to hear him say, "I love you", just one more time, but he is just as broken. He just does not know that he can still color. He still thinks that once something is broken, you throw it out, but me, I know I still color. That is the catalyst. That is what has pushed me into my greatness. Knowing that I still color vibrantly! Knowing that I have an impact. Knowing that I am worthy. Knowing that I am valuable. Knowing that I am ENOUGH! Knowing that I am the prize. **This Broken Crayon Still Colors!!!**

If you have recently ended or just got out of a toxic relationship with someone with narcissistic traits like I just did, you are likely dealing with plenty of hurt and confusion, even when you know, deep down, that you were not to blame. You may be wondering what you could have done differently to prevent abuse. We know the relationship is not healthy. We are aware they mistreat us. But it is very hard to shake the memories of how we feel in the beginning and the good times we had. These memories might lead us to crave their company and feel like we would do anything to earn their love and approval again.

Abuse is often deeply traumatizing, and the healing process can take some time. If you are feeling lost, the tips below can help with the steps to seeing a brighter future:

Acknowledge and accept the abuse.

Recognize that you did experience abuse, whether from a romantic partner, family member, or friend. In the beginning of the healing process, you might have difficulty setting aside rationalizations and potential excuses for the other person's behavior. In fact, you may feel perfectly willing to take blame on yourself, as long as it means you do not have to admit someone you love has intentionally hurt you. This is normal and completely understandable. Denial can protect you, in a way. Strong romantic love overshadows reality for many people. It is also tough to accept that some people just do not seem to care when they hurt others. Denying what happened prevents you from addressing it and healing from it. It can also set you up to experience more pain in the future. If you know your loved one experienced emotional distress of their own, you might empathize with these struggles and want to give them a second chance. Compassion is never wrong, but mental health issues do not excuse abuse. You can always encourage them to reach out for support — while creating enough space to keep yourself safe. Learning to identify tactics often used by people with narcissism can make it easier to come to terms with your experience.

Set your boundaries and state them clearly.

A lot of times people often recommend cutting off all contact with your ex-partner after ending the relationship, whenever possible. Going no contact is not just a boundary for them. It is also a boundary for you, but not possible in every situation. Maybe you have children with them, or they are a family member you will see occasionally at gatherings. If so, think about what you want and need: "I deserve to be treated with respect." Then turn that into a boundary: "I am willing to have a conversation with you, but if you shout, swear, or call me names, I will leave immediately." To create essential space and distance for yourself, also consider personal boundaries, such as not sharing personal information.

Prepare for complex emotions.

Most breakups involve painful feelings, which include: grief and loss, anger, shock, sadness or feelings of depression

After ending a relationship such as narcissistic abuse, you might experience these along with other types of emotional distress that may include: anxiety, fear, paranoia, and shame.

The trauma of a toxic relationship can also leave you with symptoms of post-traumatic stress disorder (PTSD). People with toxic behaviors can cause a lot of pain. But they also have a knack for getting you to believe in their reality. So, while you may have sustained some deep emotional wounds, you might still question your own actions. Your love for them can, convince you it was your fault they manipulated you and mistreated you. Breaking off these toxic family relationships can also trigger feelings of guilt or disloyalty. These are normal emotional experiences. Working through them alone is not always easy, especially when you feel confused by manipulation tactics. Find someone that can offer support as you begin navigating these complicated feelings.

Reclaim your identity.

People with narcissistic traits often expect others to behave in certain ways. They harshly belittle or criticize people for failing to meet these standards. Here is what it can look like:

Your ex said your hair looked "stupid and ugly," so you changed it.

Your ex said you are too flawed, so you believe it.

Your parent regularly told you how "foolish" you were for "wasting time" on music, so you gave up playing the piano.

They might try to control your time and keep you from seeing friends or participating in activities by yourself.

If you have changed your looks and style or lost things you used to value as a result of this manipulation, you might feel as if you no longer know yourself very well.

Part of recovery involves getting reacquainted with yourself, or figuring out what you enjoy, how you want to spend your time, and who you want to spend it with. You are healing, after all. Make sure to self-explore and rebuild your relationship with yourself.

Practice self-compassion

Once you acknowledge that your relationship was, in fact, abusive, you might have a lot of criticism for yourself. But remember, no one deserves abuse, and their behavior is not your fault. Instead of blaming yourself for falling for their manipulation or judging yourself for allowing them to mistreat you for so long, offer yourself forgiveness instead. You cannot change the past, and you cannot change their behavior or actions. You only have power over yourself. But you can use this power to make the choice to honor your needs, like respect, happiness, and healthy love. When you feel down on yourself, try repeating an affirmation like "I am strong," "I embrace my flaws," "I am loved," or "I am brave." Understand that your feelings may linger. Love can be difficult because you cannot really control it. You cannot always stop loving someone, even someone who hurts you. After ending the relationship, you might still hold on to positive memories and wish you could somehow experience those days again. It is important to recognize you do not need to stop loving someone to start healing. Waiting for that to happen can stall the recovery process. You can continue loving someone while recognizing their behavior makes it impossible for you to safely maintain a relationship with them.

Take care of yourself.

Good self-care practices can make a big difference in your recovery. Self-care involves meeting your emotional and physical needs. That might include things like: getting enough sleep, relaxing when overwhelmed or stressed, making time for hobbies and other activities you enjoy, connecting with loved ones, using coping skills to manage distressing thoughts, eating balanced meals, and staying physically active. Your mind and body help support each other, so taking care of physical needs can help you feel stronger and more equipped to work through emotional distress.

Talk to others.

Opening up to supportive friends and family members can help you feel less alone as you heal. The people who care about you can: offer compassion, validate the pain you experience, help distract you or provide company on difficult days, remind you the abuse was not your fault.

Some people in your life may not offer much, if any support. Some family members may take the abusive person's side. Mutual friends might support an abusive ex. This can cause confusion and hurt. It is often helpful to set boundaries around your time with these people as you work to recover. You might, for example, ask them not to mention the person around you, or to avoid sharing their opinions about the situation with you. If they do not respect those boundaries, consider limiting the time you spend with them. If you found it difficult to leave the person abusing you, or already have thoughts of giving them another chance, a therapist can help you identify reasons behind these feelings and create a plan to avoid unhelpful choices in the future.

You can heal, though it may not happen right away. Just because it has broken you, you can still color. And by coloring you can heal. Once you heal you become whole again. Let it go. Start anew. Color again.

About Stacy

Stacy Bryant, also known as (Coach Stacy), is the founder of The Stiletto Bosses Network™ and The Free Hope Foundation for Domestic Violence. She is the host of Candid Conversation with Coach Stacy on 108 Praise Radio. Coach Stacy is also the CEO of ICU Coaching Academy. She is a Retired Veteran of the United States Army and she devotes her life to empowering others. Her goal is to assist and empower people all over the world by instilling and expressing confidence in themselves. Her focus is to empower people by helping them with their finances, relationships, entrepreneurship, health, faith, and life.

Stacy is a Certified Master Life Coach Trainer, Best Selling Author, Speaker, and Radio Personality. Her passion for inspiring and encouraging others has made her a sought-after Inspirational Speaker and Coach. She is the author of Building Self-Confidence and the Her Story Series. Coach Stacy is also the co-author of the "Will to Win" with Brian Tracy. Stacy has a bachelor's degree in Business Administration and is currently pursuing her MBA.

Stacy has walked the road of an overcomer her entire life and is passionate about personal development. She is dedicated to helping others rise above their circumstances. Her mission in life is to encourage and empower others to explore and find who they are inside and out. From there, she believes they will be able to create the life they have always dreamed of.

IN THE NAME OF ALLAH, MOST GRACIOUS, MOST MERCIFUL

Chapter 2

Unstoppable

BY SHAKIL ALI

I read once that by the sixth month of pregnancy and sometimes earlier, the unborn child is living an active emotional life. The child can see, hear, taste, experience and even learn. Most importantly the child has feelings. The period from conception to birth is critical to the formation of that person because the fetal consciousness is an observer and recorder of all the mother thinks, feels, and does. Through that fetal consciousness I heard my mother's cries, I felt my mother's pain. Right from her womb I knew I had to protect her.

My conflicts as well as my trials and tribulations started right there in her womb.

Life always begins with mama; mine loved me, but she loved me in fear. She was a mere seventeen-year-old-- scared, lost, and abandoned, in love with a verbally and physically abusive man who controlled her life's existence. My mother was afraid all the time because she did not know when that day may come that her husband might take her life.

She was a gentle woman; she drank a little, smoked a little, and she loved to dance. Often in our home, her and my father would entertain their friends. They would stay up all night playing Bid Whist listening to the likes of James Brown, The Isley Brothers, Earth, Wind and Fire and other musicians from the 70's.

You could hear them laugh and sometimes they would call me in the room to dance for the guests. I couldn't wait to demonstrate the moves I had learned from watching Soul Train.

When the night had ended, and the music stopped, my home turned into a battlefield. My father would often strike my mother for some unknown reason. This physical abuse would often spill over to me and sometimes against my grandmother who was my father's mother. He would verbally abuse everyone in the house. He would break up dishes, turn over tables, breaking up anything he could get his hands on. The next day My grandmother and my mother would be cleaning up the mess and my mother's face would often be swollen. A child should never see his mother like this and seeing this made me cold, it made me heartless, and I knew there would come a time when I would make sure that this monster of a father would never harm me or my mother again. My mother had to wear two faces. She always wore a smile for her friends, but she was miserable on the inside.

She was constantly occupied with the needs of my father, so much so that I felt unloved and unwanted. When you feel unloved it is virtually impossible to love, so I found myself at war with my community and my family. I became that child that mothers told their children to stay away from.

My mother was beautiful, inside and out, but like many young women of her statue she was held captive by love, or the thought of love. I do not have early memories of hugs and kisses from my mother. What I have though is life lessons, invaluable lessons that cannot be found in universities. I am so blessed, so grateful to have a mother that God Allah designed just for me, and to share time and space with such a remarkable woman. Never during my entire existence had there ever been a time when she was not there. What I am today is because of the strength and the prayers of a mother. Those prayers and wise counsel continue today.

It has been over fifteen years since I last looked into the face of my father. Life was not kind to him. Life has a way of making you reap what you sow. My father was a short man but a proud man all the same. He was a man who wore a suit every day. His shoes were so shiny that you could see yourself in them. He once told me to always look like you have something even when you do not. He spoke his mind regardless of the consequences. He was not educated but he was smart in many ways. He understood the importance of work and providing for his family. In spite of his flaws, we as a family never went without. There was a dictatorship in our house and my father was the dictator. He could look at his children and we all understood what that look meant. He suffered from alcoholism and would often come home so drunk that I would have to assist him in getting upstairs to the bed so he could rest and get to work the next day. Ironically regardless of how drunk my father came home he would always get up and go to the same job for 36 years. I never loved my father, but a time came in my life when I understood that life is hard, and sometimes it is mean. The universe does not treat everyone equally. My father was full of anger and he took that anger out on his family. One night my father came home drunk, and he and my mother were in the kitchen arguing. I had placed a knife under my pillow because I had made up my mind that I was not going to let him ever beat me again. I heard my mother screaming telling him to stop so I grabbed that knife and went in the kitchen and stabbed my father in the back. He turned around and knocked me to the floor. I began to fight back. I made sure he understood that if he ever put his hands on my mother again, I would kill him. He never struck my mother again, so I reckon he got the message.

Soon after this event, my father checked into a rehabilitation center in North Carolina. The last week of my father's stay in rehab, my mother and I drove to North Carolina. We spoke to counselors as a family and individually. During a session with my father, I remember the counselor stating to my father that he spoke as if he didn't like me and my father said, "I don't like him." The counselor screamed at my father and told him to get out. She asked me how I was feeling and after all these years I remember distinctly my response. I said, "I'm fine, I don't like him either." Those words did not affect me at all because I hated the man.

My father was bipolar, and although he had never been diagnosed with this mental disorder, he displayed all the symptoms of this manic depression. When I look at my siblings, we all have a piece of this man in us. We all have some sort of phobia or disorder as a result of growing up in a dysfunctional home. We all suffered from his alcoholism. My father was a very angry man, and as the oldest of my three siblings, I caught the brunt of his anger and his abusive personality. Once my mother had gotten fed up and moved out, taking my younger brother and sister with her. She left me with my father, and I resented her for this. She was well aware of how this man had treated me and she left me there and I held this over her head for a very long time.

My father pleaded with my mother to come home and she eventually obliged, and I was happy just to have my brother and sister back home. My father soon put me out because I would not conform to the rules of his house.

Homeless and in survivor mode, I began preparing for prison. I had learned how to steal at a very early age. Once my mother came home with a pair of new sneakers for me and I was so excited to go to school the next day to show off my new shoes. What I did not know was that those shoes were purchased from a bin at the local grocery chain.

When I arrived at school, the kids laughed and teased me because these shoes were not of the finest quality, "boloney soles" they would call them, and they had a square toe to top it off. Humiliated and confused, I went home and asked my mother why she would buy me such shoes,

I did not understand that she bought me what she could afford. Our family lived in poverty for a long time.

It was on that day that my criminal enterprise began. I vowed to never wear another pair of cheap shoes in my life. I went inside of the Army Navy Store and politely removed a pair of Converses that we referred to as 'Chuck Taylors' without paying for them. It was too easy. I began boosting shoes, clothes, jewelry, etc. It became addictive. I was eventually arrested and sent to the juvenile detention home-- my first taste of prison. They made us go to school during the day and would allow us an hour for recreation. Other than these two activities we were locked in our cells. I did not talk to the staff or the other prisoners except for my homeboy from my neighborhood.

My daily thoughts seemed to center around how it was possible that adults would permit children to be placed in cages like animals. Just to exist inside of these tiny cells calls for some heavy psychic readjustments. This place was simply preparing us for darker days ahead.

One night while asleep my cell door miraculously came open. I did not move. Soon my homeboy appears and tells me, "Let's go".

"Go where?" I asked.

"We are breaking out."

"We? Who the hell was 'we'?" I wondered, yet I found myself heading towards the exit. I saw several other kids ready to leave. It never occurred to me to inquire as to how they got those cell doors open so as we were about to leave, I noticed the guard lying on the floor bleeding and my homeboy said he had hit him over the head.

I don't know why, but I just couldn't leave. I told them to go ahead. They left, and I stayed to help the guard. Soon the police arrived, and I was returned to my cell. I remained there until trial. By the time my court date arrived, all of the escapees had been captured except my homeboy; he was still on the run. When I got to court the Judge looked at me and said that he was informed of my heroics at the facility and dismissed all charges. Since I could not go home, I was released to my father's sister's home. It was rough living there because my aunt had four kids of her own and she also housed foster kids. I loved my cousins, and I loved my aunt, but what no one really understood was that I needed psychological help. Prison destroys the logical processes of the mind and just because they called it a juvenile detention facility. It was still prison.

I was captured again at the tender age of 26. My criminal enterprise had moved from boosting to bank fraud and forging checks. I was sentenced to fifty years in prison with forty years suspended, which meant I had to do ten years. While in prison I lost my heart and soul, my paternal grandmother, and my best friend Shaky. I was hurt and bitter. What kept me from going insane was my counselor and therapist who still to this day is a pillar in my life. After spending two years in prison, I was released.

It did not take me long to start my enterprise back up. It was all I knew how to do. I was sick. Working a 9 to 5 was not an option. I had managed to get my hands on a money order machine and like clockwork, I put it to good use. I lasted about three years before I was captured again.

The authorities offered me a plea deal if I would return the machine. The plea was for two and a half years but I knew that I still had forty years over my head and most likely I would receive every year of it or at least a large portion, so I rolled the dice, snake eyes. I was found guilty and was sentenced to 48 years in prison. I realized that sentence was not a reflection of what I did, but an accumulation of what I had done, things I had gotten away with, people whom I had harmed.

Naturally, no one receives this much time for forging checks, but it was life informing me that I was not exempt from the universal law of reaping what you sow. My understanding of life came from the streets. It was not until I entered this hell that I began to discover myself. There are 86,400 seconds in a day. How you use those seconds are critical. Les Brown said it does not take any effort to be a loser.

I realized that the world is short and every breath I took was taking me closer to my death. Just as I began preparing myself for prison, I now was determined to prepare myself for the next journey. During my prison stint I had two skills that made me popular on campus. I could cut hair and I was always one of the best basketball players on the compound, if not the best. My basketball talents led me to the nickname of Mr. Unstoppable. I embraced this moniker fully but not just on the court. I began to apply it to everything I wanted to accomplish. I truly wanted to be unstoppable.

My first transformation came when I was introduced to books. Authors such as John Henrik Clarke, Alex Haley, James Baldwin, Dr. Francis Cress Welsing, Amos Wilson, and countless others; however, the most profound book I have ever read in my life was The Holy Quran.

The Quran softened my heart. It transformed me from being an animal to being a human being. It taught me to spend more time treating my heart, hastening to correct and purify it from sickness and all sin.

I had to acknowledge my wrongdoing, I had to pray for forgiveness. I had to learn to become firm and patient, in pain or suffering and adversity, and throughout all periods of panic. I had to stop my evil doings. I wanted to win back God's grace. I wanted to become a man of upright moral character. The Prophet Muhammad said, "There is nothing heavier in the Scales on the Day of Judgment than good character." From this point on I always wanted to be in the right place at the right time doing the right thing because there is no right way to do the wrong thing.

The path of this physical existence is merely a means for reaching the ultimate purpose of real life. After all I have been through, I am still here. Resiliency.

Today I am living proof that broken crayons still color, that you can reinvent yourself. You can rise from the ashes of failure, heartbreak, trauma. I am an author; I currently sit on the board of two non-profit organizations. I have received certifications as a life coach, a national peer support specialist, a forensic peer support specialist, an advocate for prisoner's rights, as well as a mentor to the youth. I am proud of the man

I have become. It was not easy, but through struggle comes ease. All Praise is due to Almighty God.

Shakil Ali

About Shakil

Shakil Ali is the President and CEO of T.R.A.P. (Total Reality Approach Process) that is committed to ending systemic racial injustice, ending mass incarceration of African people, and protecting human rights in the U.S and beyond.

Shakil is a well-known advocate for criminal Justice Reform, he has spoken in front of the Virginia General Assembly challenging Delegates and Senators to eliminate archaic laws that continuously incarcerate hundreds of thousands of precious poor, black men, women, and children.

Shakil served 24 years in Virginia's penal system and during those years he experienced solitary confinement, around the clock lock-ins, racist staff, no contact visits, prisons with no programs in which to grow. It is where he states he grew into manhood.

Shakil is now a mentor for the youth, runs various programs in the community such as Real Men, Real Talk, A Peer Recovery Support Group. He is a youth Basketball Coach. He sits on the board of Directors for the "Help Me Help You" organization created to assist in poverty reduction and the reintegration of returning citizens into the community.

Shakil is a National Peer Support Specialist, a Certified Life Coach, a Forensic Support Specialist, and a leader in the community for Social Justice Change.

Chapter 3

Determined

BY DELORES L. PRICE

Mother to Son
Well, son, I'll tell you:
Life for me ain't been no crystal stair.
It's had tacks in it,
And splinters,
And boards torn up,
And places with no carpet on the floor— Bare.
But all the time
I'se been a-climbin' on,
And reachin' landin's,
And turnin' corners,
And sometimes goin' in the dark
Where there ain't been no light.
So, boy, don't you turn back.
Don't you set down on the steps.
'Cause you finds it's kinder hard.
Don't you fall now—
For I'se still goin', honey,
I'se still climbin',
And life for me ain't been no crystal stair.
Langston Hughes

I remember reading "Mother to Son" by Langston Hughes as a 'tween. I remember how much I identified with his words of truth. I mean, sure-- I was not a mother, but life for me was not a crystal stair. I recall some of the tacks I stepped on at that age, and a few splinters that got caught on my heel. Honestly, at that age it felt like my whole world was a facade. I was hurt and quietly dying on the inside.

I wanted to be daddy's little girl, but instead I was mommy's baby. There was nothing wrong with that. My mother was simply amazing. She was a single mother of three, raising her babies on her own and she did it with grace, strength, determination, and heavy reliance on her faith in God. Nonetheless, I wanted my father. He lived five minutes away from me, but even that was five minutes more than he had for me. I rarely saw him, and that was devastating to my self-esteem. I was a 'fluffy' kid, and I saw myself as fat. I wished that I was light complected because brown skinned girls with brown eyes were not in big demand. All the boys wanted the light skinned girls with light eyes, and that was not me. I had long kinky hair and no matter how often I was told that my hair was beautiful, it didn't matter. Why? It was not "good hair" --you know, the kind of hair that you can get wet, and it curls up right away. Man, I wanted hair like that! Everything that I saw in the mirror was wrong. I thought to myself, "God did not mean to make me this way. If my daddy does not want me, then these boys out here do not want me either." And guess what? Neither did I! Praise be to God. I have never thought about killing myself, but my thoughts and actions lead me to self-destructive behavior. Between middle school and my freshman year of high school I had "danced on the boards all torn up".

For the next few years, it was calm for the most part. During my senior year of high school, however, it felt like the carpet had been snatched from beneath me. My father was diagnosed with lung cancer, and at that point I felt like I was living the words of Langston Hughes' poem. I was walking, running, and dancing on "places with no carpet on the floor".

After his diagnosis I saw my dad a lot more often. I have always been a thumb sucker. He would do his best to get me to stop sucking my thumb on the occasions that I did see him. I always told him that the day he stopped smoking cigarettes, would be the day that I stopped sucking my thumb.

In all my years of doing sports and dance he was not present. Finally, he showed up to the most important volleyball game ever. I was so excited to have my dad there! It was the city championship, and I was playing in the left front position, where I knew my father would certainly have a great view of me as I played. As our teams faced off, my defining moment arrived. The ball was tossed up, and the girl hit it, hurling it in my direction. I thought it was going to be in, but it was floating out. It touched my arms, and I shanked it. The other team won the game, and I was blamed for losing the game. I felt defeated in front of my teammates, and worse, in front of my father.

My father passed a few months before my high school graduation. I remember the day like it was yesterday. My dad's health was slipping away, and he called me over to his bed one night and talked to me. To this day I cannot recall what he said to me. Now, that memory cuts like a knife. I would give the world to remember his last words to me. The next day it was storming outside, a storm unlike any other. It felt heavy and weighed me down. It was pitch black outside; it made me feel so uneasy. My mom was on the phone and her call was disrupted by the loudest rumble of thunder I had ever heard. It startled me so much that I stopped dead in my tracks, and I knew that it was over. Shortly, after the phone rang and I saw the look on my mother's face. It was confirmation that my father was gone to a better place. Something left me that day. Exactly what it was, I can't say.

I think during this time I was walking on bare boards with splinters and tacks intertwined. There are things that happen in life you wish you could forget; however, I remember this day vividly. I had met a man, and we had been talking for a few months. He was older than me, and he wanted to take me out to dinner. I agreed to go out with him. After all, he appeared to be an absolute gentleman.

The dinner was awesome, and the night was perfect. We went back to his home to chill and watch a movie. He wanted to move a lot faster than I did, but I thought he understood what I was saying. I was not ready for that type of commitment, I told him we should take things slowly. In the moment I felt slightly uncomfortable and the vibe in the room was changing. It was an indescribable feeling that came over me. I automatically knew it was time to leave, but my exit was delayed as he started to move closer to me. The gap between us no longer existed. He went from his arm being on my shoulder to him touching me in ways that were not invited or wanted. The word "NO" is supposed to have so much power, but in this situation my words were meaningless. He disregarded my pleas and took what he wanted, despite my objections.

When he finally permitted me to leave the room, I exited as calmly as I could. My mind became set on survival. If he could violate me in the manner in which he had, I wondered what else he was capable of. Once I was securely in my car, I locked the door, started the engine, and began to weep violently. I made my way home, driving through a torrent of tears. Once I was safe at home, I called a friend and told him what had happened. I remember hearing the anger in his voice and I felt foolish, stupid, and ridiculous. He comforted me with his kindness and reassured me that it was not my fault. I cannot express how happy I was that he lived in another state, because if he had been closer to the situation, he would have caught a case that day.

As for me, I was angry at myself and disgusted with my attacker. I blamed myself for being raped and I fell deeper into the dark, bottomless pit of depression. I had already lived in depression for six years before the rape. As my sense of hopelessness grew, I thought to myself, "heck, let's just add a few more months to the madness."

At this point you may be asking, "How long did he go to jail?" "What did your family say?" "Did anyone know you were so depressed?" Well, he did not do any jail time. I was too scared to tell anyone. I could not bring myself to tell my mother. I was terrified of how she would look at me and above all I did not want to break her heart. When it came to depression--Honey!! Halloween occurred daily for me. I wore different masks when I needed to. Rarely did I let my guard down so that people could see me for who I was. If I didn't like myself, surely you would not like me either; at least that's what I told myself.

It was in the middle of this darkness that I made a decision that was a slap in the face of God. I am not sure if you have ever been in a situation that you know brought tears to the eyes of God, but I have. Faced with an unexpected pregnancy, I believed the additional stress of a baby in that period in my life would make things unbearable. I already had a one-year-old child and having another baby was more than I could handle, I told myself.

I did not want to do it, but I did. I walked into the waiting room alone. I carefully surveyed the room and wanted to run out of there but could not. I had no clue what I was getting myself into. They called my name, and it was my turn to be seen. I recall shaking from terror and disappointment. I felt like I was being gutted like a fish. The procedure hit a slight complication. The baby would not detach from my womb. A few more minutes of tugging and pulling and it was all over. I was taken into a room filled with other girls and women. Some were upset and being comforted. Others were expressionless and ready to go. As for me, I sat in my chair alone sobbing and upset with myself. How could I have done something like this. It went against everything I stood for. God gifted me with something so precious, and I threw it back at him in the most horrific manner possible.

I asked God to forgive me, and I begged him to give me back my baby. Shortly thereafter, I became pregnant. I was overjoyed, but my joy did not last long. I was having severe cramping and ended up losing my baby. The pain I felt after losing my baby pierced my heart in an unimaginable way. I learned that day what it felt like to have something snatched from you that you desperately wanted, without the chance to fight for it or to keep it. God allowed me to feel how he felt on that day.

Throughout this journey that we call life, we will experience amazingly great moments as well as some very grim moments. Sometimes these grim moments greet us unexpectedly and sometimes we create them. Nonetheless, no matter the circumstance, we can determine how we respond to these situations. This does not mean that we are not going to feel pain, sadness, and disgust. We will feel the side effects of life's situations, but you do not have to give up. You are that box of Crayola crayons. Each color represents your many gifts, talents, hopes, dreams and even your purpose. Sometimes we allow life circumstances to break one of our crayons and in that moment, we toss our dreams, hopes and purpose to the wayside. I encourage you to keep coloring. Do not allow anyone or anything, stop you from creating your masterpiece and do not forget to share it with the world. Your story is meant to be shared. Someone in this world is waiting specifically for you. Do not be selfish. Open yourself up and color boldly. I share my story to encourage others to let them know they are not alone, to encourage them to keep coloring and try to prevent others from making the same mistakes. Why? Because this broken crayon still colors!

Determined

The situations I have lived through,
Including self-inflictions too.
Have shaped me, molded me,
Helps me color more vividly.
I create a masterpiece,
From thought provoking canvases to inspirational tapestries,
I am love, and I love thoughtlessly.
The sniper contracted to end my life,
Still plots and plans to cause me strife.
He fails to see my desire, my strength--
No more solitary pity party,
I'm fighting back harder.
Like a virus that mutates when used to penicillin
Sniper bullets and tactics are no longer winning.
My response is different during this fight.
2.0 is about to take flight.
This broken crayon is nowhere near done,
You better ask somebody.
You found the right one!
Delores Gaines-Price

About Delores

Delores L Price is a proud graduate of The Ohio State University where she graduated with her Bachelor of Science degree in Special Education. She is currently a 7th grade Intervention Specialist where she teaches math and science. Delores specializes in encouraging, empowering, and supporting visionaries as a certified Life Coach.

Along with being a Life Coach, Delores has coached various athletics for 10 years. Helping her athletes see the connection between athletics and the realities of life brings her great joy. Delores is the owner of Sweet Nellies Bakery which creates delectable desserts. To add to her various accomplishments, she is now an International Author.

Delores's greatest accomplishment of all is being the mother of 4 amazing children. She is a firm believer that her visualization will become her actualization through manifestation.

Chapter 4

Daddy's Love

BY ILYASAH SIMPSON

"Prostitutes come home earlier than you", his words were searing. For a long time, my name was "stupid bitch". I was called that so much, I thought that's who and what I was. My self-esteem was extremely low. I doubted my every thought. I was afraid to execute any mental plan imagined or written on paper. I couldn't think; I felt defeated. I felt mentally paralyzed and plain scared to move. How does a person get away with putting that much fear into another? At that time, I was not able to identify my feelings. I did not know then that fear was an emotion created in our own minds, allowing it to take over our own thoughts.

It was a bright brisk Saturday. I had to go to the doctor. I came home to an array of bags on the curb. Naturally, I assumed since it was Saturday, it was garbage day and that was garbage on the curb. Something told me to look again. I looked harder at the bags. My eyes zeroed in not just on the bags, but the piles of clothes that were wrapped in twine. I saw a coat that I purchased just a few months before. That was not garbage. I ran to turn over the piles of clothes. It was everything from my closet.

My mind shifted. I became lost and bewildered. I began to ask myself what is going on? Why are my belongings out for garbage? Within a blink of an eye, he rolls up, jumps out the car and yells, "bitch give me my keys!"

I looked at him as if I was seeing a monster. My entire body went into a frozen position. I could not talk.

He yelled again, "Give me my keys right now!"

He ran up on me, yelling in my face and for the third time, "Bitch. I said give me my keys!"

My natural response was to step back. I stepped back and threw the keys over his head. Oh, he thought I would hand him the keys nicely. I was not about to be nice. He was yelling at me like a stray dog from the street. After I threw the keys, he ran to pick up the keys in the middle of the street. Turning Ito collect my belongings. I threw all my clothes in my car and left.

That is exactly what I did and in that order. More yelling and cursing came along as a result of my actions, of course; however, all I heard was, "You will never ruin my marriage," and the rest was, ".... *whaa- whaa-whaaa*". My ears totally shut off and shut down. In a split second the man who I thought was my biological father just became a regular man in the street who had lost his mind. The man who I thought was my father immediately stopped being my father. I was now his enemy. The man who I never knew to be my father entered his spirit into mine and began to move within my body.

A voice came to me as I loaded up the car and began to drive and said in a strong tone, "I am your father, and I will take care of you."

I knew something was going on at the time. I just could not identify what it was, but I just went with the flow. Life started moving fast after that day. I realized that bright brisk Saturday was the first day that I met Jesus.

I was born in the Nation of Islam. As a child, I remember going to the mosque on 116th Street in Harlem, New York, wearing our uniforms. I remember going to the mosque on Sundays. We lived in the Bronx then. My parents moved to Long Island and life in the mosque seemed to stop. We practiced the ways to eat and to live and that was about it.

However, as I began to grow into my own as a teenager and young adult, I realized Islam in my house was not practiced the way it was supposed to be. I grew into using my own mind, not the mind of my dad. From experiences in my own life and watching others, I now questioned and doubted the ways of my household. My sound mind was able to identify his characteristics of being an abuser, a gas lighter, and a narcissist. I interfered with his territory. Trust me I get it. Quite naturally I am 19 years old. I am not going to let you abuse my mother in front of my face. So, trust me I get it. I was a standup act.

Emotional abuse, verbal abuse, physical abuse. Abuse is abuse. My mind could not escape it. When abuse happens, it is similar to the movie, 'Invasion of the Body Snatchers'. Once you have been free of the environment, it is a process to become free in your mind. I get PTSD from the thought of that bright brisk Saturday when my father ripped the carpet from underneath my feet. I was never upset at what he did, it was how he did it. Me growing into my womanhood was a threat to him When he put me in the street with all of my clothes, I packed up every item never to return. From that day on my life was never the same. The soft me grew a hard shell on the outside and inside.

Some people never become free from the abusive chains, but I was determined to work on myself. I used self-talk to encourage myself to step out of the box of chains that I mentally carried in my head. I constantly battled in my mind with my worth, value and purpose. It felt like agony. I became determined not to ever lose my identity ever again. I carried a posture as if I were made of steel and nothing of harm could ever penetrate me. My soul became ice cold. I moved forward in life with determination. I became a strategic thinker. I watched, listened, strategically planned, and then made my move. My only agenda was to outwit others. I told myself that every single day.

From then until now I was consistent with my behavior. I felt it was me against the world and I refused to be defeated. If you had a plan of manipulation over my life trust me, I saw it. I watched your every move. I let you think you had me and then I checkmated your ass. Ask somebody who experienced me. They would definitely tell you: "Don't do it!!!!"

I am the coolest person you will ever want to meet. I am a quiet woman who keeps to herself. I am not the everyday chatty kind of woman. Just do not come into my personal space if you are not invited.

Moving forward with my life, God ordered my steps. I have experienced life on a variety of levels. I am fortunate to say that the day my father put me out of his house was the best thing he had ever done for me. I became free from his mental bondage. My heart was always caring. I never wanted to see people suffer. For any situation that showed up, I was there to assist. I had wisdom to handle the circumstance. Whatever I went through, I knew I had a remedy to move differently the next time. There are times when the same situation would show itself but this time, I was ready. No more wet behind the ears for me. I had the experiences going through the fires already where before it felt as if I had lost my mind. I grew a mind of my own. I experienced life for the rawness that life could deliver, and I am still standing. Life is what you make it. It is not how you fall. It is about how you respond to every fall. I fell forward. Every fall was an experience that I learned from. With experiences, you either learn from them and keep them as wisdom on a shelf or continue the behavior and fall harder later. Me, I am the type that it only takes me one time to feel the pain and I am good. I put all my experiences on my own bookshelf. I made it my business to always share my experiences.

It is this thing called life. Life will beat you up if you do not prepare or embrace yourself for what lies ahead. Funny thing was I looked at situations for what they were. I called a spade a spade. If it was blue, then it was blue. I never would change my perception to turn blue into light blue with purple lace. I never wanted to create a lie and live in it. I avoided that course of action for the reason of growing up in a home that covered up what was actually going on. The exterior appeared to be one way but in essence there was a different pot of chicken cooking on the stove.

Your father is the first man in your life that displays what love should be in your life. I do not have the rags to riches story. My father was an excellent provider. I wanted for nothing in my eyes. At least before I viewed him as a man and not as my father. No, I did not grow up in a household that lacked anything. As a matter of fact, we had everything a child could want. We were the first to have whatever came out new. The newest sneakers, the latest coats, shoes, clothes etc. If there was lack in the mind of a child, it was hidden and all I saw and could say was we as children, had it all, materially speaking.

Daddy was very strict on us. If we disobeyed, Daddy would bring us to the couch in the living room to give us these long sermons that would last for hours. One thing is for sure, my dad taught us right from wrong. His stories actually prepared us for the life ahead that we had no idea about. My father was quite the historian. He was very knowledgeable in politics, black history, and current events. He was a great writer. He expressed himself both positively and negatively. Dad had his ways, but he was an amazing provider. He educated us with culture. He taught us how to enjoy and experience life as best as he knew how. We traveled from infants. He taught me well. I hear his voice even today on the How To.

He always said," Whatever you do, just be the best. Work hard, do better. You are not average. You are above average."

I live by those words daily. He said it so much it is embedded in my head. Looking back, I never felt he did not love us. I finally learned to understand he did not know how to love. He never learned how to love. Tender love and care were not an added ingredient to the recipe for love. Depending on the age when you met him was his mental state of the man or boy you received. I just so happen to get the guy that tried, but still had the chains from his past attached to him. He never escaped. He lived in his own mental prison. He just pushed his bags of chains onto whoever he was with at the time.

At the end of the day, my father was a troubled man and his frustrations from his own life led him to be abusive to others. Hurt people hurt people. That misery oil drips. That evil oil drips. That abusive oil drips. That scar tissue oil drips. That vulnerable oil drips. The oil drips and creates generations of chains and mental bondage.

As life moved forward for me, I have learned you are a product of your environment. With that being said, each man I became involved with was older. In addition, I went through abusive relationships. I thought that was love. I realized it was not the man I wanted but the father figure that I desired to love me. Yes, even as I am an older young woman, I wanted the love from my father.

There were points when my father treated me as if I never existed. He even kept my mom from associating with me. I will never forget how my father would come to Queens from Long Island to get food from the Spanish restaurant directly across the street from my shop and not come over to say hello. It is devastating when others would see and mention it. That is when you feel like blood is running from your heart pouring out as if there was a hole in it.

I would sit quietly as someone says, "Yas, isn't that your parents across the street? They come all the way out here and not say Hi? "

That is the moment when you want to disappear from the room. I just cannot make this stuff up SMH. My takeaway from this experience was once your father hurts you, no man's pain can cut you as deep as your father. My motto is and always will be when it comes down to loving intimately in a relationship is to never give a man your love 100%. Give them 95%. You will need that 5% to save your life. Yes, I was broken but I STILL Color.

About Ilyasah

Ilyasah A. Simpson is a native New Yorker. Ilyasah is a single woman and a mother of an awesome young son.

Ilyasah has 15 years of experience working in the area of Mental Health with a Master of Social Work from Adelphi University.

Ilyasah is an author: *So, You Think You Can Pray*, and a co-author of, *I AM A Woman Empowered*.

Ilyasah also known as Minister Charge was ordained as a minister in 2019. This minister also holds an Associate of Arts in Biblical Studies. In addition, Ilyasah is a Board-Certified Christian Counselor by the National Association of Christian Counselors.

Ilyasah has a ministry called The Charge Room Incorporated. The Charge Room Inc. is a platform men and women built to provide a safe zone and strategic interventions to allow broken hearts and broken souls to reconstruct, renew and reform their minds in order to surrender their old selves to awaken and receive their newness.

Ilyasah is currently a radio talk show host for The Charge Room show on iHeart Radio.

Ilyasah is a Certified Life Coach where she defines herself as Coach ILLY, "The Relationship Strategist". Ilyasah specializes in individual or group coaching while utilizing effective evidence-based strategies to assist one to identify, modify and reinvent who they are, where they are, and transform them to where they desire to be.

Just an additive, Ilyasah is a Certified Culinary Professional, a world traveler as well as a lover of creative arts and music.

Chapter 5

You Better Tell It

BY ANNETTE JACKSON

For the most part I grew up in a two-parent home. My mother was an educator. She taught junior and senior high school students. My dad was in the military. Much of his time was spent deployed on a ship. My mom was really into church and serving the Lord. She was the church organist, secretary and played for different gospel ensembles including her own. I remember anticipating when the ship would come in so I could see my daddy. When we could not be at the port, just the sight of him walking up the sidewalk of Dennison Ave in Chesapeake Bay meant the world to me. My dad loved to drink so one of the things that would happen when he got home was all his buddies and their significant others would come over and party. My dad would be so drunk by the time everyone left, it was frightening. It was frightening because when he was like that he and mom would argue for hours.

I recall one of his deployments where he had been in the Mediterranean and when in port had a life-sized doll made to look like me. He made sure that I had the matching outfit. He gave her to me when he returned home. That same night I changed into the matching outfit as my doll. As usual, daddy's friends came by. They partied and left. Dad was in his usual state of drunkenness. I had placed the doll in my bed and sat on the floor in the living room against the wall. Daddy and mom began to argue. It appeared daddy did not like mom being around the church, specifically other men and mom did not like him getting drunk. Somehow the arguing escalated, and my dad began throwing things around. I was too afraid to move and before I knew it, he had grabbed me and threw me across the room. I was in the hospital for months after the incident and I didn't get to see him again for years. I remember making a promise to myself that I would never be in a marriage like that; even though there was a lot of good, there was equally a lot of bad and ugly. There was a lot of hurt and open wounds that I was too young to understand. Despite the drinking, the fighting and going to church like nothing had happened, I was a broken little girl who loved her daddy.

The years went by and my mother continued to teach and play her music. Sometimes after concerts we would go to my Aunt Ivy's farm to eat, play, and fellowship. Often the quartet or members of the chorale were invited. There was a particular Sunday evening I recall where we were all gathered at my aunt's house. We had eaten, played and were in the house singing as mom played the piano. One of the men in one of the groups would always play with us kids. He would chase us and flip us upside down and would hold a few of us on his lap. On this one evening it was just me on his lap. I could not make out what was going on with all his movement. He put his hand under my dress, and I found it hard to break loose. He had whispered in my ear not to say a word or else. I was terrified. I was scared for my mom, my sisters, and my brothers. I wanted my daddy, but he was not there.

A few weeks had gone by and my Aunt Alberta had noticed that I was different. She noticed that every time there was rehearsal I would disappear. She had asked my mom if I could spend the night with her so she could talk to me and see what the matter was. While crying and shaking with fear I told her everything. I also told her that I wanted my daddy. That was not something she could give me because he was deployed again. She called my mom, and they notified the police. The police came and I had to get checked out. I guess the word got out quickly about what had happened. People were disgusted and outraged. As my mom continued with her groups and regular work, they had to put the word out for a replacement in the group. They now needed a bass vocalist. I thought nothing of it because members of the group would change from time to time, but this new person, Mr. Rambo was always around. He sang in the group; he came to my aunties house and would do drop by visits to make sure we were okay. He was around for over a year and then we did not see him anymore. I later learned that he was the officer assigned to watch over us until the culprit was caught.

My parents later divorced and added to my trauma, I would no longer have my daddy at home. Who would keep me safe? My daddy and I wrote constantly. When he finally settled in a port where he would not be deployed for a while, he would call me. In my mind, with everything that had happened between him and mom, me being violated and now the divorce, I was clinging for dear life. My parents both got remarried in the same year just months apart. My daddy married another church lady, and my mom married a preacher. I objected to both marriages, but my voice was not heard. My stepdad was ex-military, mean, selfish, very demanding, and abusive.

I had become a "PK", short for "preacher's kid". Most people had the perception we were either extremely sheltered or totally off the chain. I can say that both were true, but most of us were like any other kid who was just trying to figure out how they fit into the world. My life was very calculated, sheltered, and structured.

We had gender specific roles when it came to rules and chores and the rules were not the same for boys and girls. I was a tomboy, though, and that presented a problem. It was instilled in me to always be lady-like, play with girls and dolls and be in the house early. I climbed trees in my dresses, caught bugs and played football. I was placed in charm school and entered beauty pageants. I guess this was to bring out more of my girly side and it also would provide some scholarships for college down the road. As a result of my disobedience and having pushed the limits, I would get my behind torn up. Oh! The golden rule was "what goes on in the house stays in the house," hence what happened to me or any of us was to never be talked about.

My stepdad was physically and verbally abusive. I saw him hit my mom and cuss at her like it was a normal thing. He had to be fed first and we got what was left. He had children from a previous marriage who were his pride and joy. He gave them everything and gave us nothing but hell. We had to wash, vacuum and shine cars we would never get to drive, staying out of sight until he was done eating up mom's time. We had to sit in church and listening to sermons from the same man that was oppressing us. Every Tuesday evening, he would call me into the orange room to talk about girls not having sex. I would always feel like I had been violated when leaving up out of that room. Each Tuesday evening, I felt like I was being primed for something and so I told my mom. They had a big fight about it and from that time on it was more tension in the house between us. I had said at an earlier age that I would never be married where there was drinking and fighting. I began to refer to him with the nickname "IT". The rules contradicted the conduct of "IT" as I had come to call him, but there was this pretense that was being upheld like all was well in the house and it was really in ruins. I felt like "It" was up to something and it was going to be ugly. I was afraid. I was afraid to get sick and afraid to be home alone. I felt if the right opportunity arose, he would try something.

Consequently, I started getting sick and as it turned out I had to have my tonsils removed. This meant that I was going to be home alone after being released from the hospital to recover. My bedroom was right across the hall from theirs. I kept my door closed all the time because I did not want him to see me doing anything and I especially did not want him to see me laying in my bed. My mom would give me my medicine before she left for work and then would return at lunch time to give me my next dose. I remember hearing him leave for work and then my mom. I fell asleep and was faintly awakened by what sounded like the front door closing, I could not talk because I had just had surgery. It was "It"!" He had returned. I heard him coming down the hallway and going into their room, then he came out of their room, paused, and opened my door. I felt wetness and whiskers on my back and jumped up trying to scream and fight. He took off, I called my mom at work and was trying to cry for help. She came home and found me in a frenzy. When my stepdad "It" got home it was a fight like no other. He was fighting my mom and then turned to fight me saying that I was a liar. I had no reason to lie, He was nasty, abusive and a pervert. What does love look like between a husband, wife, and family? I was confused and still determined that my life would not be like this. The kind of rigidity and abuse sustained left me naive to a fault and unprepared for life. This was the beginning of my end for living at home with my mom and stepdad. It was also the beginning of my self-abuse. I began to take handfuls of one-a-day vitamins each day so I would stay awake, and I began to drink vodka. This was my coping with what I could not talk about and a way of numbing my pain.

When I left for college, I had never been on a date, let alone an unsupervised date. I was underage and did not know what kinds of things awaited me on campus life. I had never been in love or had a strong like for a boy because I was not allowed to have those kinds of relationships. Mind you I am now popping pills and drinking. The first part of my first year of college was spent at Baptist College at Charleston, now Charleston Southern University. In the winter term I transferred to Ohio State University. I was sixteen, book smart, and street dumb. I was immediately labeled as "jailbait" on campus because I was underage. I began to try to figure out this life of freedom with no guidelines. I had never been on my own or made independent choices.

I met my best friend Skip in my first political science class. He was eight years older than me but was great company and polite. He was a Muslim and protective. He had a way of helping me to feel secure in my surroundings. He had a discernment about him like I had never seen. He became my manager for the pageants that I would enter that year. He was strict in a good way, and remember I said he was discerning? One day in the student union he called me out. He challenged me to stop drinking. I challenged what he thought he was seeing. I conceded, accepted the challenge, and told him everything. He told me that I was a winner and that now I could really face the interviews with confidence, and grace the stage commanding the attention of the entire room. The first pageant was a success, and I was first runner up. That secured me a little more scholarship money.

One day Skip introduced me to a friend of his from his hometown. The three of us talked and ate lunch. Skip shared that his friend was a fine art major and was preparing for an art showing. Skip's friend invited us to his apartment to see some of his latest paintings and so we went. We arrived at his friend's apartment and they began to smoke weed. There were others who had stopped over to see some of his paintings and they all smoked. I had never smoked before. It was not my thing. My friend Skip called to me and said, "I have to go and take a test; would you be okay staying here until I get back?" I said sure. I stayed and one by one the others left. The smoke was so dense in that little apartment it was like a fogger had been set off. So, it was me and Skip's friend left alone to look over the art and his friend fired up another joint. What I can remember is that I ended up having sex for the first time with a stranger, someone I neither loved nor really knew well enough to say I liked. I knew instantly that my life was changed. I could feel something happening within me that was altogether different, yet familiar. Skip finally returned and then got me safely home.

The next day while sitting in class I became ill. I was nauseous and dizzy. Skip got me to the hospital, and they could not find anything wrong. They gave me a prescription and sent me on my way. I told my mom what had happened and that I had the prescription. Once she saw it, she flipped. She asked me if I was pregnant, and I told her I did not know because I had just had sex for the first time the day before. She immediately called her OB/GYN to set me an appointment the next day. They drew blood and I was indeed pregnant. The course of my life was changing so fast. I was about to lose part of my funding for school, I was pregnant by someone I neither really knew or loved, and my mom was livid. I was in a state of shock, disappointed, underage, and felt like I had no choices. My mom did not haste to make plans to confront the boy and get me married off to save face. After all, this was a Christian family, the preacher's kid who is now pregnant. Before the weeks end, I was married to someone I did not know or love.

My husband was verbally, emotionally, mentally, and physically abusive. I was afraid, alone, and without help. I was hungry, locked in an apartment on the third floor with no way out. I would pray so hard for God to forgive me for my wrongdoing and to keep me alive. I prayed so hard for the hunger pains to go away and for the abuse to stop. My mom would never admit to seeing my hair chopped off by him and the patches that were missing or the lack of weight gain during my pregnancy. Finally, my oldest sister saw him and said that Tamra, my niece, wanted to see me because it had been a few years. She never came back with Tamra and I now had a five-year-old and was married to everything I said I never wanted. He was a drunk and a drug abuser. He would leave me locked in for weeks at a time. Even once I had our first child and could go to work, he would pop up and watch me to make sure no other man would say anything to me. There were times when I would leave work and get jumped by him at the bus stop. He would not allow my best friend to see or have any kind of interaction with me. One day Skip showed up outside our apartment door and just talked to me through the door. I tried telling him what was happening, and he promised me that he would help me get out of the abuse. It was years later and three babies in before I would see any light.

My Aunt Helen was heading back to Ohio from Kentucky and she said the Lord had put me on her heart in a way she could not shake. Heeding that unction, she came straight to my apartment. She said that once she was out of the car all she could hear was me screaming for help, babies crying and him beating me up. I was determined that if I was going to die that it would not be without a fight. I was in the fight of my life, for my life. Hearing the fighting and screaming, my aunt called the police. My landlord arrived, talked to my aunt, and got his master key for the apartment. As he was opening the door the police were arriving on the scene. I was told that it took quite a few officers to subdue him. I did not get to walk away. I was carried out on a stretcher. I was hospitalized with a fractured neck. I had months of recovering and therapy ahead of me. Upon being discharged me and my babies were transported to Virginia where I would continue in therapy and have help with the children. I was scared and felt like he was still lurking about watching my every move and calculating his next move. After months in Virginia, I was able to return to Ohio. I got back to Ohio and the first news I got was that he was out of jail. I was riddled with fear.

With the help of my aunt and best friend I was able to relocate into a new apartment on the other side of town. I was finally in a new place, new surroundings, and neighbors, with an older couple who adopted us as family. I finally got the courage to tell them my story and they assured me that they would make sure we were safe. They took me to file for a divorce and I was finally starting to piece my life back together, so I thought. After months of living in our new place, fall was about to turn to winter. I had fed the kids, bathed them, and tucked them into bed. I showered and hit the bed with such exhaustion. It felt like all that I had been through was finally being released and my body's response was fatigue. I was in a deep sleep when I awakened to being raped. He had found out where we lived, broke in and raped me while I was sleeping. As I was getting my bearings and fighting, my newly adopted mom and pops heard the noise and tussling. They came with triggers cocked and apprehended him until the police arrived. I was taken to the hospital and underwent the rape kit procedure to confirm that it was indeed him. Again, my world had been rattled and I was shaken to the core. Is there no end? I wanted healing and wholeness, I wanted freedom and happiness. Let me tell you, it was hard to find joy on this next leg of the journey.

I missed my cycle, and I was devastated. I was once again pregnant and what this meant was that my divorce was put on hold until after the baby was born. This was a baby I did not want. I did not want it because of how it was conceived, and I did not want it because of who it was. I was angry and I was becoming bitter. My mom told my dad what had happened, and he called me and pleaded with me not to get an abortion. Somehow in my mind getting an abortion meant getting rid of him and that was the farthest thing from the truth. I finally promised my dad that I would not get rid of the baby.

The time came for the baby to be born and I named him after my dad and my adopted dad next door. They championed me through this entire pregnancy and never let me forget I was worth more than the hand I had been dealt. They reminded me that my worth was not chained to my choices and that I would learn the true meaning of love, overtake my fears and to love living. I did not have to hide anymore! They helped me to see me in my children and not just their father or the reminder of how painful my life had been. They helped me to see the unwavering and undefiled love in its purest form through the eyes and the heart of my babies and the people who were my support circle. They helped me to be courageous enough to tell my story one day because it may just help someone navigate the rough waters of their life coming out of abuse. So, I say to you my dear reader "you better tell it!" You can have the best examples and still make all the wrong choices. You can have the worst examples and make all the right choices, but tell it, whatever it is and whatever you have been through because a concealed wound never heals, and a broken crayon still colors a beautiful picture.

About Annette

Annette Jackson was born in Bath, Maine. She grew up primarily in the south as a "military brat" which has afforded her to live in many places. She is the founding Pastor of the Church of Columbus located in Columbus, Ohio. She serves as the Interdenominational Women's Ministerial Association Vice President, Manifest in Me Board of Directors & Executive Committee, Northern Regional Apostle for Empowerment Covenant Worldwide, Vice President of the Issachar Council. She is a very passionate Transitional Life Coach for ex-offenders is a conference & motivational speaker. She offers leadership development & empowerment to others. She is a published contributing author and community servant. She has been a co-host for both the "Anointed to Win" weekly radio broadcast & Anointed to Win Christian Women's Talk Show and serves as an ambassador for Strong Confident Woman, LLC. She attended the Ohio State University majoring in Human Relations/Family Development. Graduate of the ACLD Pastoral Program, has a Bachelor of Arts from Ohio Christian University in Leadership in Ministry and a Master of Arts Ministry & Practical Theology. She is currently working towards her Doctor of Education & Organizational Leadership. Annette loves to cook; she is not a baker so don't judge her, she loves to shop and travel.

Chapter 6

Black is Beautiful

BY CHANDA E. MCGUFFIN

Born in 1971 to Charles and Carolyn McGuffin, I did not enter this world alone. Approximately nine minutes prior to my arrival, my twin brother had paved the way for me to enter this crazy world. According to my mom, the doctor said, "it's a girl and she's being stubborn". That stubbornness would serve me well. My twin would be my protector and best friend. Growing up having a twin, you always have a playmate. Growing up, and to this day, he is affectionately known to me as my BoBo. We have a brother seven years older and we saw him as a father figure. We loved him like no other person in our lives.

I know that my biological parents were my heart, but I was my Godmother's heart. God brought me to the world through Charles and Carolyn, and I was God's gift to "Doey" (how I first was able to pronounce Doris). My Godmother, which I shortened to "Mother", loved me just like I was her daughter. My mom could not do hair. That would be my Mother's first duty. We spent countless hours getting my hair done and talking. My mom entrusted us to her care. You recall I told you I am a twin? My mom took all the help she could get when it came to raising us.

I loved being with her. As I grew up down the street, I would yell up the street if I could come up there. She would stand on the porch watching me come up the street and tell me when I could cross. One time the mailman carried me up the street and delivered me with the mail. We moved across town, but my mom kept taking me back to visit. A foot of snow fell one time, and I worried my family so bad that my oldest brother told me to put on my boots and coat, and he walked me over there.

Most of my childhood, 'til about the fourth grade, I have blocked out of my mind. The stories that I shared about Doris were from stories shared with me. I only remember the snowstorm walk.

My father was an alcoholic and abused my mother. On one hand I hated my father and on the other hand I loved him. I hated having any love for a man that hurt my beautiful and angelic mother. I had an internal war within myself all the time. To protect myself in that traumatic home environment, I found safety at Doris' house, and comfort in food, leading to a lifelong battle with weight issues.

My father became sober when I was probably seven years old, but the violence did not stop. As I got older, I started to stand up to him in my own way. We would have "family meetings" and my brothers would say "no matter what he says Chanda just say OK so we can get out of here!" Did I listen? NO, I was always determined to have the last word or damn near close to it. As I am writing this, I just have to chuckle, because my son has this same trait, and it burns me up! Sorry, I digress for a moment.

I was broken because of the violence in my home. I believed I was ugly because I was overweight. I felt like I was a horrible person because of my strained relationship with my parents. I decided I was going to end my life. I was so down and defeated at college when my academic advisor saw me in the mail area one day and asked me to come see her. Instead of talking about classes, I began to share about my brokenness and not wanting to live. I will never forget the love she showed me and invested in me. My healing journey began that day in 1990.

My academic advisor became a personal counselor. She taught me that I am the captain of my ship, and my mom was the captain of hers. I had to allow my mom to live her choices and stop trying to save her. My mom was not my responsibility. It was just that I loved her so much that I wanted her to be free of a painful marriage.

I found out I had another brother during my senior year of high school, and I met him for the first time my sophomore year of college. I was so angry at my father, and those old feelings of resentment began to resurface. I wanted to save my mother again from this hurt. The truth is, you cannot save anyone but yourself. So, I focused on getting to know my brother and loving him the best I knew how. It was not my brother's fault for being born. He did not deserve to be rejected any longer. We are still close to this day. I am my brothers' keeper.

During my college years, I met my girlfriends for life. My closest girlfriend is the first one I met on my first day on campus. When she took me home with her, for the first time in my life, I saw what a family should look like. Her father was a man who loved and honored his wife. Her family welcomed me in just like their daughter and sister. It just felt right. It felt like love. I memorized their address. For me, that address was etched in my mind because for the first time in my life, it felt like home. She and I have been through new relationships, lost relationships, births of children and the death of my father. We are more than friends. We are sisters.

I tell young people "this is the time to be selfish! It is just you and it is your time to pave your way". I spent my college years doing just that. To this day, they are the best years of my life. I grew into womanhood. I found who I was, and I accepted who I was. I was and still am Black and beautiful. I color my life Black not because of anything downtrodden or depressing but because of my strength, my tenacity, and my courage. NO ONE can take away who God made me! I embrace all of me.

Over the next 25 years, I had a rewarding but challenging career. I remained in my conservative and confederate hometown. I was an educated and highly intelligent Black woman with a degree from the beloved James Madison University. I would not be denied upper management roles. I had the audacity to apply for a Bank Manager position never working from the bottom up. However, I nailed the first interview and the second and was offered my first Bank Manager position in 2004. For the next 14 years, I moved up to Assistant Vice President, Financial Advisor and Peer to Peer Coach. They hated me, but remember I color my life Black and beautiful!

Right before starting my banking career, I lost my dad. Although my childhood was tumultuous, as I grew up, I became close to my dad. He doted on me. He protected me with everything in him. I never doubted he loved me. He just did not know how to be a father or husband. Then, he compounded it by drinking. Alcoholism will destroy a family. My father had great strength and resilience. He poured himself into AA for the next

25 years before his death. I did not realize the lives he truly impacted until he passed away. Many would come to me in the months following his death to share with me how my dad never gave up on their sobriety. They felt they owed my dad so much.

I remember feeling those words so deeply because he had done the very same thing for me. He had given me the nickname "Lil Warrior" during my college days. It was time for me to tap into the warrior inside of me. I guess that is why I did not think twice about going into banking where very few Black people make their career. Life was going to be different. My mom was coming to live with me. It really was not a second thought. It was my time with my mom. We could start repairing and healing our relationship. It seemed natural for her to be with me.

Then we got the surprise of my life-- I was pregnant! Doctors had told me for years I could not have a baby. Because I was pregnant with my son within the first year of my father's passing, I will always believe my dad sent me a piece of him back to the earth.

I remember telling my mom I was pregnant. She was not happy at all. She said "Chanda you're not tying me down with that baby. I have been set free to do what I want, and I am not keeping this baby." Well, September 6th came, and my baby boy stole his Ganny's heart. I had to ask for time with him. My son had his Ganny wrapped around his finger. They still have a close relationship. My son protects her with everything in him. Without my mom, I could not have answered the call on my life. I am forever grateful for her love, guidance, and prayers.

When my son arrived on the scene, everyone in the family adored him. He was given my two older brothers' names. I had no other name for him. It seemed that he was a rebirth and opportunity for great family healing. My brothers were so honored. From day one, my brothers have helped me to mold and shape my son. He has truly been a blessing to our lives. I always tell him," … I know you will respect me after I carried you for 9 months, 6 days, 19 hours and 18 minutes and the last 3 months were total bed rest". Now, he can repeat this almost simultaneously as I say it. I am so proud of the young man he is becoming. I needed him as much as he needed me. He has helped me to find a new side of myself and learn true unconditional love. Being his mom is the greatest gift God could ever give me. I thank God every day for choosing me to be his mother. It is a true honor.

In 2006, I went back to school for my MBA with my son in my lap or playing on the floor beside me while I worked on my schoolwork. Five years after receiving my MBA, I completed my Master of Education Program. Let me stop here to clarify this point-- my education did not make me. My education helped me not be denied roles that I was qualified for.

My father had taught me that piece of paper that I earned could never be taken away from me. I do not knock anyone who chooses not to go to college. That is your story to tell. For me, college saved my life. Being a life learner empowers and encourages me. I absolutely love learning!

Near the end of my banking career, I became extremely ill. Every doctor kept saying I had asthma, but my symptoms were so different than asthmatic people that I had known. Not feeling well, I went to work one day, and the Regional Executive visited my branch (this never happens). She heard me wheezing. Over time, I had started to become embarrassed by the wheezing. She turned to me and said "Chanda, I want you to go find out what "that" is. I need a doctor's note before you can return."

Long story short, I went to an ENT specialist who informed me I was suffocating alive from scar tissue that was growing over my windpipe. My health condition is called sarcoidosis. What is unique about my sarcoidosis is it was attacking my throat instead of my major organs. I had to have emergency surgery to clear the airway.

Two months after having surgery, I was in a head on car collision. As the truck was barreling toward me, I began to call out to God begging "please let me live for my son. Please don't take me today." I knew after that second encounter with death, I had lived for a reason. I was spared in order to fulfill my purpose. Two years later, I needed to have my airway opened again. This time I stopped breathing on the operating table. They had to revive me. My doctor said I fought hard. He said something in you would not allow you to die. I thought to myself...my son and my purpose. Really, they were one in the same.

Over the next year and a half, I progressively got worse. I needed medication that I could not take because I worked 60+ hours a week. My health was deteriorating. I was having severe dizzy spells. My primary care physician said after the third surgery on your throat I cannot allow you to go back to work. You have got to heal. You are going to kill yourself or someone else during one of these dizzy spells.

This was devastating. I had built a stellar career. I had fought racism and discrimination for so long that it was part of the course. I felt that accepting a disability was like me giving up. I went into a deep depressive state. I felt defeated for the second time in my life. The Lil Warrior was lost without her career that had become Kryptonite. Now what?

My doctor recommended I find some volunteer work that I was able to do in between my doctor's appointments, recovery, and medication regimen. My business partner and I decided to start a social justice organization in early 2018. I began to pull the networks I had obtained over my career together to garner support from all over Virginia and eventually all over the country, including many supporters we have never met in person. So, I turned my attention and heart to the venture, pouring my energy into building RISE.

The children and their parents become a RISE family. Within the first couple times of being with us, their parents see vast improvements. My business partner and I give them a safe environment to learn and thrive. We remember as children hating our school. Our Black children go to public schools every day that they do not feel as though they belong or that they are safe. We want to give them a place that they want to be.

One thing we are most proud of is opening Virginia's first Black library right in my hometown. That same town and area I have fought racism and discrimination my whole life is now embracing RISE. Never say never!

There are days I cannot get out of bed. There are days I have to walk with a cane. Some days, my body may be racked with pain. However, because of the grace that God has shown in my life and answering my prayer not to take me from my son, I press on to answer the call that is on my life. My baby boy is 15 and I often wonder if he realizes what I do is for him to have a better world? He answered that question for me in a Christmas card in 2020, he said "Mom, I cannot wait to see how you change the world."

Before finishing my story, my Mother, my Doey, my son's "NeNe" gained her wings. For three weeks, Doris fought, and doctors fought for her, but for some reason in my spirit, I knew this was the end. I was really spoiled by her. She began baking peanut butter cookies for me for Christmas (I always said they were for me, but they were for everyone). I grew up on them. Christmas 2020, I announced I was not celebrating these pagan holidays. She texted me, saying, "well since you're not celebrating Christmas, I can skip your cookies". I said, "no, no just bake them earlier as peanut butter cookies". We laughed. She baked those cookies the weekend before she fell ill. When my God sister bought them to me and I turned to walk back in the garage, I heard God tell me, "these are the last cookies you will get". I shrugged it off.

The next three weeks would be long. NeNe coded, and God bought her back. She told my sister to call me because she wanted to see my face (that means FaceTime NeNe). I said, "wow, you look good! You are awake and talking". I said, "now, don't rush the doctors. Get completely healed before coming home". As I said that to her, I heard God say, "those are the last cookies". Sure, enough on January 5, 2021 at 8:43 P.M., she gained her wings. Memories of my entire childhood flash across my mind, as well as the memory of my high school prom, where she bought my dress and fussed the whole time about me being expensive. My high school and college graduation, she was there. My 30th and 40th birthday celebrations, she was there. The birth of her second grandson, my son, she was there to visit him his first day home. The reality of my 50th year of life and on, she will be my guardian Angel. Her time here on earth was over. I will be eternally grateful for her loving me all my life. For a woman to love you like her own child because she chooses to be is my blessing. I'm so glad she got to see my son become a respectable young man.

When I tell you broken crayons still color, I am a walking testimony. Coming from an alcoholic home to becoming the vice president of the bank, then becoming the co-founder of a social justice organization, I continue to color Black is beautiful regardless of if the crayon is broken. Mother my crayon is broken without you, but I will continue to make you proud of me. My mess has become the message for my people to regain their voice and hope. Black is still beautiful!

About Chanda

Chanda McGuffin (AKA "Lil Warrior) is a native of Waynesboro, VA and still resides there with her mother and 15-year-old son. Her professional career has been in the finance industry and business management after graduating from James Madison University. She received her MBA in 2006 from Capella University and her MEd in 2012. Chanda is a certified Life Coach who, co-founded RISE in May of 2018. Although the organization is new, the work that she does in the community has spanned most of her life right in the Waynesboro and Staunton community.

Chanda has worked with at risk youth all of her adult life through education and leadership conferences. As a motivational speaker, she speaks on race relations, anti-racism, building effective teams, leadership, and conflict management. Her true passion and calling is to tap into the warrior inside everyone and encourage them to be the best version of themselves. Her hobbies include reading, writing, praise dancing and yelling at a basketball or football game as she watches her son play. There IS a warrior inside all of us and when you tap into the warrior inside, you will find what truly motivates you.

Chapter 7

The Variations of the Color Blue

BY MARY A HAMBRIGHT

From the personality side it states about the color blue...

You are sensitive to the needs of others and caring with your close circle of friends. It is a symbol of depression, which is associated with trustworthiness and reliability. In a blog from Psychology Today, "...if blue is your favorite color you love harmony, you are reliable, sensitive and always make an effort to think of others. You like to keep things clean and tidy and feel that stability is the most important aspect in life."

I must completely agree with this information as I look back over my life, recalling the hurt, pain, suffering, lonely nights, and broken promises from relationships that I gave my all to. Does this sound familiar to you? This is the depression represented by the blue crayon. So many days I smiled and laughed, holding my outside physical self together, while on the inside I was melting down like a lit candle turning into hot wax.

Although I was broken like shattered glass, I never wanted anyone to see me as weak. I continued to smile, and I never disclosed what I was going through. I was military minded, no emotions, and no excuses. I knew I had to carry me, and be strong not only for myself, but for those around me, they would not see weakness and could easily confide and trust me.

My roots are from Alabama, that's where my family is from. From the time I was old enough to understand my roots, my heart will forever be "south". My mom's side is from Bessemer, AL and my dad's side is from Greensboro, AL. However, I am a product of Michigan, born May 15th, 1970. The foundation of our family is everything. Serving God, hospitality, love, support, integrity, and joy were all the things that family was built on. Helping one another in time of need.

You see when I was a young girl, about 6 or 7, at the impressionable stage of life, I watched how my mother took care of our home and my father as a wife. Being born in the '50's in the South, my mother's generation of women were quite different from my generation today. They were more submissive and did what it took to raise their families. My father worked in a factory, building cars for General Motors until the day he was killed on his motorcycle, on June 24, 1992. My mother would get up at the crack of dawn to assist my father with getting ready for work. She would make him a hot breakfast, fix his lunch, iron his jeans and shirts. At that early age in the 70's, I did not know exactly what he did. But as I got older, and found out what he did, (and what she did), I thought back to those childhood years; who needed ironed jeans to go into a filthy, oily car plant to get dirty? For my mom it was not about the type of work he did, it was her love and loyalty for him that made her do what she did for him. He always came home to a clean home, dinner hot out of the oven and nobody ate before him. It was not punishment of us as her children, it was the respect she had to him as the breadwinner and her husband.

As a young woman, I had my first relationship when I was twenty-two. I fell in love and we moved in together. We had a son, and I felt like I was on my way to having the kind of family I grew up in. I started doing all of those things I had watched my mother do over the years with my father; I did the cooking, cleaning, and ironing. I would even get up on Saturday mornings and hand wash his car. I was very loyal and waiting for him to love me in the same way. Every year for 6 years, I waited for a ring. hoping he would ask me to marry him. Instead of a ring, I got cheated on. My hopes of wedding vows were replaced with repeated broken promises. As a result of his actions, I spent a night in jail, with 2 years of probation and biweekly appointments with a psychologist for my behavioral issues. We finally broke up and we both moved on. I felt a piece of my heart had been removed and I would never love anyone else at that point.

It was some years later when I met someone I would give my heart to. I was returning home to Michigan from a motorcycle road trip that I took every May to Myrtle Beach, SC for bike week. I remember stopping to get gas and ran into a friend of the family. We chatted briefly. He introduced me to a guy that was with him, that I thought was very handsome. We exchanged hellos, and my friends and I departed. About a week later, I ran into that same family friend, which relayed to me, that the guy with him wanted to meet me. I was really excited, so I took his number and I called him the next day. We talked for hours on the phone; coincidentally, he lived in the same neighborhood as my mother. We became very acquainted and started spending a lot of time together. A few months later in August, he asked me to marry him, gave me the ring and in my mind, I was finally about to get the life I had yearned for in my heart, after all of those lonely years. It was extremely charming to find out he had asked my mom if he could marry me. My mom had approved of him, and we were now discussing our future.

Every day, I could not wait to get off work and spend the day with him. He was fun, and adventurous, everything was going great. A few months later, on Christmas Eve, things changed. He was at work, and I had the day off, so I decided to do some holiday cooking and decorating at his place, as well as some overdue housekeeping in his room. As he came in from work, I mistook the look in his eyes for excitement, instead it was pure rage. He proceeded to his room and retrieved his handgun, demanding to know why I was going through his belongings. I explained to him I was not, that I had only cleaned it. He then went into the kitchen and dumped all the food I was cooking down the drain. He unplugged the decorated Christmas tree and threw it across the floor as he started pulling all the decorations. I was so confused as he grabbed me, and we struggled to the floor. He pulled his gun and told me he was going to kill me. I went into survival mode. I remembered a movie I had seen where a lady was in danger, and she played on the psyche of her assailant. Instantly, I started telling him how I love him, he makes me so happy and we just needed to talk about it. I kept reassuring him that I should have asked to clean and decorate. His demeanor became calmer, and he let his guard down. Once I saw that he had let his guard down, I knocked his glasses off of his face

63

and I ran out the door. My older brother's girlfriend lived about a ¼ mile down the street. I did not know if he was there or not, my instinct and adrenaline had me running in the cold and snow, wearing only jogging pants, a thin tee shirt and socks on my feet. When I got there, I began beating on her door, angry, wet, and cold. I stood there crying, and still confused as my brother opened the door. My brother went and retrieved my things. I could not understand why all of it had happened.

I had so many unanswered questions, because of what had transpired. I started doing a little research on him and found out he was from another state. He left because he was on trial for attempted murder of his ex-wife, whom he had thrown out of a window. I also found out he had a daughter at the time. I believe she was about seven years of age. He lied about it in our early conversations, telling me he did not have children and had never been married. Needless to say, I felt betrayed, used, with another piece of my heart being removed.

I guess it is safe to say, I felt at this point there was not a need to have a relationship. I decided to casually date for a while. Then in 2005 I met the guy who would become my BFF. He was in the military and had started a motorcycle club overseas. We met over the phone through a mutual friend, and exchanged numbers, agreeing to talk later. When we finally talked, we discovered we were both headed to Raleigh Durham, NC for a motorcycle event. We met and had the best weekend ever and traveled back to Michigan together. Over time, I fell in love with him, with my whole heart. It felt like I had regained the broken pieces of my heart. I never had anyone who commanded my attention with his smile, his confidence, his persistence, social intelligence, and his intellect like he did. It was all on another level. He was extremely dependable. Whenever I needed him, he was right there, or he made sure someone got me what I needed. He would just call sometimes in very few words to ask, "You OK?" When we talked, he was full of laughs and I could just be myself with him. We had fun while we were together, doing what we both loved to do, riding motorcycles. If he talked trash to somebody, or vice versa, he knew I was always right there to back him up.

One day I realized although he had the BFF title, it would be the only title because he was not ready to settle down, and give me what I wanted, or needed. I knew we could not be in a real relationship, because he was that guy who demanded attention from women. He was smooth talking, a showoff in his own way and very mischievous. Funny thing is, everybody knew about us, but he always made me feel like his world was mine.

We eventually ventured into business together. In 2012, we joined an MLM, and I met someone who got my attention. The image was everything I imagined; he was not a cheater, he was fun, and his IQ was out of this world. We spent five years together, and I finally got a ring on my finger. We were planning our wedding on Aug 11th, 2018. I came home one day from work July 23, 2018, he had moved out. When I found this out, I never shed a tear. I was more confused, wanting answers. In my heart though, I was glad it was over. I just wanted to know why I was strung along for five years. Was it that he wasn't in love with me?

Was it that he did not want to be married? I just wanted to know. I had to admit that getting involved with this person, had not felt right from the very beginning.

November 19, 2018, I moved into my new home, and the guys broke a bulb while moving my furniture. The blessing of that broken bulb was revealed in an unexpected way. A mutual friend suggested I call an old acquaintance who had an electrician business. I had known him for 16 years, but we had lost contact with each other over the years. I called him to repair the wiring. From the moment I saw him climb the ladder, it stirred up old feelings. We started seeing each other regularly. We had conversations that I have never had with anyone and out of respect for us both, we did not rush into a relationship, but it turned into one. The relationship was tested along the way with infidelity and unreliability. When he would disappear without explanation, he returned to find me still there. As bad as I wanted to retaliate, my love for him wanted to understand why he was not satisfied with me.

We went away for a weekend, and later I found out he was texting a woman telling her he needed her, he loved her and wanted to be with her. This is where the blue crayon broke.

Depression set in because the one person that I thought loved me had managed to leave me heartbroken again. I felt like my world had been shattered. This man had captured my soul. I wondered if you could truly love someone after they have snatched your dignity. Does true love offer you only friendship without a romantic relationship? Is that true love? Does true love withhold parts of a person? Is it true love to settle for some love and not all of love?

I don't pretend to have the answers, but for the first time I am emotionally okay with having a friend without a relationship, because I know I deserve a man who will love all of me. A man who will love my flaws and let the world know that I am still the love of his life and all the woman he will ever need. I deserve a man who will be everything I need; he will not just offer some of himself and be okay with me settling while he continues to chip away at my heart. I am no longer confused or give anyone the power to leave me depressed. I will always be loyal, trustworthy, and reliable.

Did you know that according to the UCLA Department of Atmospheric and Oceanic Sciences; Blue is the hardest color to see as more light energy is required for a full response from blue-violet cones, compared to green or red. You are sensitive to the needs of others and caring with your close circle of friends.

Now I understand what it means to be sensitive to the needs of others. I love people past their pain and mine to let them know somewhere in life, somebody genuinely cares about them. When others feel no one else is there for them in the midst of their color blue, I show up to give them hope, praying that they will see me.

Same as crayons, color hearts have meaning too. The yellow heart is for friendship. I will now offer this first, knowing when to keep my distance and not let my feelings get prematurely involved. The red heart is for true and long-lasting love. I only have one red heart left.

I am still awaiting my knight in shining armor. A purple heart means physical attraction. I see this has gotten me in situations before, being attracted to the outer appearance, even though we should be attracted to those we want in a relationship. I will not let this lead my feelings. A green heart is for nature and St Patrick's Day. I will only pass those out, if someone is lost in the woods or on the holiday. The black heart emoji stands for sadness or a dark sense of humor. I never anticipate wearing or passing out Black hearts. They are the colors I have left.

In the Bible, blue spiritually signifies the healing power of God. It is mentioned nine times in reference to a gorgeous gem known as Sapphires! This is how I have reminded myself to see me in the mirror daily. I may have been broken, but I am healed, and I will forever leave myself open to love.

About Mary

Mary "The Mindset Mentor" Hambright, is the founder of B.O.L.D., Building Outstanding Ladies Daily, a mentoring group focused on young girls to millennials. Mary's deep passion for helping others heal mentally from circumstances which have affected their lives, inspired her to create the organization. As a Mindset Mentor, Mary is also committed to promoting financial literacy and assisting individuals in starting their credit journey to a better relationship with their money. Not stopping there, Mary connected with the SheEo District of Atlanta and was recently promoted to Director of New Members. Mary's natural leadership abilities made her a perfect fit for the organization, as she continues to help women disrupt the norm by changing their mindset as a graduate of ICU Coaching Academy, as a certified Life Coach, she is rising above mediocrity. She has co-authored a book "Broken Crayons Still Color" in the midst of it all, understanding that all things should have an order and cleanliness is next to godliness, Mary also is the founder and owner of "A Generation of 3 commercial cleaning service". Mary resides in Michigan, where she loves to spend time with her family and friends. Traveling the world every opportunity that she gets, amongst her other hobbies of riding her motorcycle and boating whenever the weather permits.

Chapter 8

The Brokenness is Necessary

BY OLYMPIA PRINGLE

I was a broken little girl-- confused, angry, hurt; my innocence stolen, I was full of shame, and guilt. I was a victim of identity theft addicted to pleasing others at the expense of self. I did not understand my worth and value, had low self-esteem, and was always looking for validation from others. Amid the fragility, there was a will and drive to succeed because failure was not an option. My identity became attached to what I could do instead of who I was meant and created to be. Because of the trauma, there was an internal dialogue of defeat. People would never know what was happening inside because from the outside all appeared perfect, but there was a war taking place.

The things I would say to myself were debilitating. If my thoughts had a play button, these are the things you would hear, "You are useless. You are not worth much. You are NOT enough. You do not have any value. No one will understand you. You do not have anything to offer. You are not good enough. You are not confident enough. You are not loud enough. You have low self-esteem. You are depressed. You are fat. You are too dark. You are not pretty. You are not articulate. You are not like that person or this person. No one has ever done this in your family. Do not rock the boat. Stay in the boat. Stay comfortable. Keep safe. Stay common. Stand, but do not fly. Fly, but do not soar."

"Death and life are in the power of the tongue…" (Proverbs 18:21, KJV)

While personally speaking death, others would speak life. Words are very powerful. What I believed about myself and what others would say was very different. They would say things like, "You truly are a blessing. You are so sweet. You are anointed. You are a great listener. You always provide the best insight and advice. You are so talented. Thank you for challenging me. Thank you for believing in me. Thank you for supporting me. Because of you, my life will never be the same. Thank you for never giving up on me. You are the best. You have accomplished a lot. Everyone loves you. I am jealous of you. You are amazing. Nothing seems to bother you. I admire you. You are so confident. You are so bold. You have it all together. Your future is bright. You have so much to offer. I want to be like you."

This was the constant war that I faced. I had an internal dialogue of defeat, self-doubt, fear, unbelief, shame, rejection, and self-hatred. On the other side, I had people giving me encouragement and praise. but my shield of defeat blocked me from receiving and believing what others spoke of me. I never had anyone say the negative things that I believed and would say about myself. All I could see is what happened to me. All I saw was the rejection, the molestation, and the rape. I was full of shame and guilt. I didn't feel lovable or good enough.

I never lacked for anything I needed or wanted, but what I longed for was to be loved and accepted. Yes, my parents loved me, but because of their own brokenness, they were not fully able to provide the love and acceptance that I longed for. I did everything I could to be accepted by others and looked for love in all the wrong places and found validation by success. Seeking validation from others and not from the one who created you, causes an ambition and drive that will leave you empty with a void that will never be filled.

How broken was I really? I became promiscuous at a young age. I was willing to accept toxic relationships, but thought I was in control because I viewed myself as powerful and having control, a "player." I entered a mentally, emotionally, and physically abusive relationship and after I broke it off, I became the side chick. But of course, my mindset was "he is with me more than you and calls me when he needs something." That is an excuse that broken women use to continue to be used and manipulated because of low self-esteem. That song by MoKenStef comes to mind: "He's mine, you may have had him once, but I have him all the time." Smh—so broken.

While in college I suffered from depression and suicidal thoughts. I did not love myself. I did not like myself. I rejected everything about myself. It was not until I met the best thing that ever happened to me that my life changed forever. October 1999, I had an encounter with the King of Kings, the Creator of the universe, the true and living God. That is when every empty place in me was filled. I felt a love that I never felt. I had a peace that surpassed understanding. I had joy even though none of my outside circumstances changed. I was free! **"...So, if the Son sets you free, you will be free indeed."** (John 8:36 NIV)

As I reflect on my brokenness, I thank God that I was brought up in church. I do not recall missing a Sunday or Wednesday night bible study. I was on the usher board. I sang in the choir and was involved in other church programs and events. I was part of our community drill team and gospel choir. I was always surrounded by people that encouraged and challenged me. I loved school and was very active. I took my studies seriously. I was a band geek. I held various leadership roles and was always pushed to stand out and not just sit in the back. Other people always recognized my leadership capabilities. I enjoyed being influential to my peers and others. People let me know how blessed they were by my gifts and talents. I thank God that He was always there. Now I clearly see that God was there even amid the rejection, rape, molestation, low self-esteem, depression, and suicidal thoughts. He says, **"...I will never leave thee, nor forsake thee."** (Hebrews 13:5 KJV) I know if it were not for His grace and mercy, I would have been destroyed and not just broken. He has given me beauty for ashes.

I would like to be able to say that once I made the commitment to be in a true relationship with the Father that life became a bed of roses, but please remember that roses have thorns. I was now on the most wanted list of the enemy and he used the person closest to me to keep me bound. That person was me.

The scripture says, **"... we wrestle not against flesh and blood, but against principalities and powers."** (Ephesians 6:12) My inner me became my worst enemy. I did not understand my worth and value. While the enemy used my past trauma, pain, insecurities, doubt, and unbelief as weapons against me, God, in His wisdom and power, used me to bless people despite the war raging on the inside. God allowed me to impact my peers and strangers through prayer, words of encouragement and starting a women's ministry while in college.

The battle would be very strong at times. I went through moments of overwhelming fear-- I was paralyzed to speak, think clearly, or even sleep at times. I would not wear bright colors because I did not want to stand out. I would not speak much because I felt stupid, believing I could not articulate or communicate clearly. I would hide in the back for photos. I dared not volunteer for leadership roles. I tried to dim my light, I tried to not take up space, but God continued to elevate me and use me to touch the lives of others. Ironically, I even held positions with incoming and new college students to help them to recognize and maximize their potential.

God has a sense of humor because I did not even recognize my own potential, but I would quickly see it in others and would correct them when they would speak negatively about themselves. I never quit pursuing my goals. I never quit encouraging people even when I was discouraged and even depressed. A lot of times it would be in those times that everyone would come to me for encouragement. It would be in my darkest moments that God would use me to be light to someone else. So, if you wonder if broken crayons still color? The answer is an emphatic yes!

One other lie I want to expose is, "I do not need anyone." I was guilty of the Miss Independent syndrome, "I am strong, and I can do it by myself." That mindset kept me in a very lonely place. I lived a very closed, isolated life, which always kept me in the mode to always be perceived as perfect, but I was so broken. I chose to accept the role as a strong and independent woman, so I did not make room for people to see my weaknesses or to help me when I knew I was falling apart. Without other people still coloring and seeing beyond my "perfection" complex, I would not be able to share my story. Each of our unique stories, aid in the forming of His-story. No one color is greater than another. Individually we have a purpose, and we need each other.

God used my brokenness to bring healing and strength to others. I have come to realize that my brokenness has never been about me, but it was for others. What the enemy meant for my evil God turned it around for my good. **"…all things work together for good to them that love God and are the called according to His purpose."** (Romans 8:28 KJV) I love the Lord and want His will above all things, so over the years, He has helped me to gain a new perspective of the details of my life. Only the creator of the masterpiece sees the true beauty in his creation and understands that there are no imperfections. To the craftsman, the imperfections are imperfectly perfect and add value.

God is the author and finisher of our faith. He already knows my ending from the beginning, but I must walk it out and trust that His ending for me is beautiful. It has taken years and is a continuous process to understand that I am enough. I am valuable. I am wonderfully and fearfully made. I have a purpose. I have a destiny. I am perfectly designed, nothing about me is a mistake. I am powerful. I am a difference-maker. I am a world changer. My light is meant to shine bright. I am meant to be here. I will not hold back. I must keep going. I cannot quit. My crayon must keep coloring and its color will make an impact because I am blessed to be a blessing. I am broken to bring color to the lives of those I am meant to impact. My brokenness will leave a legacy because I am determined to help others realize they still color too.

Exhortation

Broken is defined as shattered, damaged, or altered by or as if by breaking. Brokenness doesn't feel good. Brokenness does not look good. But brokenness is a necessary process that we all will go through and must go through. When you go through a season of brokenness, from it will flow a color that is richer and deeper than before. Brokenness is also not a one-time ordeal, you will be broken again, but hopefully, when you go through it again you understand that it is for a purpose.

When you are operating in your purpose, you do it often without even realizing it. A crayon will always color whether broken or whole because that is what it was created to do. God created us and He will do whatever it takes to get out of us, what He purposed to be on display for His glory. Jesus said, **"The thief's purpose is to steal, and kill and destroy. My purpose is to give them a rich and satisfying life."** (John 10:10 NLT) Jesus's body had to be broken for us to have access to the Father. Jesus took the little boy's lunch and blessed it and then broke it so that the multitudes could eat, and even after that, it was leftovers (ref John 6:1-13).

Brokenness is a necessary process, but it does not mean it is the end. Sometimes it will lead to your beginning. In the bible, it states, **"Though we experience every kind of pressure, we're not crushed. At times we don't know what to do, but quitting is not an option. We are persecuted by others, but God has not forsaken us. We may be knocked down, but not out."** (2 Corinthians 4:8-9 TPT)

God makes all things new. He is the Potter, and we are the clay. He specializes in restoration of broken lives; sometimes He may have to break it more so that He can smooth it out just right. It is all about perspective. You are still here, so you might as well purposefully and intentionally make and leave your mark. The impact of the mark is up to you. Go through it. Glow through it. Color through it!

Some truth and affirmations:

- A crayon will always color no matter if it's broken or not.
- You have always left a mark; now is the time to realize it.
- Color and make your mark on purpose.
- Be intentional!
- Believe in you, God does.

"He heals the brokenhearted and binds up their wounds."
(Psalm 147:3 ESV)

You have always shined, so keep on shining. You are a difference-maker. Your imperfections make you more valuable. Accept you, be you. The brokenness was never about you; it was for someone else. God knew what would destroy others would make you. The brokenness caused your true purpose to be revealed.

"Trust in the Lord with all your heart, and do not lean on your own understanding. In all your ways acknowledge him, and he will make straight your paths." (Proverbs 3:5-6 ESV)

My prayer for you is that you will come to know that you are loved, you are valued, you are special, you are important. You have a purpose and a destiny. You are not an accident, nothing about your life has been by happenstance. You are not forgotten. God knows your name. Everything that the enemy has meant for your bad, God can and will turn it around for your good. God has a plan for your life. I speak healing, peace, wholeness, and joy over you. You are a part of a bigger picture and only you can fulfill your part. Your color is needed. Father help them to see life from your vantage point and reassure them that You have been there all along. You are needed, my dear brother and sister. Be blessed and encouraged. Amen.

About Olympia

Combine the heart of a worshiper with the love of Christ, empowering grace, and a contagious spirit of freedom, and the result will be none other than Mrs. Olympia Pringle. It is with a faith-over-fear mentality that she moves forward in her God-ordained purpose of helping hurting individuals to become healed, delivered and abounding in freedom. Although she grew up in the church, it was an encounter with the Lord during her early college years that shifted Olympia from religion to authentic relationship. This experience served as the catalyst to her journey of healing and freedom. Since then, her mission has been to walk with others from brokenness to wholeness.

Olympia is both anointed to deliver the Word of God and equipped to lead others along the road to success. In addition to being an ordained minister, author and recording artists, she also has over 10 years of experience in higher education. Olympia Pringle earned a Bachelor of Science in Middle School Education from Murray State University followed by two Master's Degrees: first Guidance & Counseling and then Human Development and Leadership. Whether in ministry or academia, as a seasoned mentor or certified life coach, Olympia has a zeal for helping others to maximize their potential for their good and God's glory. It is with patience and keen discernment that she seeks to empower people to overcome past hurts and present chaos to walk in victory.

Olympia Pringle is the author of Embrace: Embrace the Pain of the Past, the Chaos of the Present, and the Uncertainty of the Future and the founder of Embrace Life Coaching. A native of Milan, Tennessee. she now resides in Clarksville, Tennessee with her husband, Willie. The Pringles are passionate about God and dedicated to using their gifts, talents, and skill sets to advance His kingdom.

Chapter 9

My Pain Became My Purpose

BY KEISHA MARIE SPENCER

Have you ever wanted to quit life? Have you wanted to throw your whole life away and everybody in it? Yeah, I know, it seems a bit extreme, but I was there. Now, let me tell you how I was led to feel that way, and how I have overcome it.

I will not call myself a survivor, but I am a conqueror. I have been broken many times, but able to put myself back together with the help of God and my own personal motivation. Depression had found a home within me. Everyone attached to me felt the negative presence of my spirit. My depression affected my job, my relationships, my weight, and my personal development. I had pretty much given up on life. I was the one that was functional daily, walking around with a fake smile, but broken on the inside, and cried out every chance I got.

Breaking Point

In 2017, I had reached my breaking point. I had come to a point where my marriage was failing, my health was not the best, and nothing seemed to matter. I wanted to quit life. The only thing was, I was too cowardly to take my own life. All areas in my life were complicated. I had been prescribed anti-depressants, anxiety pills, blood pressure medicine, and many other supplements to help balance my life. I gained more weight than my body was accustomed to bearing. I felt ugly and unworthy. Outside of work, I did not want to be bothered, nor did I want to affiliate with anyone else. I filled my days with duties to avoid my problems. My friends did not recognize me, because I had lost my bubbly personality. My finances were not in tip-top shape, yet I was still taking care of everyone around me. Honestly, I don't even know how I was managing.

Breaking Point

Although it is hard to see the end,
There comes a time when you must depend,
On Life itself and how it ends.
Although your mind is completely through,
The strength can always be renewed.
Just trust the process, and take it day by day,
You may have reached your breaking point, but you lived to see another day.

Marriage Chronicles

After 11 years of being in a relationship with the person whom I thought was my soulmate, everything had come to an end. However, the depression did not happen after the breakup. It began during the relationship. You know the old saying, "When a person shows you themself, you better believe them". Yeah, I failed. I ignored everything because I was just trying to force a situation that was not healthy.

Not to mention, I was in my second marriage. My first marriage was a huge mistake because I married for all the wrong reasons, and that caused me to marry a compulsive liar and cheater. I met him while I was pregnant with my first son and he came into my life during a difficult time. I was only attracted to the way my first husband treated my son and I, but he had no plans on being faithful and honest with me. I was 20 years old and trying to be grown. I had my first son at 19, so I was focused on making a home for him. That relationship did not even last two years. After being married for 6 months, it was over.

A year after we separated, I met my second, most recent husband. The goal was an eternity, especially after the epic failure of the first marriage. In my mind, he was my end game. We had a lovely relationship. We were both young and learning. The only thing is, I was already established, but he was not. That was not a problem for me because I saw the potential, and he was overall a good person.

The same year my first husband and I separated; my oldest son's biological father was killed. That broke my heart because my son lost two fathers in one year at the age of 2. When my most recent husband and I started dating, we both had a son, and everyone blended perfectly. He has always been a wonderful father to my oldest son, and the two children we now have together. However, he was not always the best mate in terms of supporting me. For years we struggled financially, as a result of his inconsistency. That led to me carrying a lot of the load. I found myself taking care of a grown individual. On top of that, I had very demanding jobs. I went from managing retail stores to teaching. Both fields required my full attention as well as emotional attachments to my job responsibilities.

I thought I would at least find peace within my home, but it was far from peaceful. There was no structure, nor balance. I dressed it up for outsiders because everyone adored our relationship. We were together 7 years before we got married, and I honestly thought getting married would motivate my significant other to do right by his family. Unfortunately, the old saying, persevered. Things were good one minute, then things would fall off. His inconsistency formulated a pattern. We operated for years using one car, one phone, one income and it does not take a rocket scientist to figure out who those things belonged to.

I never experienced physical or mental disrespect from him because he was not that type of person, at least not with me. However, he did become dependent. That weighed heavily on me. He was taking my generosity and compassionate nature for granted. I found myself in a busload of debt, leading to bankruptcy because "I was robbing Peter to pay Paul".

I could not do what I wanted to do for myself. All the sacrifices I made were for my kids. My friends became upset because I would always say how I could not do certain things because my finances would not allow it, when I was making the money, just was not reaping the benefits because everything fell on me. I went through a year of hell during our marriage due to hormonal issues that led to me having a hysterectomy. My husband was not supportive during that time, in fact, I felt that he distanced himself from me. Our sex life became rocky after that. Partially, because I was not mentally or physically in a space to feel sexual. He used that against me and made me feel like us not having a romantic relationship was my fault. However, he was not trying to do anything to support my healing process. Nor did he make it a priority to date and romance me. I felt like I began to beg my husband to think of me in a special way, as I did for him. His excuse would always be, "You know my money is not right, and I do not want you always paying for everything." This was true because, the majority of the time, our dates were on me.

He was fine just sitting in the house doing nothing. Wow! That is crazy, now that I think about it. A year and a half before we separated, my husband had an accident in my truck. Until this day, I am being affected by that incident financially. However, after that blow, our relationship took a major shift. Things went from bad to worse. We argued about everything even to the extent where it happened in front of the kids. I became terribly ill in my body and vomited daily for about 4 months. Doctors said it was stress causing my acid reflux to flare. I wanted out but could not pull myself to leave. I did not want to give up. I was committed to my vows, but I was miserable. God knew that my husband had done so much to me throughout the years that I had forgiven him for, and the only thing I was holding on to is the fact that he had not been unfaithful or abusive.

At that point, I did not want to be a wife, a mother, a daughter, an employee, or a friend anymore. I was done. In December of 2017, I surrendered my will to God. God said, "That's all I wanted from you, my child, was to surrender your will."

In March of 2018, I discovered my husband had been unfaithful, and I was given permission by God to leave and restore my life. Since that time, I have been walking in my purpose.

Untitled

Sometimes we hold on to things that are not meant to be kept.
But were placed in our lives for a season.
No matter what the assignment was, you know there was a reason.

Never get so caught up in making others more of a priority than yourself,
Because at the end of the day, you are all you have that is left.
When all is done, look high to the sky,
Ask God to restore, for you shall live and not die!

The Lesson

In general, people assume their current situation is triggering their emotions; however, it is deeper than that. Once I realized that I began to heal.

From childhood, I had a life of confusion and contradictions. Although I had a family, felt isolated. My actions were overlooked, and my body had been violated. It was if everyone lived in a world of their own. I did not have a great representation of how a man is supposed to treat a woman. My father was active for the first few years of my life and then he disappeared. He left behind my mom, my oldest brother, and myself. My mother, the woman I adored, seemed so strong, but so helpless when it came to men. From that time, I witnessed my mom being involved with men that did not treat her well. I also witnessed my older brother fall into the same cycle as the men my mom had dated.

I maintained a toxic long-distance relationship with my father. He had a pattern of jumping in and out of my life. As I got older, the tales of my father's behavior began to surface. He battled alcohol and drug addiction. As a revelation, I realized that my relationships were an extension of everything I was trying to avoid.

I have never suffered from domestic violence, and I owe that to a strong sense of discernment, after witnessing that behavior with loved ones. Not every wound is physical. I allowed myself to be taken advantage of in other ways. If you do not deal with the things that hurt you to your core, they create a disease you can't recover from. When I finally submitted to God, is when I began to heal. That is when I became mature enough to handle the harsh reality of my past and began the process of forgiveness. I am not my pain, but I am my purpose.

My Present

After 2 years of rebuilding, I am now a single mom, but my children are not lacking for anything. I have invested in myself. My bounce back body is amazing, my health is in excellent shape, and my mental stability is intact. I have become a Certified Life Coach to motivate and educate others on creating a healthy balance, sustaining emotional stability, discovering their gifts, walking in, and profiting from their purpose.

The goal is for everyone I touch to grow mentally, physically, spiritually, and financially through submitting, healing, investing in self, all while accepting accountability to move forward. I have founded a non-profit organization that provides mentorship to high school seniors, in order to reach them at a pivotal season in their life to provide direction and resources for success. I also have a program for mental health and social-emotional awareness, where the goal is striving to restore, influence, and vamp emotions to get to a place of peace and purpose. As I continue my journey in life, my goal is to maintain my freedom of peace and completely fulfill my purpose, while helping others along the way.

From Pain to Purpose

And it hit me, back-to-back, from a child to an adult.
Were my feelings valid, was I overlooked?
How could the people I love hurt me the most?
I would have been content with being a ghost.
My life did not seem to have a meaning,
but self-doubt and pity are only the beginning.
The power of forgiveness is always tough, and you cannot restore it until
you have had enough.
Everything you go through does not have to be in vain.
Although it has caused you a lifetime of pain.
Broken crayons still color, not one trial is greater than the other.
Face your pain and rise to a healthy surface.
For your pain can very well become your purpose.

– Keisha Marie Spencer

About Keisha

Keisha Spencer, also known as Coach K. Marie, is a local citizen of Memphis, Tn where she was born and raised. She is the proud mother of 4 beautiful children and take pride in parenting. Keisha has devoted years to training minds, nurturing gifts, and making people feel good about themselves throughout the years in her profession as a manager, educator, and personal stylist. She learned about coaching when she hit a roadblock in her own life and was struggling to move past it. The techniques she developed were so successful that friends and family began asking me for help with their own challenges. This motivated her to turn her passion into a full-time career.

She became a Certified Life Coach in the spring of 2019 after healing and changing her mindset. She also became a wellness advisor in February 2020. Those two areas in her life became very pivotal to her purpose. From that time, she has launched her thriving business "Fit for a Purpose Nonprofit Organization" which was designed to help nurture the minds of young adults transitioning into adulthood and also raise awareness of the social-emotional and mental health illness, as a result of anxiety and depression, or simply an overload in the mind. She is also a Senior Director in a Women's Empowerment Organization known as the SheEO District. She is definitely a woman of multiple layers, unraveling piece by piece as she aspires to help others unravel their gifts, connect with their inner peace, and completely walk in their purpose. Keisha aspires to grow her business, "A Better Me by K. Marie", as an established Professional Life Coach, known for her captivating spirit, passion for purpose, and desire to change lives.

Chapter 10

Dim Stars

BY LORI MIER

I used to believe that the greatest experience of loss in my life had been written in the stars, forming the pattern for my life, both the dim stars and the bright ones.

I believed that my constellation was pre-designed and scattered across the night sky like cosmic glitter long before I was born out of the stardust that birthed me. That belief is what allowed me to cling to the awe in my story and begin to find my healing path.

I was never suicidal, but I daydreamed a lot about my own funeral as an adolescent and young adult. Who might show up and what powerful stories about my life might they tell?

My parents' lives were cut short at an early age, they were 20 years old, and 23 years old at the time. I was a three-year-old toddler when I lost them. I have kept the newspaper clipping in a folder, inside a box, all these years. The headline reads:

"Pickup Plunge is Fatal: Parents Die, Tots Survive."

I survived, with my sister, overnight, alone in the rugged mountains of Oregon. That became the defining moment of my life, at least for me for so many years and into my adult life. What about surviving the rest of my life? And what about living it?

I wasn't at my parents' funeral, and no one came to the slew of funerals I had for myself over the years, either. What I mean by that is no one showed up to assist me in how to grieve after they died. People physically showed up, but the invitation to grieve was left at the door, thrown out the window, or just never extended from adult to child. It is my assumption now that they knew little about grieving their own losses, so how could they help me.

Back then I had no control over who stayed in my life and who did not, and the grief that was mine was secretive and misplaced. It was secretive because no one asked, and because I was three years old. And still, in the years that followed, no one asked, and I felt that I should not talk about it. And even when I decided to tell my story I ended up feeling worse because what I saw in the faces of those who I told, was either shocked that I survived or momentary awe of my strength. What they saw in me had little to do with what I was going through and who I was in that moment, someone seeking depth and love and friendship, someone seeking connection. If I am completely honest, when I first began telling my story I mostly told it so that others would see me, and I would be noticed. I longed for anyone that would help me begin to witness first and then bury that loss or any of the losses that came before or after the fatal accident so that there might be something left about me that was good to know.

I wanted a witness to and to bury the times that I was locked in stairwell attics and thrown into walls. To bury the image of me as a "terror" in my early grades and classrooms. I wished for just one person to recognize how intense the ending of that physical abuse was when it had stopped, as I entered middle school, and I turned inward and began pulling my hair out (known as Trichotillomania) and talking to a star each night that I associated with my lost mother and father. The beginnings and endings of these significant things I had lived held so much weight and I knew little of grieving them. When I had difficulty with friendships, I misplaced the loneliness with hair pulling and later alcohol. When I became a woman, I kept it a secret and I was unable to grieve, honor it, or to feel joy about it.

When I had sex for the first time, I kept that a secret too. When I was raped, I told myself I did this to myself. And when I heard the story of my molestation, which I was too young to recall, or that I lived in a car for a period of time before they had died, or the numerous other stories of family trauma, I had no idea how to digest it all and so they just became facts in my story that I carried somewhere inside of me knowing that they hurt but that they were not accessible. The stories of molestation, rape, abuse, alcoholism, and denial throughout generations were nothing more than facts I was to know and live with as opposed to things I could heal, or we could heal. The few times when I was approached with conversations that were of some depth and understanding of my adult mistakes and healing it was too late to feel anything except that it was solely my responsibility to rise above and be independent in my own healing and happiness. No one else has the power to make us happy, and we need to own our choices is what I had always taken away. I did that; I owned them and became a somewhat responsible adult. I took myself to therapy. I quickly chose my life over alcohol. I bought into the idea that no one was to blame for my mistakes but me. And on a surface level I blamed no one. I forgave. I understood that trauma repeats itself when it is not healed, and I had empathy.

What I still held onto, however, was that I had once been a child that needed to grieve. I had once been a child who witnessed grief on a large scale that unfolded in unhealthy ways by the adults in my life. They were heroes to me because they showed up in physical form and did the best that they knew how in the given circumstances. My pain is my own but what I have allowed myself is a chance to grieve what could have been-- someone offering my child self a chance at feeling seen and loved deeply.

What I needed was to bury first ceremonially and emotionally, the death of my parents, and second the other hard things that came up, with a supportive hand on my back. Maybe most of us experience some or all of childhood and adolescence this way. Maybe there are very few who have not a clue about what I mean because there were those adults who were both present and supportive in their lives. I am not special in my pain or my healing, but I have known that I am the owner of my story for a very long time. It is what I have seen as the innate wisdom in myself since I was a child. This wisdom is what allowed me to talk to the star, as a way to grieve and connect with my parents when I was a lonely child.

It allowed me to join AmeriCorps and travel alone to India. It allowed me to give up alcohol for good after only a couple of years of heading down a path I knew I did not want to be on. It is what took me back to school as an older student and for the very first time, graduate with honors. So, I learned that the greatest loss of my life, at such a young age, is part of my story, but-- it is not the whole story. I believe that people who see me now know that there is more to me than that day my family's pickup plunged off a ridgetop road in Oregon. I had to find a way to grieve all of the years that I felt like I was nothing other than my family's story on that horrible day; that I did not have to lose them to become the person that I am today, so my path to healing brokenness began here:

Wonderment interrupted dread

A story that reassured my meaning of what had happened to me took place less than two weeks before the fatal accident. With all the money she had, my mother drove across the country to return home to Illinois with my baby brother so that her side of the family could meet him for the first time. During this visit my mother asked her older sister some version of this...

"If something ever happens to me, please promise me that you will take care of my children. Okay?" My Aunt promised that she would.

Less than two weeks later my Aunt was in Oregon and quietly put us on a plane while everyone else talked about who and where we would go to.

This exchange had solidified my predestination. This story was haunting and powerful. My mothers were not particularly close in their large family. Perhaps she intuitively felt that their deaths were shortly upon them. I questioned many things last year when I opened myself up to more. Was this fatal accident on purpose? I quickly decided that I did not need to go down that path of thinking.

When I returned to Oregon in August of 2020 to reunite with rescue workers, my father's family, and my parents at their resting place, I understood why I became so at home surrounded by the Appalachian Mountains of Virginia, where I had moved to in my late 20's. They closely resemble the landscape of my first years and the place in the mountains where I survived, and my parents did not. This was a pivotal connection in my cluster. I realized just prior to this reunion, that when I was 11 years old and talking to a star, I had begun my healing journey without recognizing fully that I was beginning a lifelong path of reconnecting and healing. This brought me full circle 28 years later.

Once, my only narrative was that I was in awe of my story, it was a miracle I was alive, people involved were heroes, it was meant to be, and I survived because I was meant to be significant in some way. Over time and experience, however, I moved away from 'it was meant to be' and 'everything happens for a reason' thinking (my constellation was pre-designed) into 'it was tragic' and 'I create my own meaning' thinking which also brought on some periods of depression and unhealthy choices. In the last few years, I have danced around and in between these two rationales for my life, deciding that there is the possibility of truth in both.

What I lean into is this: I have purpose and set before me by a higher power are fragments of choices that could lead me to the best possible outcomes for living that purpose. As I exist, I create my meaning. As I exist, I attract others that align with how I want to live and vice versa. The higher powers have shown me the stars, but it is I who must decide, every day, how to cluster them to create related things and meaning to reach that purpose. There is now a deep need to look at the question of how I got arrived at this point, because my intention sometimes proves to be the opposite of my ideal self; in other words, it is self-centering. I can no longer fail to acknowledge that I have been given an unearned opportunity to become that "responsible" adult, searching for depth and meaning. I look back at my days in AmeriCorps, my trip to India, and the social work degree, realizing that those were all attempts to connect and become someone who inspired others. I had to design those powerful stories that would be told at my imagined funerals. I had too much ego and I see now that it was saviorism. Sometimes I get it right. In fact, I think each year that pass I get it a little more right. By right, I mean seeing what I have been blind to and getting closer to living with purpose that is not only about myself but about all of us. Our systematic macrocosm was not created for this, but I believe that we are. So now I dig deeper to heal so that I can get it right more often. This takes a lot of honesty that frankly I lacked for many years of my life and I have only just admitted this in the last two years.

There is a part of me that still holds on to the heroism in my story and I will always hold on to wonderment and awe. I am both in the stars and planted firmly on the ground these days. The years of self-doubt, self-sabotage and saviorism have taught me that it was time that I was honest with myself and others. There is no direct way to heal the heavy, difficult stuff inside of me and I must make a daily choice to no longer ignore it or replace it with what I described above. It is not a magical transition I have made; it is a work in progress. I must choose every morning when I wake up, and sometimes, I still get it wrong, but I am doing the work because I have believed for my entire life that brokenness is not an end, that the dim stars in my life clusters (made dim by others, by circumstance, or by my own doing) still shine and I can still return to them to make them brighter. This returning repeatedly led me to write this chapter in this book, as well as publishing my first children's book about that very star I talked to as a child. It has me in community for the first time, with people who choose to be in my cluster. Mutually, we teach one another how to turn our dim stars brighter. It is what led me to begin creating my own art, my own business, reimagining my marriage, becoming a more present mother, using my own voice, and living daily an anti-racism plan. We are all on a healing path, unique to our own clusters of stars. My story on that mountain in Oregon is unique but not because I was pre-made as more worthy of an inspirational and purposeful life but because of what I have chosen to do every day with my life since it happened, returned again and again to the dim stars to find ways to get them to shine brighter, so that I can be a better person.

I do not know if I know how to teach that; I think that it is seen and that is enough. What I can leave you with is the idea that I am healed is nonexistent for me because my healing will never be final; I will always need to grieve, mend, adjust, listen, and choose honesty about who I am in this world. I will always need to grow because I am human. If I know this, I will strive to seek learning from those that also know this and those who do not yet know this. Crayons will always break. Dim stars will always be a part of life clusters. I am made strong by my daily choices, the belief in my own innate wisdom and the capability to challenge the nonsense that we were created a certain way and we cannot change that.

I no longer wish to heal at another's expense, and so I choose to try not to. Maybe those before me did not or still do not know how to heal, but they can always choose to revisit their dim stars over and over in an attempt to make them brighter. When I choose this, I find a more authentic path, a community, and a less self- centering purpose. Dim stars or broken crayons, one still shines, one still colors. You can always return to them. I will keep returning to mine because that is what I do. Let us witness and support the need for our children to grieve and keep returning.

About Lori

Lori is the creator and owner of her story. She also loves Chai Tea.

Broken Crayons Still Color: Life After is the first book by Author, Lori Mier. She is also the author of Merin and Her Very Bright Star: A story of resiliency, a children's book that was deeply inspired by Lori's own story of loss and healing. She has a degree in Social Work and currently works independently as an Ecotherapist Guide, Life Coach, and nature photographer, combining all three to offer a unique and healing experience. Her healing nature photography has been published on the cover of AT Journeys magazine as well as travel brochures. Lori lives in the Shenandoah Valley in Virginia with her husband and son, and with her husband, created the not-for-profit program, Through Hiking, for young adult foster youth and agencies. Under the leadership of black women, Lori is daily trying to engage civically and passionately to do what she can to dismantle systemic racism. www.linktr.ee/Lori_mier_author

Chapter 11

Surviving the Quiet Storm

BY NICHOLE CHOATE

September 2014- November 2014

I woke up in the middle of the night with a horrible pain in my left breast. It felt like a burning and throbbing sensation. I could also feel swollen lymph nodes under my left arm that were painful to the touch. I also noticed a protruding area underneath my collar bone on the left side that was not really painful but very noticeable. After thinking more about it, I decided to go ahead and go to work thinking that maybe I had slept wrong or the deodorant I use was irritating me. Later on, that afternoon due to the unbearable pain I left work early and headed to Grant Medical Center Emergency Room.

After hours of x-rays, testing, examinations, blood work, and tons of questions by the nurses and doctors, I was discharged and referred to a breast specialist. The ER Dr had discharged me stating that he could not find a specific reason why I was hurting and after performing a breast exam could not feel any kind of lumps that would be causing the pain. He also examined the protruding area underneath my collar bone and stated that he thought it may be a swollen gland and maybe I had some kind of infection. The next day I scheduled an appointment with the breast specialist that was referred by the ER Dr and was able to be seen soon thereafter.

During my visit, several exams were performed including a mammogram, as well as a breast exam including the area under my arm and beneath my collar bone. I gave all of my health information including family history of cancer and advised that my family on my father's side was prominent for cancer. My grandmother passed away from cancer at the young age of 38, my aunt Doris was diagnosed with breast cancer at the age of 49 in 2000; my father, grandfather, and uncle were all diagnosed with prostate cancer and several first and second cousins were battling breast cancer.

After my initial examination and negative result from the mammogram screening the breast specialist told me that she thought maybe I had nicked myself under my arm while shaving. She could not explain the pain I was experiencing in my breast or the protruding area underneath my collar bone. I was prescribed an antibiotic for 30 days and was given a follow up appointment date to check my progress.

Later, I was seen for my follow up appointment. The pain in my breast and under my arm was still there and still as bad, if not worse than the previous appointment. The protruding area beneath my collar bone was still present. During the appointment I was scheduled for an ultrasound of my left breast and underarm and given another prescription of antibiotics. I was told that they did not know what else could be going on. I was then referred to my primary care physician for a follow up.

I went in for my follow up appointment with my primary care physician. By that time, I was extremely frustrated and upset. I was confused that 2 months after feeling this pain, no diagnosis had been given, only antibiotics, a lot of testing. I had missed work, and doctor bills that were starting to rack up. My primary care physician ordered an ultrasound which I had already had and another mammogram. I told her what the ER doctor and breast specialist had told me and that I had been on antibiotics twice for 30 days each. Once my mammogram and ultrasounds both came back negative, I was prescribed a 3rd round of antibiotics and was told that maybe the infection had gotten so bad that another dose was needed. I started the antibiotics and after the 2nd week of taking them, I knew that whatever it was that was causing my symptoms was not being cured by the medicine I had been prescribed three times in a row. By this time, it was late November and I still did not have any relief from my pain or diagnosis as to what was going on.

December 2014

My mother who had been very worried and concerned about the fact that I was unable to get a clear answer on what was going on referred me to Dr. Sickle-Santinello's office for a 4th opinion. I scheduled an appointment for December 3, 2014. During my visit I discussed with my Nurse Practitioner everything that had happened, starting at the beginning in September. I advised her and provided documentation of my previous appointments, testing, examinations, etc. I was overwhelmed with emotions and terrified because deep down inside I knew that there was something horrible brewing.

After reading all of the information I had given her and talking to me about my family history, my nurse practitioner examined my breast, under my arm and underneath my collarbone. She also did an ultrasound to see if she could see anything. She looked at me and said due to the pain you are experiencing, the lymph nodes being swollen and the area underneath your collar bone, I am going to be honest with you and say that I feel we need to do a biopsy. Now I had never had one done, but I heard from other people that they were pretty painful, but I wanted to find out what was going on, so I agreed. After signing some paperwork, she performed the biopsy right in the office. (I definitely have to say it was very painful, little did I know this would be 1 of 5 biopsies that I would have before there would be a solid diagnosis). I was told that the test would take a few days to come back but that she would rush it. On December 5th I received a phone call and was advised that the tests had come back, and they requested me to come into the office on Monday Dec 8th to discuss the results. I was literally terrified.

On December 8, 2014, I was diagnosed with Stage III Breast Cancer, Lymph-node exposure and the BRCA2 gene. (BRCA2:

A gene that normally acts to restrain the growth of cells in the breast and ovary but which, when mutated, may predispose to breast cancer and to ovarian cancer. BRCA2 mutations have also been discovered to be responsible for a significant fraction of early-onset prostate cancer.

The first breast cancer genes identified were BRCA1 and BRCA2. Mutations of BRCA1 and BRCA2 account for about half of all cases of inherited breast cancer. These tumors tend to occur in young women. BRCA1 and BRCA2 are usually not involved in breast cancer that is not hereditary).

Fear and anger ran through my body like ice cold water. My head began to hurt, and my body felt numb. I did not understand what was going on and as my health care provider was talking, her voice started to trail off as if she were fading away. "*This has to be a dream*", I thought, but as I slowly came back to reality, I realized that it was not a dream; it was in fact a nightmare that was going to play out for a long time. The last thing I heard clearly was, "We need to get you to an Oncologist and start treatment as soon as possible".

At first, I did not know whether I was coming or going. As my doctors were still trying to piece everything together, what was known for sure was that I had a small tumor in the nipple of my left breast and several painful & swollen lymph nodes under my left arm and collar bone. With that information in hand, chemotherapy had to be aggressive and start immediately.

January 2015-July 2015

In January 2015 I began the 1st of what would be sixteen rounds of chemotherapy that would end in July 2015. While my body began to go through physical changes from the treatments, I also went through severe mental and emotional changes as well. The chemotherapy was harsh, and very hard on my body. I was so sick and there were days I was unable to get out of bed. The pain was unbearable at times with everything hurting from my head to my toes. I was very nauseous, and vomiting was an ongoing thing. My energy level was a -0 at all times making it hard for me to do my normal activities and take care of my children. I can say it literally felt like I was in hell, although I do not know what hell feels like; I imagine it was what I was going through.

My doctors had already warned me about the side effects of chemotherapy. Hair, eyebrows, eyelashes, etc. would begin to fall out. So, I knew it was going to happen and I tried to get myself mentally and physically ready. I went ahead and cut my hair short so that when it fell out, or so I thought, it would not have a huge effect on me. Boy was I wrong. At about the fourth week of chemo my hair began coming out as a light shedding when I brushed, combed, or ran my fingers through it. Next it would start coming out just by a slight tug, when I took my headscarf off, or when I washed it. Then it began to come out in handfuls and patches. Ultimately, I would have my significant other shave it off. It was such a traumatic feeling.

I felt as if my world was falling apart. I could not come to grips with how I was going to live without having any hair. And to make matters worse my eyebrows and eyelashes had begun to vanish as well. I began to sink deep into depression and wanted to hide from the world. I can remember my significant other and my mother telling me "It's just hair", "It will grow back". But at that time and moment I could not see past the loss of my hair. I felt that no one could understand what I was going through if they had not gone through it themselves.

My hair, to me, or so I thought at the time, was what made me a woman and I felt as if I had lost a part of my soul. I felt ugly and wanted to hide from the world.

For those who have never been through chemo or know anyone who has, it is a life changer. No one goes through it the same and it does not affect everyone the same. For me it was severe. With each chemo treatment I began to feel worse and worse. My body felt as if it was breaking down on me and mental trauma was just as bad. The nerves in my body became agitated and I ached all over. Sometimes the aching was so severe the pain would keep me up all through the night. I had a hard time walking or getting up from a sitting position and it was almost impossible to do any kind of housework no matter how light it was. I became very frustrated at times because I felt so bad it started to interfere with my day to day living. With 3 children, a significant other, a job and a dog, I felt helpless that I could not be the woman of my home and take care of my responsibilities. I felt as if there was no end in sight. My days seemed to be long and my nights even longer. I was on disability from my job from January to May during the harshest chemotherapy and once I started the lighter doses, I was able to go back part time while having my treatments once a week. Though they were still bad, they were not as bad as the first doses.

I completed my sixteenth dose of chemotherapy in July of 2015. It would take several months for the medication to fully exit my system and I would finally get some relief from the side effects. On July 30th I had the first of several surgeries. This one would remove my left breast and thirteen lymph nodes. My surgery was a success, and I went home after my second day in the hospital with two drain tubes, bandages, and an overwhelming feeling of incompleteness. I could not look at myself in the mirror for several weeks without my surgical bra and again became depressed. I cannot describe the feeling except to say I felt that everything I thought made me a woman was being taken away from me. Even though I had made it through the roughest part of my illness, I could not help wondering why me. I hurt all over. My left arm was very sore and had limited mobility.

Ultimately, I was diagnosed with Lymphedema, swelling that generally occurs in one of your arms or legs. Sometimes both arms and both legs swell. Lymphedema is most commonly caused by the removal of, or damage to your lymph nodes as a part of cancer treatment. It results from a blockage in your lymphatic system, which is part of your immune system. The blockage prevents lymph fluid from draining well, and the fluid buildup leads to swelling. Because there is not a cure for Lymphedema, I began therapy three times a week to help reduce the symptoms and give me some relief with swelling and pain.

July 2015-August 2020

I have spent the last several years recuperating from chemo, more surgeries, many, many procedures, and tests, and undergoing therapy for my arm. Living in constant pain has become an everyday thing for me now and it doesn't look like it's going to let up any time soon, if ever. I think the main things that have kept me going are my children. Fighting for them is what motivates me to never give up though there are some days I truly want to throw in the towel, I cannot. I have to live for them.

During this journey I have been through so many emotions. It has been such a mental struggle to stay positive and keep moving. There were days when I felt so lonely, there were many people who said they would be there for support but in time they drifted away. My significant other was there by my side to go through every step; so many days I questioned whether he would stay or not. I felt ugly, and less of a woman. Especially after my surgery to have my left breast removed. I asked "How could a man stay in love with a woman who has been through so many changes?

The emotional stress was sometimes so unbearable that I would just sleep through the days.

With the support of my family, friends, significant other, medical team, and other cancer survivors I was determined to live and make it through this storm. My mother had instilled the belief that God will not put more on me than I could bear and though in the beginning I questioned it, I realized that it was true. I was given this battle to fight for a reason. There were so many days when I did not want to go to treatment. So many days when I just wanted to say, "I am done", but I knew that giving up was not an option. Even though it would have been easier, I knew that once I made it through, I would be stronger than ever. That saying, "what doesn't kill you will make you stronger", is the truth.

This has been one of the toughest fights I have ever had to endure. I've experience mental, physical, and emotional strain from the beginning, and continue to battle these issues daily. The treatments broke me from head to toe and I can truly say it was the worst experience of my life. I didn't know what it meant to be stripped down to nothing or broken down to the bone until this journey. Although the road has been rough, I survived the storm of my life with GOD, the love and support of my family, friends, medical staff, and other cancer survivors.

I learned that in order to stay strong and fight as hard as I could I had to find a way to stay positive. The negative thoughts are what puts doubt and stress on you, which causes your body to work against you. Keep those negative people away, keep those negative thoughts away. No matter how hard it gets, stay positive and fight! People will say all the time "I know what you are going through" or "I know your pain". But unless they themselves are going through it, they really don't.

The word cancer is a very scary word, and the first thought of the word is "death." The reality is cancer is NOT always a death sentence. I am living proof that you can beat the odds against you. *I am a survivor by nature.*

About Nichole

Nichole Choate is a Cancer Survivor, who beat the odds and won the fight against Breast Cancer. Nichole was diagnosed with Stage 3 Breast Cancer with Lymph Node Involvement and carried the BRACA gene in December 2014. She is a Mother of 3 amazing children and has worked for the City of Columbus for the past 10 years and is a Certified OH State Notary. While fighting cancer she decided she wanted to be a voice for other women with this deadly disease and started to journal her journey. Nichole has wanted to be an author all her adult life but never could seem to settle enough to start writing until her illness. She has a passion for helping people and believes someone can benefit from her journey. Her desire to build, motivate and help those struggling with coping, fighting, and living with Breast Cancer, has inspired her to enroll and study to be a certified life coach. In her spare time, she loves to spend quality time with her children, family and has a passion for motorcycles "YES she rides" and loves to sing, read, and watch horror movies.

Chapter 12

God's Not Done with Me Yet

BY CHETARA BRISBON

As a child, I struggled with depression, which followed me into my adult life. I can remember the numerous times I fought internal battles of believing I was not good enough or not pretty enough. I felt unworthy of love, alone in a world surrounded by people who were loved. Multiple suicide attempts led to psychiatric stays in the hospital and long therapy sessions followed by bottles of pills to suppress the hurt. This is not meant to be a sad story, rather a story of encouragement and overcoming life's obstacles.

I remember when I was 10 years old, lying in bed with a knife under the mattress, waiting to slit my throat at any given moment. I had my suicide note written next to it, so if anyone found it, they would know why I no longer wanted to live. I would down bottles of pain pills at one time to make my heart stop beating, only to have my stomach pumped at the hospital. One night, I decided enough was enough and I wanted to end it all. I wrote my suicide note, explaining that no one loved me, and I would not be missed. I wanted to be cremated so no one could see how ugly I was. Voices in my head kept telling me to just stab my chest like they do in the movies. The knife under my bed was used to slice the meat, so I knew that it was sharp enough. Tears rolled down my face as I wrote. My hands shook and my stomach turned. I put the knife to my chest with the sharp end right above my left breast. I pushed the knife in and felt the sting. The pain began to be too much, and I dropped the knife. Thoughts raced through my mind that there had to be an easier, less painful way to die. I just knew that I did not want to live anymore.

Growing up, many of us were told to repress feelings and keep things that happened in the house to ourselves. Talking about mental health was not only exhausting but there was a stigma surrounding people that struggled with depression. Therapy sessions triggered events that led to suicide attempts but never really focused on the root of the problem. I turned to God to beg for healing. I was not overly religious, but you could say I was spiritual. I had a relationship with God, prayed daily, and went to church. When I felt myself falling into an episode, I would hurry and pray to shift my focus. It was a temporary fix, similar to just putting a band-aid over a deep cut. The wound was still bleeding and needed to be healed. Faith without work is dead. You can have all the faith in the world, but if you aren't actively working towards that goal or accomplishment, the situation will still remain the same. I realized I had to dig deep and really work for healing.

Digging Deep

In order to heal, I knew I had to dig deep and find the root cause. When I say deep, I mean DEEP! Why did I have so much hate for myself? Why was I so hard on myself? Why did I push people away? Wasn't I good enough or worthy enough? I pondered the thoughts over and over in my mind. I knew that my childhood was tainted and there were people that I still needed to forgive in order to overcome trauma.

I did not grow up with both parents, just my father and stepmother. My older brother and I were in foster care for four years (ages three and five). I rarely saw my mother, even after we went to live with our father. There was no relationship with her, other than the few encounters we had once or twice every few years. It was not until I was an adult that she wanted a mother-daughter relationship. Deep down I felt unwanted. The love from a mother is supposed to be pure and unconditional. The fact that I felt unwanted from my mother made me feel like I was not good enough. I hid that pain deep inside for years. For years, I took that hurt and pushed people away. It was the reason I was so hard on myself.

I remember my mother calling one day to pick us up for the weekend. Me and my brother excitingly packed our bags. We sat by the front door waiting for her to pull up. The day turned into night, still waiting, and no phone call to let us know what was going on. The disappointment set in and it was not until days later that she would call with an excuse as to why she did not come. This behavior became normal to the point that we just did not have high expectations anymore.

The Turning Point

Something in my life had to change. I felt myself going further into a dark hole and my life had been heavily affected. My friendships and relationships were short and anytime anyone became 'too close', I would push them away. I felt as though people were going to ultimately walk out of my life at any given time.

The turning point was not until after my daughter was born that I really found my 'why' in life. Although I was spiritual and prayed daily, there was still a piece of me that was not filled. In several dreams, she would appear with a blurred face. I knew it was a sign from God that he was not done with me yet. In June of 2015, I found out that I was pregnant. Pregnant?! I was filled with mixed emotions from being happy, to wondering what type of mother I would be, to questioning my worth. When I heard her first cry at birth, tears fell down my face as I lay on the operating table, waiting to get the first peek. I knew from that moment that I had something to live for. Life was no longer about me, but rather about caring for her.

I am not inferring that having a child is the answer, because I know it is a sensitive subject for many. My revelation came from within. I had to start with me and redefining who I was. It was an internal battle that initiated from childhood trauma that led me to believe that I was worthless and undeserving of love. I had to forgive others, as well as myself. I knew that I had to really forgive my mother for abandoning us. I had to be the mother that I needed her to be for me as I grew up. Holding on to past hurt burdened me with extra weight and baggage that transferred into the relationships I had with others. I distanced myself and always carried the notion that others would leave if they knew me (the person I incorrectly believed I was). Friendships were short for that reason and relationships usually ended after about three to six months. I also had to learn how to love myself in order to really love others. The old saying that states "you cannot love others if you do not love yourself" held true. I had to get around people that were aligned with greatness; people that gave positive energy.

I can truly say that today, my life has turned around. I am in a much better space mentally and every day I am reminded of my blessings. I no longer have thoughts of suicide or unworthiness. Every day I speak positive affirmations, along with a daily prayer. I keep my mind active to remain focused on positivity and productivity. It has been a journey full of ups and downs, but it has been one worth taking.

You Are Loved

So many people deal with depression and suicidal thoughts every day. Many are saddened by life's hurdles and would rather end their lives on their own terms. We all know at least one person who suffers from depression, anxiety, or even low self-worth or personal image. I am here to assure you and those that suffer, that if you stay the course and keep pushing, dig deep, and align yourself with greatness, your future will be bright. You are loved and you are worthy. God was not done with me, just like he is not done with you. He would not allow me to die when he knew my life was destined for greatness.

Deuteronomy 31:8 states, **"The Lord will be with you; he will never leave you or forsake you. Do not be afraid; do not be discouraged."** Even if you are not religious or spiritual, just know there is hope for you.

I hope my story inspires someone who is going through what I experienced for decades. Life is full of ups and downs and we must learn to ride the waves. There is hope in your situation and always remember that someone loves you. Your next blessing could be right over the obstacle(s) you are experiencing right now. I pray you keep pushing and never give up. God Bless!

About Chetara

Chetara Brisbon is a financial coach and business education coach who enjoys teaching and motivating others to reach their full potential. She uses her experience to teach others to overcome obstacles and think outside the box to reach goals. She has an extensive educational background to include a Master's in Business Administration, several insurance and financial certifications, and currently pursuing a PhD in Leadership with a concentration in Business Administration. Currently she resides in Columbia, South Carolina with her daughter and fiancé.

Chapter 13

I Know How to Say, "I'm Sorry"

BY JEFFERY L. MILLER

It was always one of my goals to be a husband. I always saw what my father did and wanted to emulate it and keep the tradition he established alive for the next generation. When I got married the second time, I knew it was going to be something special. I can remember the first time I saw her. She walked past me, and I told the person sitting in my office, "that's going to be my wife." I was in management at the time, so I went to HR, just to make sure before I approached her that I was not violating any company policies. The HR lady looked at me and said, "Nobody has gotten her attention. She just comes in and goes home. None of the guys have had any luck." I looked at her and I said confidently, "I'm not one of those guys." She laughed it off.

A few months later, I paid a visit to the HR lady, and asked her to reach out to the young lady and have her come into her office. I wanted to prove that I was dating this young lady. No one in the office knew we were dating and spending time together outside of the office place. I liked it that way. In the office everyone thought that I was this funny quirky nerdy type of guy. They didn't know that I was pretty savvy when it came to approaching women and suited me just fine.

After we dated for a while, I got to know her, her family, and her son. I decided to introduce her to my family. She met my daughter and son, and eventually we all moved in together. It was pretty cool. We had good conversations, and our kids all fell in stair-step age wise with each other.

Eventually, we got married. We became a family. I will never forget the ceremony. She was stunningly beautiful as she walked in the room, I could not see anything but her. I remember her father and her mother looking at her and her brothers and sisters looking at her and how happy they were. After the wedding, we went back home to rest from the long weekend. There were so many things that we had done and so many people to thank, but we just crashed and did not wake up until the next morning. The glow of love was intoxicating.

Then the recession hit. I lost my job because of corporate downsizing, but in the midst of that, I remember thinking, "no big deal, I'll find something else". I cashed out my 401k and kept right on paying the bills. I had a decent amount of money saved up, and since she was still working and earning a pretty good salary, the money wasn't scarce. I knew that I would find a way. I didn't and like millions of others, my savings ran out and my ideas of having a new job quickly dissipated. When the money was gone, when the job prospects were low, when no one was calling me back, I found myself slipping into a depression. I wasn't depressed because the bills were not paid because they were getting paid. We were living off her salary. I found myself depressed because I was not doing what I thought that a man should be doing-- leading the household.

I was still going out doing odd jobs here and there, working on things for family members so that I didn't have to ask for money. I was able to do things with my artwork here and there, but it did not bring in the revenue that I was used to. So, after those odd jobs dried up, there were no other prospects and the only thing I was left with was a face that reflected my depression. And that look was cold. A cold vacuum void of ideas, manhood and escape. This took a toll on me but even more so on my wife. I gave her a mountain of dependability and when she came home from a hard day at work, she was looking for that strength. It was gone. When she came home from a hard day, she was looking for intimacy. It, too, was gone. When she came home from a hard day's work, there was still food there that I cooked (I would not dare have her come home from work and not have done something around the house), but she could feed herself.

She needed a different type of nourishment. She needed her husband. She needed the man that she had been used to for the previous years of dating. She needed the man that was her strength, the man that made a way for her to be completely feminine, the man that allowed her to be who she was. That man was gone. The husband she had known was starting to push her away. It was subtle at first, but I was pushing her away with actions that showed that I no longer believed that I was worthy of a woman like her. The depression was winning.

It is human nature that after getting pushed so much, to push back or to walk away. She began to push back simply because I pushed so hard. And when she pushed back, I justified myself because of my sadness, completely sabotaging that relationship. I had to feel in control of something. I had lost control of my income. I lost control of my confidence. I lost control of my dignity. The only thing I could control was my love affair with my own fear, sadness, and depression. In some perverse way, it was a relief. A relief from the responsibility of not just being a husband, but from being "her" husband. I could feel her reaching out to me at times, talking to me at times or reaching out to be intimate and the coldness of my body stopping me from responding. I can remember her coming to me and sitting behind me while tenderly whispering words of encouragement in a way that men dream of, and my inhospitable heart rejecting them while my lips mendaciously said, "Thank you." The depression was winning.

After doing everything possible to sabotage that relationship and that marriage, it ended in the most spectacular way. Not even soap operas could rival the drama. Some friends reached out to try to help, or to encourage me. Many of them did this out of genuine concern. Many others enjoyed it. Those frenemies reveled in the fact that our perfect picturesque marriage was over. They seemed happy about the fact that she and I crashed and burned in a spectacular fashion. There I was, adding, "another failed marriage" to my marriage resume, and on my relationship report, "living with a harlot called depression"; she had nothing for me. No kind words. No warm kisses. Nothing to feed my soul. Just an uncharitable touch and eyes as lifeless as stone.

Although I was no longer a husband, I was still a father. Divorcing them was never a thought so I had to figure out a way to take care of them. They didn't deserve the utilities being turned off every week. They did not deserve one being turned on and shortly thereafter, another utility being turned off. They were in high school and they did not deserve to be embarrassed. Now, I had to reach out to family members who had their own set of responsibilities, just to put food on the table. I stood in line at food pantries. I stretched every dime that I had just to make a way. One night while depression was holding me in her cold embrace, I said enough. My children deserve better than this! I'm better than this! Even though my marriage was over, I knew that my relationship deserved better, and I should have done better! I was determined to make changes! The depression was not happy.

I began hustling. I began calling people that I knew; I began calling jobs that had opportunities. I just began calling and calling and calling and calling. Then one day I drove by a building with a huge "We're Hiring" sign saying, "Opening Soon." Once I got home, I saw that same company posted in a Facebook story. A friend said she had just been hired there and they were looking for qualified people. I printed off my resume and I drove there the next day. I walked in with bold confidence and said, "I'm here to talk to someone about an opportunity with the company. They directed me up the stairs and they asked me if I had filled out an application online.

"No," I said.

"Well how did you hear about us" the interviewer asked.

I said, "I was just driving by and I saw somebody post something online."

They took my resume, and I knew what was coming next. They looked at my resume, they looked at me and said, "we want you to go and take this assessment".

I scored something like a 98% on the assessment.

They looked at each other and they looked at me and they said, "Do you know that this job only pays $10 an hour?"

I said "I understand that. I'm just looking to get my foot in the door. I will not be in that position very long."

They looked at me again. They looked at each other, and then said, "Well, we don't think that you're the right fit for that type of position. We are looking for managers. We think your skill set is better suited for the position of management."

I took that opportunity and I started working really hard. I wanted everyone to understand that this was not an opportunity that was going to be squandered, this was my life! This was an opportunity that I was going to take every bit of advantage of, because this was my time to reclaim my manhood.

My masculinity was tied up in my ability to make a way, not tied up in the job. And I had abandoned that at one point because I had a relationship with depression. But depression had been served divorce paperwork!

After roughly a year at this company, my ex-wife was looking for an opportunity. She reached out to me because she knew that I was in a management role now. Having worked with her before I knew what her worth was, and I knew that she would be a really good fit at this company. I asked her to send me her resume and I helped her get a job with the company. I remember her walking in. I remember everyone, turning and just looking at her. How radiantly beautiful she is, how mesmerizing her eyes are. I remember everyone just being blown away by how powerfully intelligent she is. I sat back and remembered that I looked the exact same way when I first saw her. I found myself capturing and feeling some of the same emotions that I had the very first time she walked by me. No one knew that she was my ex-wife, and I would just sit back and watch her walk and smile. I would just sit back and watch different people, plot, and scheme on how they will try to approach her. I would just sit back and laugh and some of the men would come to me and ask me about her and make these comments. It was hilarious and it was ironic.

We worked together for roughly a year before I moved on to a different opportunity. She and I made peace and we discovered that we both are very stubborn. In the midst of our marriage falling apart, there was that part of us that was reaching out hoping that the other one would open the door. We each were hoping that the other would say, "I miss you", hoping that the other one would say, "I'm sorry". I don't believe that it was her responsibility to say that it was my responsibility. I believe that had I stood up and said, "come here" that she would have. I believe that if I had stood up and said, "I am going to figure this out" she would have supported and strengthened my resolve. I believe if I would have stood up and said, "things are going to be okay", we would still be married. I believe that I showed her what men do and I was embarrassed that I could not meet my own standard. She told me that I showed her that women deserved to be protected. Women deserve to be taken care of. Women deserve to be valued. Women deserve to be treasured because they're precious. I still value those words. We had both hoped that we would get through it together.

I told her "You know we should still be married. You know we could work those things out, and the only reason that we did not is because at that time I did not know how to vocalize it. I did not know how to say, 'I'm sorry'. I did not know how to say, 'I need you', or 'I'm hurting'. I didn't know how to say, 'hold me because I am depressed' ". Now I know how to say, "I am sorry, and I apologize." We hugged, I kissed her forehead and we left each other whole by returning the pieces of our hearts we both misused. We returned them to their rightful place in the box of crayons and now we both continue to color.

About Jeffery

Jeffery L. Miller is a certified professional life coach with a focus on coaching professional men, women, and couples. After coaching effectively for nearly 3 years, Jeffery earned his professional certification through the ICU Coaching Academy in 2019.

Jeffery has obtained a Bachelor of Science in Organizational Management and Leadership and is a member of the Association for Talent Development. With these credentials, Jeffery has facilitated learning events and served as the keynote speaker for events as small as 50 people ranging to crowds of nearly 1000 people.

Chapter 14

Broken for Brilliance

BY SONYA M. PULLIAM-PAYNE

"Get some insurance and prepare to bury your parents". The words from my high school counselor echo in my soul. My parents were hustlers, supporting a habit that would kill them both. I lost my birth father before I knew him and everyone seemed to look at me with sad eyes, you know that 'poor baby' look. The odds were stacked against me before I was conceived. I am a fighter, and I have persevered, but the battle has not been without tears or struggle.

One loss piled on top of another during that time, like a trail of dominoes crashing into each other, creating a mess where there once was order. After the death of Big Momma, the place I called "home" began to fall apart. First, it was the vehicle, then it was the deterioration and disrepair of items in the household. Eventually, even the house was no longer my home, forcing me to move what little remained of our worldly belongings into a storage space. Over time, those meager possessions were counted as loss as well. All that survived the storm of my life were the memories.

In the midst of this journey, I was pregnant, homeless, and destitute. Being homeless for 3 months, coming into this space 9 months pregnant and two trash bags to my name, I was the picture of brokenness. I gave birth while living in a homeless shelter. The shelter was a haven for youth entering into adulthood, foster kids who had been separated from their parents and families of origin, who became parents themselves. The environment was unsanitary, infested with roaches, and plagued with the mentally ill.

The population at the homeless shelter was transient, with people coming and going freely. Substance abuse was an everyday presence, whether it was drug use or alcohol, and there was a continual haze of cigarette smoke that hung in the air like a cloud of despair. There was no regard for the children who were there, or the effect these things had on the living environment. The meals that were served came from scraps of food discarded by others. It was redressed and served to us; some folks were grateful, while others clearly did not appreciate the kind gesture. Perhaps I was in shock, but I adapted to an environment that was unfamiliar. I dealt with stress through prayer and faith in God.

Holiday time was approaching, and my child and I became the poster family for the donations that year. The response was great, and donations poured in. For my family, the benefit was more powerful than the donors could have imagined. The direct impact it had on me and my family, was in the value of taking nothing and making it into something.

I was with someone who protected me and covered me from targeted racism and classicism, as it was assumed that we came from nothing. The truth is that material things cannot buy peace or sobriety, my protector needed both; as those things became a reality for my protector, I would see the fruit in my own life.

Looking back, I am sure I experienced postpartum depression along with all the trauma and loss that I faced by the time I was 19 years. It was all a blur for me.

I learned how to be a parent from my parenting, and that required me to heal or repeat my mistakes. I didn't realize how broken I was until one day when I saw the pain in my child's eyes. In that moment, I knew I couldn't hide from the truth anymore. Up until that point, I had denied it, and justified my actions. I was reminded of the scripture in the Bible that talks about passing the sins of the father on to the children. At that point, I made the decision to get to work to put the broken pieces of my life back together. I realized that it was those areas of my life that had never been confronted that were creating a prison I never asked for.

I was blessed with an example of grit and perseverance, so I was prepared to make changes in my life. I never thought twice about leaving the familiar to navigate something new and different. I left everything I knew to support someone I loved. The unknown became my destiny.

The challenge came when I tried to change, while those who were around me stayed the same. My brokenness was reflected in my relationships and my surroundings. When I wanted to blame others, I continued to see my reflection. I became a mom, college student, employee, and a wife. I recommitted myself to religion not God. No matter what I did, it all reflected my broken attempts to fix me. My best efforts for redemption turned into some of my greatest failures during that time.

I enrolled in college the following January, entering into a new world and new experiences. I tried to ease in and become who I thought I was supposed to be, I did not quite find my groove, but I pushed through a few semesters. It was a challenge being a mom in a space where I didn't feel like I fit in. I was in the minority with a priority to make the best of the situation. I was one of nine black students enrolled in an all-girls college. It was predominantly white, and it impacted the way I lived the next few years of my life.

I juggled school and employment for a brief time, finally deciding to shift my focus, making the care of my son my top priority. I left school believing it was not the place for me. I felt defeated; when I left, I believed I was not smart enough. I realize now that I was fighting a system that was created to defeat me. It took years to heal the pain of that experience.

Eventually I married, continuing to navigate many career options, trying to become a success. I didn't realize I was repeating the cycle of trying to become who I thought I was supposed to be. I fought to overcome the failures of my past. I lacked the understanding, tools, or know-how to succeed. I had little self-knowledge or awareness of my true identity or self-worth. I was still living through the eyes of how others see me.

I came to a place and in my life where I took total responsibility for myself and the many broken pieces in my life. I was driven to find out what all this meant, and how could it possibly work together for my good. I had to discover the authentic 'me' and decide based on my journey who I would become. I began to look at me and wow, did I see, know, and understand the complexity of who I am and began to see the possibility of greatness in me. It was the pain of my reality that began to push me to understand my purpose.

Embracing and accepting the reality of my needs, I walked through the doors of a therapist for the first time. The blessing was being able to unpack, declutter, throw away and reorganize my life. I learned in my 20's that the design of my life belonged to me. I learned that design up to that point was from a place of pain. I had survived and that was something to celebrate. My time spent in therapy revealed the dysfunctional patterns that had defined my life design. The more clarity I gained, the more I wanted. I finally understood I had made choices that fed my need to be safe, choices that led to the further unraveling of my reality and fed my desperation. That desperation had driven me to seek fulfillment in connection to others. This cycle of desperation had defined me, and it also broke me.

Realizing how broken I had become, I began to use the skills I learned in counseling, workshops, and retreats, as well as lessons learned from my parents, my friends and even my enemies. I began to put it all into practice.

My environment began to consume me, reflecting what I internalized. I began to declutter my life mentally and physically. Decluttering began to show me who I am, not the person I pretended to be. My clutter disrupted my growth but was evidence of my pain. Starting in my bedroom closet, I pulled out hidden things. I realized that that every hidden item in my closet was linked to a memory that was too painful to deal with. Every piece of clothing was a memory and a part of who I had become, so I struggled throughout the process. My wardrobe represented who I was, it represented my success or failure. It was a part of me, and I had to hold on. In the midst of the clutter, I lost myself, it did not represent the greatness hidden deep inside.

The trap I set for myself began to impact my physical environment, showing me the places broken. My bedroom, the place we should relax and restore became a dumping ground for the things I did not want others to see. My bathroom became anything but a sanctuary or a place of refreshing. My closet stored my deepest, darkest secrets in boxes, in bags. My spiritual walk came into question and I began to question my spiritual journey.

I survived, overcame, and even broke through in spite of feeling stuck in the middle of it all. The truth is, that my inability to release the things I thought would break me are the very things I needed to unravel. The pain becomes life lessons, and the brokenness was the platform to discovering my true self.

I realized the importance of support, and the necessity of having a coach. I continue to overcome the challenges I face asking for help. It has proved to me that in spite of all the places I am broken, every piece defines my brilliance. The moment I realized that brokenness does not define me. The defining moment is that every trial had a purpose. God never wastes a hurt. I am broken for brilliance. Yes, every dark place in my life leads me to a brilliant place. My brokenness is the foundation and as I continue to heal, I see the brilliance. The brilliance in the experience, and the message from the mess. The more I searched for meaning God showed me a picture of myself. There is brilliance in the journey especially when you are aware of the intensity of your brokenness. I became stuck in the content I felt hibernating in my sorrows, and my terror of falling deeper. I had to decide about my life, my future. I had to decide to heal and to ask for help. I had to heal enough to accept the brilliance and the courage to clear the path that leads me to a place that allows me to remove the layers of pain, it reflects in my environment and on my body. All the clutter, the weight, and the relationships, all of it represents the pain of my brokenness and leads to the path that makes me brilliant. I am broken for brilliance and in this moment every experience reflects the brilliance. I am broken for brilliance, are you?

About Sonya

Sonya Payne is a native of Richmond, VA calling Staunton, VA home for more than 30 years Sonya has worn many hats, but at the core she is an advocate to those in need and seeker of truth. She believes that the truth not only sets you free, but it heals. Staunton became a pivotal part of her transformation as she found herself homeless, 9 months pregnant and desperate for a change. This very different place became her refuge and the place she truly began to understand the power and importance of her spiritual walk and faith in God.

As a young single mom, the challenge and conflict of providing for her son placed her education on hold but not her passion for people. Her job searches and ultimately her career path led her to the human services sector to include the juvenile justice system, domestic violence advocacy and ultimately what she believes to be her true calling. In 1996 Sonya and her then husband of 3 years opened their home and heart to children displaced to the foster care system. This journey continues today, and she and her husband have touched the lives of more than 100 children.

Motivating and empowering women through inspirational writing, sharing a raw and uncut truth is Sonya's calling card. Her life mantra: Always speak the truth in love and minister grace to everyone. The people who inspire Sonya the most are her parents, Lonnie and Beverly Robinson, her greatest cheerleaders. She also attribute's her strong desire to serve others to her now deceased grandmother Ruth M. Christian affectionately known as "Big Momma".

Sonya's life path is to motivate and inspire others to recognize the power of the gifts in you, a path that she has become the first partaker. This journey alone is opening doors to opportunity she never imagined but is embracing with courage and strength.

Sonya Payne is life learner. As of late, Sonya adds to her accomplishments becoming a Certified Life Coach. This journey has helped Sonya to fine tune her purpose and business goals. She is here to motivate and inspire others to embrace their truth, trust in this process will open the door to healing with healing being the door to destiny.

Chapter 15

From Caution to Courage

BY JOYCE LICORISH

The light and the darkness found within yellow reflect the light and darkness inside of each of us. You may be wondering what is dark about the color yellow. After all, it is the most attention-grabbing color, it catches our eye first. It is the color of daffodils, sunflowers, lemons, and a busy carefree bee, and speaks to happiness and creativity, right? Yes. Yellow can also mean pump the brakes, proceed with caution, and can also symbolize cowardice.

I think there is a bit of yellow in each and every one of us. After all, are we ever really authentic? Living our plastic lives, painted faces, inflated behinds, and altered selfies plastered on the internet boasting of our successes and triumphs when behind closed doors we at times lay in shambles on soggy pillows? There are moments in our lives that bring us to our knees, moments where we can choose two courses to deal with our FEAR:" Forget Everything And Run", "Face Everything And Rise", or "False Evidence Appearing Real." There are moments where we suffer greatly in the silence of Imposter Syndrome feeling completely unqualified to walk into the destiny that is pulling at us to take action in our lives. Succumbing to 'Destination Happiness' where we think we must achieve a certain thing before we can take the leap of faith and get out of our own way to walk into our destiny. The way we handle these moments speak to our character and shape our destiny.

One such moment in my life took me to a very dark place. I remember the day like it was yesterday although it was many years ago.

The sky was beautiful that morning, the yellow sun beaming through the clouds down on my hopeful face. I remember distinctly taking a moment to take a deep breath before jumping in my car to head to the audition of my life. See, I had spent every moment for the prior 7 years preparing for this very moment. It had finally happened, after many years of singing in a cover band opening for acts such as Chaka Khan, Babyface, 112, Petey Pablo, six years of performing in the background as a chorus singer with the Indianapolis Opera, and after two more years of working under the skillful direction of a very well respected former Hollywood director in my city as a producer on his projects, and a starlet in several of his cabaret shows, and landing the role of Effie in an Indianapolis based mini-tour of the popular musical Dreamgirls. After years of disappointment and empty promises from agents and managers to make me the next big thing, I finally had an invited call to fly out to audition for a Broadway touring musical as the lead in the role of my dreams.

When the casting agent called me, they said that my YouTube video performing 'I am Changing' from Dreamgirls had gone viral and was sent to the casting director and he wanted me to fly out immediately to L.A. for auditions and that they had pegged me for my dream role as Sofia, in The Color Purple. Auditions would be held in three days at the Debbie Allen studios. They further went on to say that I could wait and come day two of the L.A. auditions when they were hosting the 'callbacks' for talent that had already been vetted. (This means after they cut out the riffraff, the performers that they really like can skip the lines and essentially be in a short-listed group of auditions). I spent the next 48 hours cramming, learning every nuance of her character, her lines, and her songs for the audition of my life. In all of the excitement, I decided to scrape together all of my money to make the trip despite all the bells going off in my head that it may not be the most responsible thing to do. See, the timing was not the greatest because at the time I had been laid off from my day job and was separated from my husband. Needless to say, as the mother of three, money was tight. The call had come with little notice, but with a little internet research I was able to book a last-minute flight, hotel room, and rental car. Booking the trip left me with less than $200 to my name but I took the leap and the flight from Indianapolis to Los Angeles. Upon arrival the trouble began, I was using a debit card and the rental car company would not take it without a substantial deposit, so my reservation was canceled. I took a very expensive taxi ride over to the hotel spending more on the ride than I had for the crappy room. Once I arrived at my room, I realized there were just five hours until my audition, so I did the research on the cab ride from my hotel location to the audition location and realized it was going to eat up another huge chunk of my dwindling funds. I decided to try a no-name rental car spot that did $20 daily rentals and happened to be within walking distance to my hotel. Back then they held a check as a deposit so I could hold on to my cash. Little did they know that check would have bounced from LA to Indiana if they tried to cash it. Nonetheless, I dressed for my audition and set out in the blazing California sun to find the rental car spot. Now mind you there was no navigation back then, so I hoofed it and huffed and puffed until finally I found the location and rented the car that looked like it had been through several wars. Finally, in the car with my printed MapQuest directions I made my way through L.A. traffic to the Debbie Allen studio practicing my music on the car ride over. I whipped the raggedy car on the lot and to my surprise only one other car was present. I approached the door and opened it to find a sweet little old woman sitting at the reception desk who beamed back at me as I rushed through the door just in the nick of time for my audition.

"May I help you?" she asked, smiling genuinely.

Without taking note that it was literally only she and I in the entire building I told her I was there for my audition. Her smile quickly faded as she relayed to me that the producers had left unexpectedly the night before and canceled call-backs because they were dissatisfied with the talent turn out the day before. Deflated, I returned to my car in shambles and cried my eyes out. I drove back to the hotel and threw myself a pity party for several hours before getting the idea to call the casting agent and relay what happened. She immediately apologized and asked if I could be in NY the next day. My reaction was a bit over the top as I recall yelling are you kidding? I barely made it to L.A. before breaking down in tears on the phone. She took pity on me and promised to make it worth my while and asked me to cheer up and she would "see what she could do". I hung up, numb, tears still stinging my cheeks. I did not eat that night, afraid that something may come up and I would now need to get another cab back to the airport the next day. I dozed off and woke up at about midnight to a phone call. It was the agent; she had arranged a flight first thing in the morning from LAX to JFK in NY and all was well. I would be able to audition in person after-all for the casting director. I was elated. I repacked my things and rehearsed a bit then showered and went to bed.

Bright and early, I returned the rental and made a deal for $15 with the owner who was a flirt, to drop me at the airport to save on cab fare. He obliged and dropped me off at the door. Whew, NYC here I come!

I arrived in NY, bright-eyed, bushy-tailed, and hopeful. I asked the concierge at the beautiful hotel they booked on my behalf for information on how to take the subway. I played it safe, beat my face to the gods and left early boarding a subway train to the theater district for my audition.

My heart was in my throat and beating a mile-a-minute. Everything was so vivid, the walls in the studio were… yellow. Hardwood floors beamed and my heels clicked louder than normal as I tried to 'walk lightly' down the hall past closed doors with beautiful voices pouring out, and open-door rooms where dancers rehearsed in front of polished mirrors. Finally, I reached the check-in location for Color Purple auditions. Within minutes my sunny disposition was flipped to being pissed… great, more yellow. When the receptionist let me know that I was to go and rehearse with the other women being considered for 'Church Lady'. No! That's not what I rehearsed, there must be some sort of mistake, I was on the call-back list for Sofia, I said in desperation. She stepped away, checked with someone, and came back and redirected me to either go in the room to be paired with a duo for Church Lady auditions or be dismissed. I was pissed. But I did not come all this way to go home. I went into the room and was paired with two other ladies, one a bright and soulful soprano the other a muddy, pitchy hot mess of a wannabe alto. I am a contralto, the lowest of the female voices. I tried to blend and harmonize on the music that was literally just placed in my hands, and we did not mesh. I was near tears. I knew this was not going to work. I asked to be re-paired and was declined. So, I sucked it up and over the course of about 40 minutes memorized the little passage and lined up to be called to sing for the casting panel. Our little slapped together trio piled into the room and performed to the panel who never bothered to look up at us until our last note. To my surprise when we were done, when I had turned to leave the room dejected and defeated, I was asked to stay. They recognized my name from the paper and the casting director finally looked up over his glasses and locked eyes with me and smiled.

"Licorish, Joyce Licorish is it?", he said.

"Yes!" I replied exuberantly, genuinely elated, and relieved.

He then apologized for the oversight the night prior and commended me for making the trip out to NY, asking me how I liked my accommodations. I thanked him and smiled as the other two singers side-eyed me on either side of me. He soon after dismissed the other two ladies and asked me if I was also prepared to audition for the role of Sofia to which I replied "Absolutely!" I was then escorted from that room to another room that held all of the Sofia contenders and Harpo hopefuls. A piano sat in the middle of the room and one by one the contenders stepped to the piano and belted out hearty "Hell No's" (Sofia's main song in the show). Now I am not ordinarily intimidated, but when I tell you my Imposter Syndrome kicked in full throttle as did my cowardice… I decided I was in over my head and turned to leave the room but before I could the accompanist called my name, and it was my turn to come to the piano. My knees literally knocked… I had to pee… my shoes felt louder than ever as they clunked on the polished floors back to the piano. All eyes were on me. Would I crack? Would I remember my notes? Was I good enough to be there? I overheard someone say this was a Union only call. I was not union. OMG! "I should just go," the voice in my head screamed.

My thoughts were interrupted when he started the song and my nerves fueled notes from my throat that I did not know existed. I closed my eyes, and I went fully into that song. I poured in all my anxiety, all my angst, my fear of not being good enough, all of my frustration about the road that led me there, and when I opened my eyes the other women in the room were all standing and applauding. I cried. I did. Right there… the ugly kind of cry. The yellow, snotty kind. Then I was whisked off to another room with the next level of contenders. This went on all day. I was there for over twelve hours. Finally, it was down to four Sofia's, and we all went before the same panel again and I was still standing. I took a deep breath and went back into the now-familiar room and this time the panel looked up and took note of my every movement and note. After I sang, I did the lines, from memory, proud of myself for committing them there within the short-time frame. The auditions finally wrapped, and the four Sofia's were told they would be notified in the next few days of the outcome. We all hugged, we were besties now as we had spent over twelve hours together, we exchanged info and went our separate ways.

I returned home beyond hopeful and utterly glued to my phone and laptop the next few days hoping to get the call, and the call never came. I was devastated and broke. I relayed my story to my "friend", the former Hollywood director and he had a brilliant idea, why not apply for the license for the show and do it on our own, there in my hometown? I ran a charity, and we could partner the charity with local high schools, use the students in the show and do a mini-low-budget high school tour of the show. The idea was brilliant. He would be the director; I would produce and star in the role of Sofia and together we would make this thing work. We applied for the rights… it took months and months to get a "yes", but when it came, we went to work immediately. I scheduled a meeting with all of the township heads of the major high schools in the city and we went in to pitch our brilliant idea. They were all on board because we had this amazing former Hollywood director participating, but during our meeting, we took a short break, and the director who I considered a dear friend walked out on me. I followed him outside and he said to me, "I don't want to do this show with your people, they're going to show up late, they are going to show up entitled and I don't have the patience. Besides, I don't need this on my resume, you do."

With that, he left me high and dry at that meeting. I held in my tears and took a deep breath and plastered a phony smile on my face returning to the room with the awaiting panel from the school board. Of course, immediately they asked where he had gone. I explained what had transpired and they adjourned the meeting expressing they would be in touch. Days later I received an email stating they were no longer interested in doing the partnership. I was devastated.

Months passed again. I was in a funk. Mad at the world. I was not performing, had not found a job and life was kicking my behind. A light bulb went off in me that said why not do it yourself? So, I followed up and asked the theatrical rights company if I could do it. They agreed. The rest is history. I was able to pool together all of the resources in my community. I called a club owner friend and asked if I could use the slowest day to run a series of fundraising concerts and he agreed. I called every singer in my city and asked if they would donate a song and each one said yes. I was able to put up 3 cabaret-style shows featuring these singers and raised $50,000 which was enough to put the show up. We held auditions and contacted media outlets to get press attached. The press was being weird about things though. One media outlet in particular straight up declined to cover the story about our upcoming production. We pressed on. The cast jumped in and sold tickets. We did an internet takeover, and everyone posted rehearsal videos and ticket information. We became an unstoppable force. Opening night came and we had oversold the house, and had to add seats to the balcony area and aisles of the cabaret-style theater. We sold out every single show. That media outlet that refused originally to cover our show now had a new Best of Competition where my new no-name theater company had placed 2nd as Best Production in the city. The local show made enough money that we were able to take the show out on the road and have a successful multiple city run. And ironically the show was so good that when we toured, we received a notice from the theatrical rights company that we could not go too near the other touring production (the very one that I auditioned for) because they were upset that we may take away from their earnings.

I pressed on. Despite the negativity, despite the bottom falling out of everything around me, despite the changes in plans, despite overhearing the rumors that that old friend of mine said, "Who does she think she is," "she's going to fall flat on her face," "she's not educated enough to do that," and "she needs to start with something smaller." Despite the fact that this same individual bought front row tickets to my show and on opening night I looked from behind the curtain to see that he did not bother to show up and the table sat empty.

I was burned by so many people during my journey to where I am today, but I chose to shift from caution to courage... Instead of worrying about who could hurt me, I decided to walk boldly forward and to take back my power and stop reacting to others' negativity. See, my broken heart from not landing the role of my dreams turned into purpose for creating opportunities for others which landed me in my dream role along with a cast of over thirty others. Now, I create opportunities instead of waiting for them. I finally chose me, and got out of my own way! I left corporate America and took on my creativity full time. I am the bestselling author of 4 books, the creative mind behind over 15 feature film and television series scripts, I produced and directed my own original play called The Birth of Soul, I additionally have done the only stage adaptation of Five Heartbeats as a musical and I am now the proud co-founder of the One Race Human Race Foundation a non-profit that allows dreamers like me to use them as a fiscal agent to fund their dreams with tax-deductible donations and the CEO of Dream Empire films and productions where our mission is to move, touch and inspire others to take on their dreams and color boldly with their beautifully broken crayons.

About Joyce

Joyce Licorish is a 4X Amazon Bestselling Author, Award-Winning Performer, Screenwriter, Director, Producer and CEO of DreamEmpire Productions. She is also the founder of the One Race Human Race Foundation whose mission is to create opportunities for more diversity in entertainment. DreamEmpire is an Atlanta-based film production company, which will focus on bringing light to new diverse talent and bringing positive and meaningful entertainment to the big screen.

Joyce got her start in musical theater, where her credits include starring in major productions such as Hairspray, Dreamgirls, Aida, and more and directing, producing, and starring in Oprah's Color Purple the Musical. She and her 'DreamTeam' at Dream Empire films over the last 24 months have created and packaged:

11 Feature Films
4 Documentary Films
3 Episodic Television Shows
1 Cooking Show
1 Reality Show
1 Game Show
Joyce may be found via Social Media at:
www.DreamEmpireFilms.com
www.JoyceLicorish.com
www.Facebook.com/JoyceLicorish
IG @SweetestMotivation or @DreamEmpireOfficial or
@JoyceLicorishOfficial

Chapter 16

Generational Curses

BY JIMESIA JACKSON

Generational curse or generational trauma, whichever it was, I knew I did not want to pass it down to my daughter. My mother came from an abusive relationship, and I heard stories from my grandmother that she did as well. Was it a surprise that I found myself in one too? Mesmerized and in love, full of self-confidence and knowing where I wanted to go in life, I eventually became a crowd pleaser, allowing others to dictate my decisions in life, putting my desires on hold, and walking in fear.

I met him in High School, at a school event. I thought he was so funny, smart-- an absolute genius. We were friends first, but our connection and chemistry brought us closer. He said I was the first girl he had ever loved and soon his actions displayed said otherwise. He wanted to know where I was, what time was I coming back, who I was with, who I was talking to and why. The first time he hit me, we were in the front yard of my house, I got home from work late, and he had been out drinking with friends. He pushed me down in the grass and started kicking and punching me. I was screaming loudly, and his friend pulled him off me. Afterwards, he apologized profusely and promised he would never do it again.

Five years later, I was twenty-three years old; I was still in this rocky, abusive relationship, and I was pregnant.

As I arrived at his townhouse in downtown Atlanta, I recognized the car in the driveway, I had seen it several times before. I knew the nature of their relationship even though he constantly denied it. He was a charmer, smooth talker, he could sell sand to an Arabian and ice to an Eskimo. Yet, I followed my intuition and turned the key to unlock the door.

Upon entering I saw articles of clothing tossed by a burning fire. Enraged and full of hurt, I forgot the fact that I was pregnant in the passion of the moment as I ran up the stairs. She must have heard me because as soon as I swung the bedroom door open, he was running out the shower as she gathered the bed sheets around her naked body. Just as quickly as I opened the door, he knocked me back down the stairs, as he begged her not to leave. Dragging me and calling me names, he ultimately wrestled the set of keys from my hand to remove the key to his place. He told her to stay upstairs, as he pushed me out the door. This was not the second or third time he had hit me, and it was not my initial knowledge of her either. She was one of the two women he kept around, besides me. He told me they were just friends and they meant nothing. When I would confront him with conflicting evidence, he said "when you look for things you find them, but everything you see isn't always black and white".

I sat in my car realizing everything that had just transpired. I was tired of crying; I wanted to just go away.

I questioned why God had given me this life, how did I end up so stupid. How and why was I pregnant? All these years, I lived off his potential, his ambition, and his apologies. What next? Where to? I had nowhere to call home, I had a bed but was living out of two boxes. It all stemmed from a misunderstanding and a physical confrontation with the first man that loved me, my dad.

After a stressful seven-month pregnancy, my daughter was born, and I was back under the roof that I once called home as a child; however, it no longer felt like home. While I lived under the same roof with my parents, I began to see a pattern. I knew my parents loved me but for some reason they did not physically show it, and I felt myself doing the same. I was becoming bitter, angry, and unable to show my daughter any affection.

The abuse from her father continued, verbally, mentally, and physically. We celebrated her first birthday, and, in the pictures, I had a black eye. It was actually Easter weekend, so I told everyone that I fell off the porch. That was the first time my dad had seen a bruise on me as far as I knew. I thought for sure my dad was going to do something, but all he said was "Don't touch her again."

I realized his understanding was, never allow the bruise to be visible. I never called the police; I never made a report. I only made excuses for him. I hung on his potential and his apologies.

My friends stopped speaking to me a little bit after that, and I felt like everything he groomed me to believe was now a reality. No one would love me, no one would want me with a baby, no one would deal with my attitude. He always told me if I ever tried to leave, he would make my life miserable. I stayed because I did not want to be a statistic, and I stayed because I wanted to give my daughter what I did not have, a loving two parent home. It was far from that, yet I was determined to get us there because I saw the potential. I was working in his family's business, living in one of their many properties.

Everything I had was because of them, he told me, and that is exactly how it seemed. They chose where my child went to school. He chose how he would pay child support-- when he would pay it. He made all the decisions for both of us and labeled them sacrifices. To this day, money has never touched my hand, it went to the private schools or towards my rent. At one point he wanted me to go out and work, so I did. Eventually, when he got tired of being Mr. Mom, he ranted and made a position for me to come back to work in the family business. No, he didn't make me take the position, I did it because the arguments made my days seem so much longer. His charm and the dream he had for the future, combined with my desire to please him, as well as concern for our daughter's welfare made me do it. Within less than a year, his plan failed, I was out of work and we were at the end of a tumultuous roller coaster ride we called a relationship.

I remembered my mom, I wondered what she felt during her time with my dad, but this was a taboo subject. Things that transpired between them were off limits unless it gave them ammunition against each other.

I started to slowly date others, first I kept it a secret, because I was so afraid of what he might do. He constantly threatened to take our daughter away from me, and because his family had money, I thought he could. I thought a Judge would look at me and see what everyone else saw, a girl with nothing. Living in a house that belonged to his family, I had only worked within the family business in the last twelve years, besides the short lived outside employment. I was convinced he would look more stable than me as a parent. Then one day I decided to just call his bluff and let the cookies crumble where they may. I told him I was dating, I let the guy come over and even spend the night.

Although I knew that relationship would go nowhere, it gave me my first taste of freedom from the fourteen-year spell I had been under. Of course, he threw tantrums, said slick comments, but he did not do anything. He never raised his hand to me again until about four years later at our daughter's birthday party. It was then that I realized that with all the counseling, the self-reflections, the will to find myself again, there was still some underlying fear of him.

I also realized that my daughter had learned the art of manipulation, at times playing us against the other. I feared.

I realized that my daughter had learned the art of manipulation and at times played us against each other. I feared that she too saw me the same way I saw myself and used it against me, or was I giving her too much credit?

The answer was "no". I realized that my experiences came from learned behavior, behaviors that I watched both of my parents exhibit and I was teaching my daughter. A few days later I had a breakdown, after thinking my tear ducts no longer worked, I broke down. I cried because I wanted to, I cried because I could and because I needed to. I was carrying years of baggage from my childhood that showed up in every relationship that I engaged in. I realized that I was walking on eggshells before I ever met him. I was always trying to keep the peace by going along to get along, a trait that I learned from my mother, carried on into my adulthood. I have always hated confrontation, so I've always been in defense mode. I have never said "no" because I feared retaliation. I allowed myself to be uncomfortable so others could be comfortable. I did it with him, my friends, my family, and my daughter as well. I had become distracted and lost so much that I started to believe that I could not do better, that I was toxic. I became unknowingly combative and defensive. I was honestly miserable but noticed that everyone else was happy because they were doing what they wanted to do, when they wanted and how they wanted, and I was making it easy for them.

Last year I found new friendships that allowed me to speak my truth without judgement. It allowed me to get to the root of what caused my toxicity and why. I found love, a love that I had known before but had given up on, out of concern of what others like my parents would think. With this love came self-revelations, both good and bad. The newly discovered realizations allowed me to speak things to those that I otherwise never would. I understand why my friends left me alone for five years. I did not like it, but I understood the difficulty of seeing your loved one being hurt. I was finally able to tell my dad that I wish he would have thought highly enough of me for me to see it in myself. I wish my mom would have opened up more then maybe I would not have had to travel that road alone and blind. I learned to be more open and honest with my daughter, all while setting boundaries.

Most of all I was able to be honest with myself.

My past mistakes have led to today's lessons. Today's lessons are paving the way for my brighter tomorrow. I learned that it is ok to say no. I now understand that I do not have to be perfect, and while my story may not be the story of others, we all have a story. I am a work in progress, I was broken for many reasons, I made decisions that were derived from brokenness, but I still serve a purpose. I will live and shine in my purpose, I can still teach my daughter and others that they too have a purpose regardless of what happened. Now that my daughter is getting older, I have decided to rediscover the woman I wanted to be when I was younger. I decided to explore what I could have been years ago if I had considered myself, despite the fears of the past or the present fear of being too old and not experienced enough. I want women like me to find their voice because your voice is who you are. Do not live-in fear, own your space, own your ambition. Leave the shame and guilt, take the lesson and the wisdom.

About Jimesia

Jimesia Jackson is a mother of two, life coach, author, and a serial entrepreneur.

Jimesia's experience as a Foster Parent, Preschool Teacher and Girl Scout Leader has guided her passion for helping women and children.

Jimesia is an avid crafter from Atlanta GA, who loves eating, shopping, and traveling.

Chapter 17

Power of Perseverance

BY CHANTYE Y. TERRY

One afternoon my job decided to give out overtime. As a backup team member, they asked me if I wanted to stay, and I was like, "sure". After my shift had ended, I decided to take a fifteen-minute break before I had to start the second half. After getting back from break I made my rounds to make sure I had enough employees to get the lines started, also to make sure all machinery had appropriate temperature range. Approaching one of the lines my friend V said, "Hey Mizz Taye come here."

I noticed a gentleman standing beside her, and she said, "Hey boo, my homie wants to get your number."

I giggled and said, "He could have asked me himself." I turned as if I was about to walk off and he asked, "Can I get your number?"

I gave him my number, but in my head, I was thinking, *I don't have time for this boy, but oh well.*

After getting out of a five-year relationship, I wasn't trying to get involved with no one else, but he was so persistent in getting to know me. After all of the texting and flirting, he finally got my attention. After conversations with him over the next several weeks, he asked me on date. So, the following weekend we decided to go out.

Looking forward to the weekend, it felt like it was taking forever. We decided to go to a local restaurant in our small town call The Depot.

He was being really sweet as we laughed and flirted.

About an hour into the date he said, "Let me be honest about what I got going on".

He said, "I'm married, it ain't what you think, we're not together and we are about to get a divorce, she is pregnant, but it might not be mines". My face expressions were like, "o my, what have I got myself into?" I liked him, but I decided to fall back; he was being so persistent, and it was kind of sweet. So, it had become a little harder to let go. Even though I was a little hesitant, I still was entertaining him. I worked first shift and he worked second on our job. He would come in early and bring me all kinds of things and I would really be loving it. A few of my co-workers would say, "Girl, he's a keeper".

I recall one Valentine's Day he came in to work a little early with a huge teddy bear, flowers, and candy. It made me feel a little giddy, but I really appreciated the fact that he would always surprise me.

After a few months into the relationship, I noticed his attitude started to change. I looked over it, I just thought maybe it was a few small things that was triggering it.

One afternoon we pulled up at the gas station to get gas and something to drink.

When I walked in the store a gentleman I knew said, "What's up Mizz Taye?"

I said, "What's up?", and I proceeded to get what I needed, checked out at the register, and headed back to the car.

After pumping the gas, he got in a car and asked me who was the gentleman that spoke to me in the store? I told him it was somebody I knew. He began getting angry and snapping off, like it was probably that I spoke to the gentlemen, without introducing and letting him know who he was. He started hitting the dashboard of the car, tearing up the glove box, and ripping off the arm rest in the car. I just sat there in silence because I was confused and couldn't believe that he had got that angry over nothing. From that day forward I started to see a different side of him. That made me start rethinking the situation. I was asking myself how he can be so kind and caring and then just flip. It had me a little concerned. A few hour later, he had calmed down as if nothing happened. He explained that he just didn't want to be made out to be a fool and that he was sorry for tearing up the car. So, I reassured him that he wasn't at fault, and I apologized as if I did something wrong. This is where the transfer of guilt began, and the emotional roller coaster started.

One night after pulling up at the house we were sitting in the car talking briefly before the conversation went left and he began to get angry about a drink or something in the refrigerator. Unclear about what the argument was really about, he had gotten so mad that he hit me the mouth.

Two days later, I got up and started getting ready for work and I noticed that my mouth is still a little sore. On my way to work, I decided to stop and get some breakfast. I was running a little behind, so I was unable to eat it. When I got to my workstation, I began to eat and noticed that I felt a chip in my mouth. As I felt around with my tongue, I noticed that my front tooth had fallen out. My tooth was gone! I began to cry in disbelief. A few years before I had paid over $7000 because of my own insecurities when it came to smiling. I just couldn't believe that he would have hit me that hard that it knocked my tooth out. I felt ashamed and embarrassed that I was with someone who had shown they no longer cared the way they did in the beginning. Upon calling him and letting him know what happened, he was so apologetic. He said he would help get it fixed, and that he did not mean to. At this point I was thinking about how to get out of a domestic violence situation. A situation that I never thought that I would be in.

Maybe I was just dealing with a narcissist. It was getting more out of hand. His actions of disrespect started to happen more frequently at home and work.

One day we were at work and he happened to be working on one of my lines. Production was going really great, and I constantly needed the tow motor driver to pick up our parts and store them. The tow motor driver called me over to ask me was there anywhere else that he could put the parts because the storage that the parts were allotted for was getting full. My boyfriend came out of nowhere and threatened the guy to get the fuck out of my face, and if he didn't, he was going to hit him. I was shocked and embarrassed. I could not understand why he would do this on my job. He just kept saying, "I don't give a fuck, we both can lose our job. But he needs to get out of your face". The tow motor driver just left it alone and continued to work. I was thinking to myself; this is crazy, and I cannot keep dealing with this. The inconsistent attitude, anger, tearing up of things and the lashing out was beginning to take a toll on me. I knew it was time to let go. Mentally, physically, and emotionally I was drained. Looking for a way out.

At one point I was begging him not to leave me because I had become emotionally confused and thought some of it was my fault. I had started blaming myself as the reason for us to be going through all this. I stopped going out and socializing because of the things I was experiencing mentally and emotionally. I was ashamed and embarrassed to talk to anyone about what I was going through.

The last incident that forever changed my life happened one afternoon while I was in my shop doing hair. I received a phone call from him, and he said to me, "Baby I'm about see my son", the one he'd been denying but looked just like him. Because of the situation between him and his son's mother, he wasn't able to see his son at the time. That, I am not going to speak on. I proceeded to ask him how that came about after knowing what was going on. But – here we go again – he started getting upset because I had questioned the situation. I understood why because he had displayed so many issues when it came to me dealing with the opposite sex. So immediately, he started getting loud-- I am talking crazy. I politely asked him if he could drop my son off at the shop. The louder he got, the quieter I became, because at that point there was no need to argue. He had completely drained me of any emotional reactions to anything that he had going on.

When he pulled up at my shop, he hopped out the car angry and very aggressive. He was yelling, "You can't stop me from seeing my son!" This was crazy when he was the reason he had not been able to see his son because of something he had done. As he continued to yell and scream, pointing his finger in my face, he hit my lip with his finger. I screamed, "I told you about putting your hands on me". I was scared, not knowing what he was capable of doing at that time. So, I said to him, "That is still your wife and your child, so go because they need you."

That really made him upset, so he grabbed my head with both his hands and started shaking my head, I guess to get me to listen, when clearly, I was over it. This time he leaned in as if he was about to kiss me as he latched on to my lip and started biting it. He was biting me so hard that I was experiencing excruciating pain. My son, who was eleven years old at the time, ran out of the shop and hopped on his back and started hitting him and screaming, "Let my mama go!" When he started to let go of me, blood went everywhere, and I told him that I was about to call the police because at that point, enough was enough. I was thinking to myself; I wasn't going to be able to recover from this like the rest. He was furious that I was about to call the police, so he pulled off, driving reckless. I remember standing right there and thinking he was about to hit me with his car. I saw something in his eyes that I never seen before.

Calling my mom before I called the police, I said, "Mommy he just bit me". My mama is a nurse, and she would be able to tell me if I needed to go to the hospital or not.

When she saw me, her reaction was, "Oh my God! How hard did he bite you?"

"Pretty hard," I told her. It was hurting so bad. I felt my lip hanging.

After the police arrived, they suggested that I go to the hospital.

The officer asked, "What did he hit you with?"

I said, "Nothing, he bit me".

The officer looked at me in disbelief, "like really, he did that?"

I remember riding in the ambulance asking myself why I didn't just leave before it got this far. I end up with 15 stitches in all because he literally almost bit my lip off.

I am very thankful that I was able to make it out of the situation a Survivor. Domestic violence is one of the things that women hide the most because of embarrassment and being ashamed. I can't say completely that he was a bad person because in the beginning he displayed a different character than the one I ended up with. After getting to the root of the problem, I realized he was dealing with things more internally that I actually couldn't see, or he wasn't telling. A part of me does not blame him after learning some of what he had to go through. I began to see that it was a cycle of how he would respond when things were out of his control.

As I forgive myself for not loving me enough to leave sooner, I have found it in my heart to forgive him and move past it. As women we see a lot of signs that a man may be insecure, controlling, demanding, and dealing with a lot of other issues. We ignore those signs and continue on with the relationship, until we are in too deep and broken. Yes, that was a time in my life where I was definitely broken. I now color again. Forgiving not only him, but myself foremost. That is what allowed the healing process to take place and give me the power to vibrate and color again. I share my story so that others will know, no matter what you have gone through or what you have had to overcome, you can heal and color again. Because Broken Crayons Still Color.

About Chantye

Chantye Yvette Terry is also known as Tha Beauty Boss. A mother of 2 children, with 1 grandchild. She was born in a small town called Springfield Tn and currently resides in Nashville, Tn for the last 22 years. Chantye is a licensed hairstylist and established owner of MizzTaye's Hair Studio in 2013.

Chantye is a certified Life Coach and certified in Vaginal Steaming. As a woman of God, she loves to study holistic living, reiki healing, chakra alignment and spirituality. In her free time, she enjoys traveling, making wigs, and working out. Her mission is to overcome the impossible.

Chapter 18

Surviving Oneself

BY CELESTA WILLIAMS

Often, I have wondered, how could I, of all people, be broken. I had two parents that loved me, right? I am a total daddy's girl, so no issues there. Or were there? Was the concept of a perfect home something I manifested in my own mind to protect myself from what was right before my eyes? What was I hiding from myself? What was I protecting myself from? What was I burying in my psyche that would leave invisible scars for wounds to later reopen and bleed all over me?

My early childhood was spent in a two-parent household, which I would later realize was not the equivalent of a happy home. Couples fight, right? They get over it, they move past it, they tough it out and stay together, right? Why were they fighting so much? Was it about money? Was it infidelity? Was it... Me? Imagine how I felt as I watched my parents' relationship fall into ruins during the first 8 years of my existence, while my sisters, being 10 and 12 years ahead of me were going off to college at the age of 18 and 20, leaving me as the only child of 3 to grow up in a single parent household. I officially became the black sheep, the odd ball, the outcast! Everything about my upbringing would be different than my siblings, but at least I did not have to deal with the fighting, right? Wrong!

Suddenly, I was not only an innocent child in a broken home, but I was also accused of causing it! In the eloquent words of my articulate and college educated sister, "this is all your fault"! WHAT? What the hell did I do? I did not even ask to be here! That was the thing though--everyone else did. Apparently, I was the Great Hope! Third time's a charm! One last chance to have a man-child to carry on my father's name. I had failed my entire family with my damned two "X" chromosomes... y, Y, why? What a burden to carry for something you have absolutely no control of. Damn those Deoxyribose Nucleic Acids. Strangely enough, every family member's long-term response to me was beyond intriguing. My middle sister continued to loathe and blame me, my oldest sister pretended I did not exist, and my mother only saw a female version of my father, including everything she loved and hated about him; however, my father absolutely adored me. Yet, I found myself trying to make up to him for not being the son he wanted.

Most people interpreted my strength and independence as a feminine trait, when in all actuality I was fighting the masculine energy imposed upon me by my family. I isolated myself. I dared not show fear, neediness, weakness, or even too much emotion. As a young adult I found myself attracted to extreme alpha males in order to counter my borderline masculinity and allowed myself to become soft and submissive. My first real relationship was of a barbaric nature. He was a brute... I was his woman... Period. Funny thing about abuse is that it can be difficult to recognize when it is not physical and leaves no visible bruises or scars. To be honest, I do not think I really cared. I could finally just be "the woman". I was so desperate to have a man take charge the way my father did, and I never could. I let him run me, rule me, dictate me, and (eventually)... ruin me. How? Those details you will have to read in the next book, but here's the spoiler alert... the relationship did not survive. I had completely let my guard down to have my heart ripped out of my chest and stomped on with infidelity and disrespect. The question was, how did I get to that point? How had I diminished myself to the point that my identity was tied up in a man?

Something about being mistreated and discarded by your own husband does irreparable damage to your psyche after giving him everything a man could ask for in a woman. You may be asking, "What makes you think you're capable of giving a man 'everything a man could ask for'?" Well, let me put that in perspective for you. Imagine a young man who was expelled from high school two weeks before graduation. The only chance at a future was to attend community college and acquire a G.E.D. Beyond that point "JuCo" proved to be a little more challenging than originally assumed. That is, until he met a certain young lady that had everything going for herself... that young lady was me. I was the sophomore class president, had a band scholarship, was a thespian, and I was in every Club and Leadership Organization on campus you can think of when we met.

Not only was I able to balance the demands of college life but I also able to take on his curriculum by rewriting his papers (from scratch), coordinating makeup assignments with his instructors, and literally making flash cards to help him study for his tests (seeing as I couldn't take them for him). This pattern of enabling led to a spiraling whirlwind of passivity, disregard, and (eventually) blatant disrespect. It would be one thing to suffer from physical abuse that you can actually see, but the verbal and emotional abuse was like a low and slow dose of poison each day that didn't actually kill me but paralyzed me just enough that I couldn't move or think for yourself. After a while, I did not even know myself anymore. Time went by, marriage vows exchanged, the children came; then he decided he was not cut out for a family. And just like that-- I was a single mom!

How could I let this happen? What was I thinking? As if I were not "damaged goods" before, what man would want me at that point? A divorcee with children was frequently seen as a burden, a woman with too much baggage, and too many scars. The deep feelings of being unlovable, unworthy, and unwanted are not easy to overcome. Especially when it started long before your disassembled marriage.

I already came into this world being treated as if I was "not good enough". No, I will never be the "man-child" my family had so hoped for to carry on my father's name; however, I am still provider, protector, nurturer, and disciplinarian to the children I brought into this world. Yes, this life has made me quite rough around the edges, savage tongued, and terribly quick witted. However, I am also soft, submissive, supportive, and loyal beyond measure. I have learned to compartmentalize life's challenges at an above average level, functioning with true emotional intelligence, in my daily life, in my professional life, and my relationships.

My past, present, nor future circumstances define what I have to offer as a woman, a mother, or a mate. No matter if I am missing the wrapper and exposed on all sides, completely dull and smooth on both ends, and severed in half, this broken crayon still adds vibrant color to any picture!

About Celesta

Celesta Williams is an extremely gifted powerhouse of talent and skill in areas of acting, singing, and writing over multiple genres of music and script. As an introvert wise beyond her years, Celesta has spent much of her life in a search for self-purpose where her compassion for people lead her to law enforcement as an emergency response Telecommunications Officer. During this time, she was able to gauge her interest in areas that she has most passion for including, but not limited to acting and music. Her recent projects include TV shows, such as, *Boomerang*, *The Resident*, *Genius* Aretha Franklin docu-series, and long-awaited start-studded feature film, *Coming 2 America*. Her exposure back into the world of entertainment has led Celesta to focus full-time on her career in arts and entertainment, as well as share her stories of triumph from a failed marriage to an ex-NFL husband, becoming a single mother post-marriage, and reinventing herself against societal odds. Her story is one of great depth and layers that she will soon share with the world through her works:
Phoenix Dynasty 2020
Where the Vision is ALWAYS 2020!

Chapter 19

Lessons and Blessings

BY KELLY ELLIS JOHNSON

If I have not learned anything else in my 46 years on this Earth, I've learned that life's journeys will be one of two things: lessons or blessings. I believe that the choices we make, along with fate determine which one we are dealt. I joined the U.S Army right out of high school. I was young, and ready to be the best version of me! My ultimate dream was to get married, have children and a wonderful life!

Life went a little differently than I anticipated. I did fulfill my dream to get married, at the tender age of 21. We met when I was 19 years old, and he was then 22. I was in the barracks at my first duty station, Schofield Barracks, Hawaii.

I had not really noticed Barry until we were at a mutual friend's house hanging out. We conversed most of the evening, and I gave him my phone number. We began dating and spent most of our time together. I guess he figured that because he was older than me it was his responsibility to teach me a few things. I was eager to please, so I was all in at first! He was good to me so I in turn wanted to be good to him. The problem with that was, it results in changing to fit someone else's ideologies, and you ultimately begin to lose yourself.

In my effort to be a good girlfriend, with the goal of becoming his wife, I began to lie to him when I would kick it with my girls believing he would be upset or make me feel guilty about hanging out with them. I wanted to portray the image that he had of me. It would feel as if he were silently scolding me whenever he seemed displeased about something that I said or did.

My response was to try and adjust to whoever/whatever he thought I should be. I wish that I could tell you that this happened during my marriage, but I honestly cannot.

He would suggest things that I could change and, in my eagerness to please him I would do it. It got me the ring but how many people know that if it is not who you truly are then the façade will be revealed sooner or later? We married after about 16 months of dating. It was a small justice of the peace ceremony in downtown Honolulu, Hawaii. We did not have a reception because the family was unable to travel for such a distance. Our marriage was healthy for a while. We would do everything together from eating out, hiking, attending luaus, watching movies, and traveling to name a few.

It was not until after our first child came that our issues began to evolve. We had changed duty stations from Hawaii to Ft Bragg, North Carolina, home of the famous 82nd Airborne Division!

I was a department supervisor at the central warehouse on base and he was a communications sergeant in an infantry unit. I became pregnant several months after moving there. We met some other couples in his unit, and we all began to hang out often.

He became really close with two of the fellas-- Nelson, and Spence. I would hang out with their wives, Reagan and Keke. During my pregnancy he would go out with them a lot more and I overheard him talking bad about me to them over the phone one day. I did not say anything or let him know that I had heard him. I just harbored my feelings of resentment and unforgiveness. I felt a sense of betrayal on his part with the way he was treating me. He was emotionally unavailable. I do not necessarily blame him; I blame myself for the woman I had allowed myself to become. Things changed after I had my son. He was a great father and became very active in his son's life. I, on the other hand, had decided that I was not taking any more of his mess and I told him as much. He began to change his ways, but I had unforgiveness in my heart, so I did not notice much. I began hanging out with friends. My girl Reagan and I were hanging out at the clubs and around town. You could not tell us we were not the baddest chicks in Fayetteville. The attention that we were getting ultimately led me to entertain conversations with other men. I was looking for the attention that I was not getting at home in the streets. I was looking for love from men instead of looking within myself and my God. I should not have needed others to tell me how special or beautiful that I am; but I did.

Things shifted when I found out that my mother was passing from stage 4 lung cancer. I went back to my hometown of Springfield, Ohio and took care of her during her transition. I watched her take her last breath.

It was hard burying my mother and I was looking for a different environment than Fayetteville at this point. The death of my mother brought my husband and I back together temporarily. I left the military and my husband had received orders to go Ft Gordon, Georgia, so I made the decision to go with him and work on my marriage.

Once we were relocated, I got a job at the Proctor and Gamble factory in Augusta. That's where I met Frank, my next relationship, and my girls' father. I met him while I was still married to Barry. Frank was loud and funny while I was quiet and seemingly shy.

I talked with a few of my coworkers but for the most part I kept to myself. I tried to stay out of trouble and avoid the attention of men by wearing baggy clothing and kept a homely look. I was doing my best to work on my broken marriage and did not want any distractions or temptations. I would often find Frank staring at me, but he never said anything out the way. Instead, he would flirt with the ladies that I conversed with.

My ego must have been bruised by his lack of attention because I changed my wardrobe, and started wearing clothing that was flattering to my figure. That insecure woman that was still on the inside of me was craving the attention of that man. My change of wardrobe caught his attention. I was not the only one at the job catching his attention, though. The ego can be a powerful thing. His Casanova ways made me seek his attention even harder.

He was a different breed than I was used to. I think that is what attracted me to him. I was drawn to his confidence and those gold teeth. Southern men had a certain type of charm and I could not seem to resist it.

He knew it too and ran with it. I was 26 years old now and heading towards another unhealthy relationship. He loved to drink, smoke and party. It is interesting how we look for love from those who are not even capable of loving themselves correctly.

Let me say this: Pay attention to what a person does; they can let anything come out their mouths but it's what they do that shows who they truly are and what's truly in their hearts.

I told myself that I just wanted to be happy. I was selfish and impulsive. My husband eventually found out about us sooner than later and came to my job threatening to shoot Frank and cutting up. You would never guess how he found out either. I had gone to a cookout with Frank and his friends on Memorial Day Weekend. My husband had decided to go without me to Bike Week in Myrtle Beach, South Carolina and after that I was convinced that our relationship was beyond repair. The petty Betty in me agreed to go with Frank because I had convinced myself that my husband wanted to go to Bike Week without me so that he could cheat on me and I was going to give him that same energy. Anyway, back to the cookout; I am sitting with Frank and there is a woman that I see staring at me when she thinks I am not looking. It turns out that she was having an affair with my husband and had been to my house and saw pictures of my son and me, so she instantly knew who I was. Talk about "Somebody's sleeping in my bed!" She had the nerve to look angry and I did not understand it at the time, so I just dismissed it. Needless to say, she advised my husband that I was at the cookout with Frank so when he got back from Bike Week, we argued, and I went over to Frank's house.

There was so much passion and excitement in being with him in the beginning. I was definitely caught up in the moment. My husband and I legally separated not long after that and eventually divorced. Frank was a fun and funny man and we had great chemistry. Outside of the bedroom though, the relationship needed lots of work. If you do not remember anything else remember this: It's not what a person says, it is what they do! There was a lot of infidelity and lies on his part and plenty of insecurity on mine. I clung even more to him for happiness and became bitter when I felt I did not receive it. Never mind me owning my own happiness! I have realized that it is not someone else's responsibility to bring you happiness: that is putting too much power in another person's hand. My

Abba Father in Heaven is the only one who will ever again have that kind of power over me.

To make a long story short, the new mindset that I had after that on again off again, relationship of over 8 years is that however a thing starts (stepping out on your significant other and committing adultery) is usually going to determine how it ends.

People such as my friends and his family asked me why I stayed so long. He was telling me just enough of what I wanted to hear and doing just enough of what I would tell him to do so that I would stay. I remember one of his family members came to me shortly after I moved out from him and said, "What did he do different?" She was right too and that made it sting even more. Truth be told even though I would complain, he never changed most of his behaviors; or he would change for a moment and go right back to doing who he was doing. He talked to me as if he understood and he cared and wanted us to work but his behavior never changed so he showed me that was not true. His actions were where his heart was. I just did not want to listen. Say what you mean and mean what you say! The more disrespect that you allow; the worst it will get. Do not continually hold on to pain and toxicity, because you are only delaying the lesson behind the situation you are in. I did many crazy and impulsive things after our relationship ended. I even went as far as to move back to my home state of Ohio.

I rededicated my life back to God. It was the first week of July at Dominion Camp meeting 2019. I heard a word, I repented of my sins and I began to live differently. That night, I had taken all of my hurt, pain, disappointments, and burdens to the altar. When I talk of living differently, one example was I went from fornicating to becoming celibate. I truly wanted to honor the word that spoke of presenting my body as a living sacrifice. I wanted to live holy for God. If I wanted to get what God had for me and for my life, I knew that my taste in men had to change as well. I asked God to change my mindset and change the type of man that I was attracted to. I told God that I wanted a saved man with honor and integrity that whole-heartedly loved me, and I would love him back. Someone that I could trust with my heart. Someone who was headed spiritually, mentally, and physically in the direction that I was. It was time to do things God's way and not my own.

I did not even try to date again for about 8 months. There was a man named Kevin who was continually trying to connect with me, but he would usually do something that made me rethink allowing him to spend time with me. He would try to contact me via social media at first and then eventually I gave him my phone number. He would ask to take me for a drink but I am not a drinker so that did not appeal to me. To be honest, it also put up a red flag that this man may know of God but was still very carnally minded. I did not want to be unequally yoked so I hesitated. I would often remind myself that actions speak louder than words so I would confront the things that I was seeing and not dismiss them. There were other things that made me feel that way as well, but I just wanted to give you an example of at least one of them.

He was persistent; I will definitely give him that. He tried from around September of 2019 until I finally allowed him to see me in April of 2020. We talked and texted often, and I was very vocal as to why I had stopped conversing with him previously and what I was looking for in a man. I was also clear that I was practicing celibacy and looking for a Godly man with that same goal.

One thing that immediately bothered me was that he would often make little sexual innuendos and if I seemed displeased would say that I should be pleased that he was so attracted to me. He eventually began to bring my guard down by encouraging me not to be so uptight. We began to spend more and more time together. We would share sermons and worship songs with each other. We would also often discuss the Bible; He was very knowledgeable of the scriptures. We would also talk about dating, relationships and how men versus women think. We talked of doing a podcast together that was centered on relationships. I found myself cooking and putting plates to the side for him. Let me be clear; this was a test and I failed again. I was this born-again blood-washed believer who was up against the same temptation. I had gone back to fornicating with this man among other things. He was spontaneous and I loved that about him. Our chemistry was dope as well.

There was one big problem. Kevin was bi-polar. He would text me out of the blue and start arguments. I found myself apologizing at first just to keep the peace. Then he would flip out on me again and again until finally I realized where this was headed. I mean do not get me wrong, when things were good, they were really good but when they were bad;

they were really bad. He was loving on me and lavishing me with compliments in one breath and bad-mouthing and accusing me in the other. I knew where these types of unstable relationships eventually led. This man had some unresolved issues that he needed to deal with. He needed a touch from God from the inside out along with some extensive counseling.

That relationship had officially become toxic. I would encourage you that when you are looking for a husband or boyfriend to ensure that you are watching how that person lives. Society says not to judge but to an extent you must in order to make an intelligent decision. Character is everything. How someone responds to things and how they live their daily lives are all clues. Is there self-awareness? How does he respond when things do not go as planned? How does he manage his lifestyle? I will not say that Kevin was not intentional towards me. He and I talked of marriage but when I noticed some of his patterns that was no longer an option for me. Remember I told you that he was persistent, which totally attracted him to me in the beginning? Well, that same persistence later turned to finding ways to come by my home as if nothing had changed. As if he had no knowledge that we were broken up. He would text me all times of the day and night and if I did not answer he would begin to say crazy stuff. It was a scary feeling. He would come by unannounced and at other times send me random and disturbing text messages.

I said what I meant and meant what I said though! I knew that God would never send someone in my life to tear back down what He had built back up! The devil is a liar! I had learned to truly love myself and that's how I was able to walk away from what I felt no longer served me. Self-love is the very best love, and I chose me this time!

What I have learned throughout my relational journey is that every relationship that we encounter is either a lesson or a blessing. I have learned to look for these key things when I consider entering a relationship with a man:

1. **Character**- What kind of person am I dealing with? Do they keep their word and honor their family? Are they dependable, caring and a provider?

2. **Accountability**- Is he accountable to self and others? Does he make it a priority to self-assess on a regular basis?

3. **Honesty**- Is he an honest man, even if it is unfavorable to himself and/or others? Does he use wisdom?

4. **Common goals**- Does he have vision? Does he have long and short-term goals? Do we share common goals?

5. **Consistency**- Is he the same man most of the time? Does he say what he means and means what he says? Is he consistent when courting me?

6. **Humor**- Does he have a good sense of humor (I can be a little uptight, so I need help y'all)? Is he easily offended?

These 6 key things are my go-to's when choosing a potential mate. They have saved me a lot of time, pain, and heartache. I have gone from being broken to blessed! God has given me beauty for ashes and wisdom beyond what I could ever hope for! What the enemy meant for evil; God turned it around for my good! God has shown me that life is full of blessings and lessons so that I will not be bitter but better! Our choices; good or bad are the canvas of our lives. It is time to paint a new picture!

About Kelly

Kelly Ellis Johnson is a US Army Veteran and mother of 3 beautiful children. Her purpose is to inspire women to become the best version of themselves. She is the former Ohio Chapter President of the Survivor with Voices non-profit organization. She is an author, empowerment speaker and healing coach. In her spare time, she loves to travel and study the Word of God as well as history. Her ultimate goal is to encourage and empower. She is the upcoming author of the fictional book titled "Finding My Way: The Prodigal Daughter" which is inspired by true events.

Chapter 20

What a Bluetiful Life

DR. MARLENE CARSON

Like the hymen of a virgin on her wedding day there was so little blood that no one noticed that I was broken. Little did I know this was only the beginning. The relationship with my father created the blueprint for every intimate relationship I would have in the future. These relationships were not built on love, trust, or happiness but on rejection, abandonment, and desperation. I was so desperate to feel alive, affirmed, and accepted that I would do anything. By the time all said and done, I had just about done it all – in the name of love.

As a mother, I now understand how important it is for a father to affirm his little girl: to take her on her first date, to send her flowers, and to buy her first diamond. I have also come to appreciate how important it is for a father to honor his son, to teach him about character and having integrity. So often we give children what we didn't have but neglect to give them what we did have, things like respect for elders, manners at the dinner table, and a compassion for people. The relationship with my biological father created severe daddy issues, even with Abba, Father God.

Different shades of blue

Although I was around 8 years old, I remember like it was yesterday. My sister and I wanted to go to the mall. She told me to go ask my father for fifty cents to ride the bus. I was so excited that my big sister was going to allow me to go to the mall with her. When I got to my parents' bedroom with utter excitement, I knocked on the door. "Daddy, do you have fifty cents?" I asked in anticipation. The voice that shot through the door felt like a bullet aimed at my heart as he growled, "No, I don't have any money!"

From afar my sister could see me crying. She came to embrace me and asked, "what's wrong?"

By this time, I was hyperventilating. "I can't go with you; daddy doesn't have any money," choking the words out.

Sister wiped my face and sat me on the couch. I don't know what she was thinking but she went and knocked on dad's door. "Hey dad, do you have a dollar?", she asked sweetly.

He replied, "Yes, bring me my pants". He rolled the dollar off of his stack and handed it to her.

She turned towards me with a smile as big as the sun on a clear blue day. She took me by the hand and whisked me off for a day at the mall. However, my heart was still at daddy's door. I didn't understand. Confusion, sadness, and rejection flooded my soul. Why would he give it to her and not me? That question sent me on a tumultuous path that I was on most of my life. My sister didn't even realize how hurt and sad I was. Like a bruise after a few days, my world turned black and blue. I just couldn't seem to shake it. No one in the family really knew what was wrong or why I started staying with my grandmother who gave me unconditional love. I thought that was the cure, but it was only a band aide.

Dark blue

While many have a textbook knowledge of the perils faced by teenage girls who are forced into sex trafficking, I know from my own personal experience. At age fifteen, I became one of the tens of thousands of girls and young adult women who are exploited daily. I remember the first time I was sold. I remember the room, the smell, who was there and the day that everything in me died. That bed became the coffin for my dreams, desires-- and I thought-- my destiny. When I got up out of that bed so much of me was left there that I didn't even know who I was anymore. I was a virgin girl, raised in the church in a two-parent household, the youngest of five siblings, and it still happened to me. I was so confused. This was a crime--a crime committed against me, but it made me feel like a criminal. Someone got paid so that someone else could rape me. Did that make me a victim? Trauma has a way of changing your perception. My innocence was stolen and there was no way to get back the one thing that I was so proud of, my virginity.

Too Little Blue

According to Bourn Creative too much blue can create feelings of melancholy, negativity, sadness, self-righteousness, and self-centeredness. Too little brings about qualities of suspension, depression, stubbornness, timidity, and unreliability. The aftereffects of that encounter with my father made me feel like a faded blue dress that had been tie-dyed with depression, suspicious, timidity and unreliability; all the while I could see the hue of who God formed me to be while fighting to understand how I could make the vision my reality. There are so many different shades of you that make up who you are. When you don't fully understand your depth, like shallow water filled with algae we see too little of the real you. In my case, I saw too little blue.

Oftentimes, we cannot fully embrace who we are because of trauma, flaws or because someone is throwing shade. When we care more about what others think of us than we think of ourselves, we will never become who God created us to be. During this thing called "life" we are trying our best to figure out the who and why of it all. We ask, "Who am I and why and I here?" Once we dive in to do an intentional search for our true identity, here comes someone throwing shade, reminding you of who you used to be, flaws and all.

Do you remember the song, "It wasn't me" by Shaggy?

Ok, I know I just told my age and the fact that I haven't always been saved. Although Shaggy was caught cheating, sometimes I just want to sing his song. See, when I was doing things with no understanding of my true identity, I just want to tell those who kept a record of said actions "It wasn't me!"

Pale Blue

My story—past, present, and future—was simultaneously known in the mind of God even before the start of my lineage. Established in the mind of God, the many transitions, private victories, and public deliverances were all a part of a process—a process that doesn't lead me to a happy conclusion, but an expected end. With that in mind, my past once filled with shadows of intimidation and insecurity has become testimony, because a shadow doesn't exist unless a light shines upon its subject—the light of God's truth. His truth that shines within the world of adult entertainment, truth that shines in abusive relationships-- truth that even shines in the Christian church shining to dispel the darkness. "And ye shall know the truth, and the truth shall make you free (KJV John 8:32). I have known the intimacy of truth, the truth that set me free from strip clubs, escort services, and pimps; pimps who hang in the darkest of motels as well as those who stand behind the most ornate pulpits. This truth healed me from years of brokenness, while causing me to realize who I am in the Kingdom of God.

Sky Blue

My grey skies started to turn blue when I read Isaiah 61:7 "Instead your shame you will receive a double portion" (NIV). Since shame had become my constant companion, I didn't know how to calculate the "double portion" or what that looked like exactly. I imagined Madea in *Diary of A Mad Black Woman* when she was calculating how much money Charles owed Helen after he put her out of her own house. Then she tripled that! See, God knows how to do it. When he said, "Vengeance belongs to the Lord and He shall repay."

He wasn't kidding. Baby listen, I never saw my life redeemed, family restored, or sitting on The U.S. Advisory Council on Trafficking – but God! There are so many promises in his Word, and I am so glad that he keeps his promises. There was one thing that I found that God could not do. After he cleaned my life, restored my joy, and put me on the path of righteousness, I would definitely concur that He can't lie!

When I began to take him at his word everything changed, but it wasn't overnight. I had to submit, surpass, and survey my options in order to succeed. This was a process that not only came with a few bumps in the road, it came with some hills and valleys as well. During this process I learned that the joy of the Lord is my strength, that I can do all things through Christ that strengthen me, and I am more than a conqueror!

I know now and that I am fearfully and wonderfully made. I am not a mistake!

Peacock Blue

Marcia Moore Designs loves peacock blue. Marcia often says, "Unlike human hair, the peacock's bright radiant coloring comes from light reflecting off the feathers rather than mere pigmentation. As a result, the exact color of a peacock shifts depending on the angle at which you view it". The peacock proves that it doesn't matter what color your skin is as long as it is reflecting the light of God. I am proud to be a black woman that the light of God shines through.

We can learn another lesson from the peacock whose colors shift depending on the angle you view it. There are so many facets to a woman's beauty, personality, and character that we can shift depending on the way you view us. So, watch us slow and see us grow.

Indigo

I could not complete my colorful journey without mentioning indigo. When I think of Indigo, I think of being resilient, rough, racy, strong, traditional, non-traditional, classy, and casual. That describes me to the core. My story is made up of so many different shades, shapes, sizes, and styles nevertheless, it's all me. I have gone from the whore house to the White House, from the streets to the C-Suite, from dropping out of school to owning a school. I've gone from my children not speaking to me to be a mother to many, from having no direction to leading, and from lack to plenty. In all this have found a peace and contentment that encapsulates the beautiful blue that I am.

Bluetiful

One of the newest colors that Crayola released in 2017 is named Bluetiful.

See, you thought this was something that I made up, didn't you? Everyone and everything can at some point go through transition. While transition is designed to take you from one place to another it is necessary for your growth and sustainability. There are those transitions that are so familiar that you can predict them, knowing how to navigate through them and even how to come out on the other side of the changes. Some of life's transitions can creep up on you and absolutely knock you off of your feet. However, there is that transition that happens in your life that no matter how you try to maintain a healthy balance it just seems to knock you off your game completely. Those types of transitions can catapult you into survivor mode and there you find yourself in a place where you are constantly trying to recover.

Do you feel like you have been living in survival mode? Let me just say, "The struggle is real", but so is the victory!

It is difficult to rise above the chaos after you have experienced an unexpected transition which could paralyze your decisions and affect your destiny. I am here to tell you that you can do it and I can show you how. If you want to know how to face your fears, confront your challenges and learn how you too can create a beautiful life? I have a few questions for you:

- Did you have daddy issues when you were growing up?
- If so, do/did they affect your relationship with God?
- Have you accepted Christ as your Lord and Savior? If not, ask me how.

Like the color Bluetiful, some say it teaches children a misspelling, others say it's "creative". At the end of the day, I have learned you can't please everybody so strive to please the Lord.

My dad would tell me that I was so black that I was *bluetiful*. It wasn't the color Crayola created but I do agree; my black is *bluetiful!*

I am Dr. Marlene Carson, Beologist.

I teach Beology-- the art and science of being.

Do you want to be the best you that you can be?

Let me show you how you too can live a *bluetiful* life!

About Dr. Carson

Dr. Marlene Carson is a SurThriver of domestic minor sex trafficking. She is a member of the U.S. Advisory Council on Trafficking, Author, Coach, and Founder of Rahab's Hideaway, Rahab's Hope of Ohio, and The SWITCH National Switch Anti-Human Trafficking Network. While many have a textbook understanding of the perils faced by victims of sex trafficking, Dr. Carson knows from her own personal experience. At age fifteen, she became one of the tens of thousands exploited daily. Through faith in Jesus Christ and sound biblical teaching, Dr. Carson's misery became a ministry. Her zeal has erected a vision that is unique in its application and effective in its efforts to break the cycle of exploitation, addiction, and poverty.

Chapter 21

Lost and Found

BY DOMINIQUE R. JONES

It's hard to pinpoint exactly which crisis had been my breaking point. I wasn't raised by my biological parents, and as a result, I grew up feeling unwanted. Then I was raped when I was seven years old by a male cousin of mine and molested by a female cousin when I was eight years old. Maybe that's when my mind snapped. Maybe-- just maybe, it was the fact that I waited all those years to walk across the stage at my high school graduation ceremony only to find out days before that I would not be able to walk and would have to go to summer school. All of this abandonment, trauma, and disappointment definitely played a part in the heartbreak from my first love and the failed relationships that followed. You know what? Maybe it was the darkness I experienced after my first divorce. The divorce that took me to a dark place, a place where I didn't want to do anything, go anywhere, eat food, or even exist. Depression is real!

Time can heal a lot of wounds, and I managed to push through it after a while; I got myself together and got back on track. I met an amazing man, got married, and thought this was the highlight of my life. Life as I knew it was pretty good. It was only temporary, though. Nine years later I arrived back at that dark spot after my second, yes-- second divorce.

The failure of my second marriage seemed to bring my world crashing down around me. I thought I had healed from all of the life-defining, life-altering events that had led to my depression in the past. The truth was, I suppressed my brokenness, and masked it all. I kept moving through life with a smile on my face convincing myself that I was okay, that I was strong and that I had it all together when in reality behind closed doors I was torn, angry, bitter, scared, fearful, hurt, and suicidal. Depression is real!

This last divorce is the straw that broke the camel's back for me. Who was I? How did I get to this place? How would I move forward and heal from this depression and become whole again?

Depression had taken over my life. I looked up one day and realized I had not washed laundry for a few months. I had piles and piles of clothes stacked all over the floor, that I would just step over acting as if they were not there. I had no desire whatsoever to clean the house. I had lost my appetite and stopped cooking. I had even stopped taking showers. Every part of my life was put on hold at that point. I stopped going to church because I could no longer hide the pain, and I was so emotional that I knew if anyone asked me what was wrong, I would burst out in tears. If you know me you know I never missed church so that was major for me, but I convinced myself that not going to church was the best thing in that season. I stopped calling my best friends and family members convincing myself that I would be a burden to them, and they would not understand my brokenness and depression. I stopped answering the phone for everyone. I just did not care. I had lost hope, lost faith, and had NO motivation to do anything! I would literally get up every day, get dressed, go to work, go straight home, turn all the lights out in the house, and get in bed. I would lay in that bed and cry myself to sleep. I was hurting, I was unfulfilled, and I was lost and broken trying to figure out HOW I got to that dark space.

First, I had to be honest with myself, and look at who I really was, and who I had become. Dominique, the church girl, the Preachers daughter, the Pastor's wife (at that time), the strong one, the one who always pushed and motivated others through their struggles was broken! I realized that I had gone through life masking things. Baby, believe me when I tell you I learned how to master masking my hurt. I would put a smile on my face, take trips thinking I was living my best life, have parties and gatherings, encourage, and motivate others, only to realize that I could not do that for myself. I wanted to fight, my temper was short, I wanted to wallow in that pain because the emotional healing and working through it would be too hard. More than anything I wanted to BLAME others but guess what, it was time for me to take my life back.

AND THEN I WOKE UP…

One day I decided I did not want to hurt anymore, and I did not want to mask my pain any longer. I wanted to heal, I wanted to feel good and be genuine. I wanted to be happy, but I knew to achieve any of this I had to deal with self. Listen, facing that reflection in the mirror and taking accountability is a BEAST!! Facing your demons does not always feel good but it is going to work for your good. I made a conscious decision to start taking my life back one day at a time. I had no clue what to do nor where to start so I started journaling and releasing my thoughts on paper. I realized that every time I did that, I would have a sense of relief because I talked about it, I was honest about it and I no longer had to hold it in. Every time I started to feel bad, slip into a dark space or entertain negative thoughts I wrote in my journals. I kept doing that until it became a habit, literally second nature for me. I then started putting the pieces of my home back together. I started cleaning my house room by room until it was clean. While I was cleaning, I got a huge trash bag and started throwing away everything I needed to get rid of that was attached to someone that I needed to let go of. Whew! What a struggle but a release as well; it was a step in the right direction. I then began to start reading about affirmations and how impactful and helpful those were.

Proverbs 18:21 states, **"Death and Life are in the power of the tongue, and they that love it shall eat the fruit thereof."**

As a Christian, I was fully aware of how powerful the tongue was, so I knew if I began to speak life into myself every day that I would begin to really believe those words and apply them to my everyday life. I created a list of affirmations and posted them on my mirror in my bedroom. Every day when I woke up and stepped out of the bed I would go to the mirror and start reading those out loud. I would read them every morning and every night before bed. As I began to believe those and apply them, I would create new ones. My affirmation time is dope!

Although I wrote affirmations, journaled, cleaned up my house and started back getting in the swing of everyday life I knew that I needed some professional help to sort out all these traumatic events that I had masked over the years. I decided to go see a licensed therapist as well as a spiritual mentor. This was one of the best decisions of my life! Therapy was intense because I had to deal with my shit and own it. I had to face my demons. Therapy helped me to really look at things for what they were, accept them, talk about them, release them, and heal! I went to therapy for about eight months, and I am so glad that I did. It saved my life! It helped me to heal from my brokenness and learn my worth. Learning who I am, and my worth were two of the best achievements to date. When you know whose you are, who you are, and your worth, you can see clearer, think better thus allowing you to make wise decisions. I no longer allowed myself to put up with things that did not add to my value. I was able to recognize toxic traits and shut them down at the door. I was able to recognize the things that triggered me so I made sure to not put myself in environments where I would be triggered nor allow others to intentionally trigger me. I learned to love myself, understanding everything about me matters. I learned that if there is something that I do not like then I am responsible to take the necessary steps to change it. I learned that I actually love my smile, my juicy lips, my love handles, the stretch marks on my body, my fat feet, my curved nails, and my dope personality. Hell, I love all of me, flaws, and all. I learned that in order for me or anyone to heal, you must start with self!

Know that you are worth it! Know that your healing is essential, but you must make a conscious decision to heal! I know first-hand about depression, low self-esteem, rejection, abandonment, suicidal thoughts, attempted suicide, being lost, broken, and hurt. I have been there, and I never want to return to that place. Healing has allowed me to learn about myself as well as gain skills and tools to help me keep going. Depression is not my identity! Low self-esteem is not my identity! Rejection is not my identity! Abandonment is not my identity! Suicidal thoughts and attempts are not my identity! Being lost, broken, and hurt is not my identity. Divorce is not my identity!

Healed, whole, free, happy, loved, joy and GOD are my identity!

Jeremiah 29:11 (NIV version) **"For I know the plans I have for you, declares the Lord, plans to prosper you and not to harm you, plans to give you hope and a future."**
#HEALSISTAKEACTION#HEALBROTAKEACTION
Do broken crayons still color? Yes, they do! I'm living proof!

About Dominique

Dominique is the CEO and Founder of Purple Butterf.l.y. which pushes women and teen girls to seek their journey towards healing through self-love and self-care and she a new author of the book entitled "A Journey to Becoming A better Me Journal" which is a 90-day journey geared towards women and teens taking time to write and journal in order to become more in tune with themselves and learn more about themselves to assist them on their journey healing. She is also currently one of the featured authors in the upcoming book anthology entitled, "Broken Crayons Still Color". In addition, Dominique Serves as the Assistant Director to the founder of Beautiful Spirited Women, Armor Bearer to the CEO of Beautiful Spirited Women and the Sargent at Arms for Beautiful Spirited Women.

On January 25th, 2020 Dominique graduated as a Certified Life Coach with ICU Coaching Academy. Dominique, better known as the "Metamorphosis Coach" will focus on depression, life after divorce, low self-esteem, healing, and everyday struggles. In August 2020 Dominique was awarded the Beautiful Spirited Woman of the Year and in January of 2021 named Gurl Boss of the week by Girl Boss Brunch USA.

Dominique has lived a life committed to assisting and serving others in many different capacities. She is fun, loving, caring, committed, loyal, honest, dedicated, intelligent and leader in many different aspects. She prides herself on remaining humble and teachable. In her eyes there is always something to learn. She enjoys helping others and prides herself on being available and ready to SERVE. Stay tuned because there's definitely more to come. A woman of EXCELLENCE is what we call her. Remember with God ALL THINGS ARE POSSIBLE!

Chapter 22

Passing the Baton

BY PROMISES R. HUFF

On November 11, 2020, my life started to change without warning...

My husband, Huff, was teaching class and he told me that his throat had been feeling scratchy and he was going to take some meds before it developed into something worse. It got so bad after his classes, I demanded that we go to urgent care because he had plans to see his mother and she had not been well. We had learned earlier in the year that she had developed Parkinson's disease and Alzheimer's, and he knew that he could not go around her sick. It had been a while since we had seen our parents, but we made a pact that if either of us had to go to the doctor or we ended up getting sick we were not going back home to North Carolina, until we were safe to be around others. With COVID-19, we did not need any underlying issues to attract that disease.

The following Wednesday, my husband was tested for Strep, Flu, and COVID-19. He tested negative for all three, but the doctor gave him a five-day antibiotic. We went home and packed, preparing to leave the next day.

We were excited to see our daughter and son-in-love and did what we normally do--we ate, laughed, and cut up! Huff reminded me that he was getting up the next morning to go pick his dad up to take him to his VA appointment. I knew he was excited about spending time with his dad because his relationship with his parents has been severely strained for over seven years, and any time spent with them would be a hit.

When Huff got up the next morning, he got up early, eager to go get his dad, and off to the Ville they went. When he came back, he complained about being extremely thirsty. Later that night, he expressed that he was starting to feel bad and wanted me to check his temperature because he was cold. The next day, he still didn't feel well, but said he was going to teach class anyway. He got through the day, but he drank so much water that it had him going back and forth to the bathroom. His appetite was at a bare minimum by then, so all he could tolerate was pudding and Jell-O. During his last class, he asked if I could call our doctor to set an appointment because he just was not feeling normal. Of course, the earliest appointment that he could get was two weeks away.

Saturday rolled around and we were gearing up to head back home. We had already planned to do all of the grocery shopping on Monday, go to my talk show recording the following Tuesday, prep and cook on Wednesday. Then Thursday before Thanksgiving Dinner, we would put on our all white and take family photos. That is something that we had been planning for a while now. Even our dog Jax got a white hoodie to wear in the picture.

Monday morning, Huff was up early as usual brushing his teeth, gargling with hot salt water to make his throat feel better. He asked me where his Keto pills were, and I told him that I thought he needed to hold off on taking them due to his throat feeling like it was feeling, and he had already begun to lose so much weight. At that, he just said, "Okay", and proceeded to walk out of the room. I followed him out of the room to mess with him like I always do, but he was in no mood to play around because his throat was still hurting. He said he felt like his throat was closing up. I immediately called my sister (she is a nurse) and I gave her all of the symptoms Huff was having. After listening to me, she suggested that I take him to the ENT (Ear, Nose, Throat) doctor so that they could better assist us, and she sent me the name and number of a specialist to call. Before I called to set the appointment, I had called to get Huff an appointment at our family doctor again, but I was unsuccessful with getting a closer date. It seems like it never fails. Every Thanksgiving holiday turns out to be for the worst. For the last 4 years, it has been ruined, now we have to maintain a sore throat for the holidays again and Thanksgiving is Huff's favorite holiday.

That day we made it to the appointment with the ENT and we were there all of 15 minutes. The pandemic had shaken things up so much that you could not sit inside of the building if you did not have an appointment, or you were waiting. So, because of that, Huff had to go in on his own, get his paperwork and bring it back out to the car for me to fill out because he was just too weak. I finished the paperwork and I nudged Huff to wake him up because he had drifted off to sleep. "Lethargic" is all I could think of. Moments later, the nurse called his phone to tell him that he could come in and see the doctor. Because of COVID-19, no one other than the patient was allowed inside of the building. So, I had to sit in the car and wait. Fifteen minutes went by and Huff was on his way out of the building. He was walking slower coming out than he was going in. By the time he got into the car, he was severely drained. I asked him what the doctor said, and he told me that he had "yeast in his throat". Thrush is what it is called medically. All he could do was take the medicine that was prescribed to him for the next nine days. Before we left the parking lot, he motioned for me to go and get a smoothie from a few doors down and I did just that. I got our favorite "Bahama Mama". The crushed ice and coldness of the smoothie was helping his throat, it seemed to ease the pain at least until I could get him the medicine to take.

Once at home, we were able to relax and unwind. After we dozed off, I realized that he had gotten out of the bed and was sitting on the floor. It freaked me out because he was slumped over. I immediately got out of the bed to check on him, he was bundled up in his hoodie and jogging pants as normal and he had our blanket wrapped around him. He said that he was trying to get comfortable and warm and nothing he tried worked. So, I turned the heat up, got him off the floor and back into the bed. As I proceeded to give him his other meds along with his antibiotic, he began to speak to me with slurred speech. He started talking about him seeing a lot of bodies lying around.

I immediately turned around and said " wait.... what did you say?"

He said, "I see different shapes and colors.... there is a lot of data processing that needs to be done".

The first thing that came to my mind was that he is either talking crazy or he has had a stroke. So, I asked him, "Boo are you ok? Did you have a stroke?"

Though his speech was very slurred, he still slowly answered, "Noooooooooooo, I am not having a stroke, I am just trying to...", and he pointed at his chest.

He seemed as though the more he talked the more he struggled to get the words out and it became frustrating for him. Soon, I began to hear his breathing change. He was long and slow and all he kept saying was, "I am trying...but my stomach."

I immediately began to pray over his body and ask God to heal him because I did not have a clue of what was happening, but I just knew that I needed for him to be ok. After I prayed over him, I rolled him back into bed and just informed him that he was going to be fine.

As Tae and I began to cook in preparation for Thanksgiving, I made Huff aware of where I was going to be, and that Nichole was going to watch him and make sure he had everything he needed but if he needed me, I was a text and a holla away in the kitchen. No longer than twenty minutes of being in the kitchen, I heard a loud thump. I dropped everything I was doing and ran to the bedroom only to find him on the floor on one knee.

"Why are you on the floor?", I asked, rushing to his side.

The best explanation he could give me was that "he was trying but he couldn't do it" and before I could ask what he meant, I looked down at his clothes and realized that he had an accident, and he was very embarrassed by it because our daughter saw it happening.

After I cleaned him up, I helped him get back in the bed and just stood by the bed and talked to him. He looked exhausted and all he wanted was ice cold water. I called my sister friend who is a nurse and asked her to come over before she went to work and assess him.

Once Lisa arrived, it was like her heart sank and I saw her entire mood changed. She asked him his name, held up a few fingers to make sure his vision was intact and just tried to ask simple questions to him to see what kind of response she could get. When she heard him speaking and breathing... she immediately said for me to give him a steaming hot bath and it would help with breathing. So, as she gave me instructions on what to do, her and Tae went to the store to get meds, tea, and broth to see if we could make him feel any better. We had already checked his temperature and he didn't have a fever, so we thought all of those antidotes and home remedies would do the trick.

I got him bathed, dressed, and helped him get back on the bean bag chair. Once he got settled, Lisa brought in the broth and the yogurt. As he drank on that and ate a little bit of the yogurt, he looked like he had gotten his second wind! He ate as much as he could, then got comfortable on the bean bag. Lisa left to go to work, Nichole took her place on the floor with him so that they could watch a movie and Tae and I went back in the kitchen to continue preparing Thanksgiving dinner. He seemed to be doing better.

Later, I checked in on Huff and Nichole, and everything appeared to be ok. I stole kisses from the both of them as they continued to try and watch a movie that was clearly watching them. I walked out of the room in confidence, knowing that everything was going to be alright. Not even thirty minutes had passed, and my name was being yelled out from the bedroom. Huff was back on the floor again and he looked like he had been fighting because he was just tired!

I looked down at his clothes and he was wet again; I rushed over to help him without saying a word and as I tried to help him, he got upset. He wanted to get up on his own, but he could not. He had lost mobility in his arms and legs and without help, he could not get up. I immediately called Lisa to come over once she was off work and thankfully, she was already on her way. God gave me supernatural strength because Huff was not able to help me at all as I managed to lift him halfway onto the bed. I got the items needed to wash him up and change his clothes again, and after I got him cleaned up, the only thing he could do was slide back down to the floor.

When Lisa arrived and saw him on the floor, she looked at me and immediately told me to either take him to the ER or have them come get him. She called two hospitals to find out how long it would be before he could be seen.

After Lisa found a hospital that could get Huff in quickly, I told her I would rather take him to the ER myself. Once he was dressed, Caleb helped me get him to the car. We got him in the car and I just told everybody to pray, gave instructions to all of the kids and I took my King to the ER.

On the way, I talked to him and reassured him that everything would be ok. He was listening, but he was just having trouble breathing and scared at the same time.

Once at the ER, thankfully, there was a male nurse at the front, and he assisted me with getting Huff inside. There was no wait, so things moved pretty fast. After giving the nurse all of his medical information, I was asked to hang out in the waiting room until they got a bed for him in the ER. For some reason, things just did not seem right, but I just began praying immediately. Moments later, the nurse came out and asked if she could pray with me and I accepted without hesitation. I must have had a very distraught look on my face, or maybe she heard every detail that was happening and just could not find the right words to tell me....

While waiting, the nurse came out and asked, if I knew that Huff was a severe diabetic. I told her no and that he has was not, nor had he ever been a diabetic. She then told me that he should have been in a coma when I brought him in. His blood sugar level was over a 1000! I didn't know anything about diabetes--I did not know if it was good or bad but clearly it was not good because of the look that she had on her face. She then informed me that his kidneys had failed and that he was not breathing on his own anymore. He was indeed breathing but he needed a little help, and they did not want to take any chances. I immediately walked towards his room and got stopped by the doctor on call. She pulled me off to the side and told me straight up, "Listen to me right now, sister to sister-- clean your face up right now. It's not looking good for him in there and if you go in there looking like you are looking, he will know that something is wrong and will be scared out of his mind. So, wipe your face and walk into that room like you already know he is healed".

I stood up straight, grabbed the tissue that she handed me and got my breathing pattern together and walked right into the room. The moment I opened the door, it felt like my heart was ripped right out of my chest as I watched my King lay on that stretcher with tubes coming from every which way, on a ventilator and scared out of his mind! I walked right up to him and immediately gave him all of the kisses and love he could stand. He looked at me with tears in his eyes because he wanted so bad to talk to me, but he was unable to. He motioned for me to come and hold his hand and I did just that. I just continued to tell him that I loved him and that everything was going to be ok. The nurse explained to me that he had to be restrained due to him trying to pull the tube out of his throat. I suggested that they allow me to stay as close to him as possible because he was very anxious and scared. Seeing me there eased his fears because at that moment, I was the protector, and I was going to make sure that he was well taken care of so that we could go back home and get ready for Thanksgiving dinner that was only a few hours away.

After getting him calm, he was sedated so that he would give his lungs a chance to rest. As time went on, the nurse came back in and informed me that he was going to ICU. They wanted him to be as comfortable as possible because from the looks of it, he was going to be there for a while.

Later in the day of Thanksgiving Day, the doctor on call came into the ER and talked with me about how we ended up there. From trying to lose weight with keto pills, to having a sore throat that was not strep, COVID-19 free, to taking an antibiotic to treat the sore throat like it was strep throat, to going to the ENT on Monday 11/23 and getting ANOTHER antibiotic for having yeast in his throat, to breathing hard and then losing mobility.

Now, we are here with a blood sugar level over 1000, being told my husband should have been in a coma when we got to the ER, but by the grace of GOD, He sustained him. I had no idea of what was happening because I was not a diabetic. I had never been around a diabetic firsthand. So, all of that was like speaking a fresh foreign language to me and as much as I was paying attention, I truly felt like I was failing at that moment.

When the next doctor came in, he introduced himself to me and told me exactly what was needed to be said. Instead of trying to paint a pretty picture, the doctor knew I needed the boldface truth, and that is exactly what I got! The doctor told me how damaged his kidneys were, and it was a long road ahead of us. Dialysis will be needed, and it will be for the rest of his life. I was also informed that there were blood clots in his lungs, and he had a stomach ulcer. I was uncertain about everything; all I could see was what was in front of me. They gave him medication that was needed to bring his blood sugar level down. Thanks to God that every time they had to check his levels; they were lower. So, something was happening, and I was excited about it.

After it seemed his blood sugar was coming down steadily, I decided to finally go home and get myself together. The staff made sure that I was contacted if there were any changes and I trusted what they said and left to go home. I was going home to take a shower, finish cooking Thanksgiving dinner and clean up so the house would be ready for Huff when he came home.

A few hours had passed, and I decided to gather the kids, say grace, and go back to the hospital to watch over Huff. I went back to the hospital with the intentions of shaving his head and cleaning up his beard so that he would not look like an old mountain man. When I checked in and entered Huff's room, he was still laying there peacefully. I rubbed his hands to let him know that I was in the room and I kissed him so that he could feel me and all of my love. He opened his eyes and saw me standing there and tears just fell from his eyes.

Within the next few hours, his blood sugar level was brought all the way down to 330. It was still high but nowhere near 1000. His levels were stabilized. While sitting with him, I noticed something odd, his hands began to feel cold. I immediately pulled the cover back to feel his feet and his legs and they were cold as well. Before I could tell the nurse, he was coming through the door, he saw my face and hit the button on the wall and yelled for help! At first, I just sat there not knowing what I should do but then it hit me that he had coded!

Code Blue! Code Blue is all I heard! One of the nurses escorted me out of the room and down the hall so that she could talk to me. When we got to the waiting area, the nurse asked me if I knew what was going on and I said, yes...he coded. She confirmed that he was definitely coding and that they would work on him for as long as it takes. I agreed that that would be the right thing to do, and as soon as she walked away from me, I immediately started to pray.

I started calling everyone that he had coded, and they were working to bring him back. We prayed for over an hour on the phone and I just began to call out the name Jesus! While on my knees I felt this cold hand on my shoulder telling me that they needed me back in the room. I was informed that they were able to bring him back, but his pulse was very faint.

The doctor came in to let me know they were sending him to get a CT scan to see what caused all of the commotion and see if they could grab a hold of the situation.

Not too long after that, the doctor on call came in and he had the most distressed look on his face. He was a Caucasian man, so he had begun to turn red, and his eyes were filled with water. "What's wrong Doc?" Why are you looking like that? He showed me a picture of what a normal brain with activity looked like and then he showed me what Huff's brain and activity looked like....

"Ma'am, based off of the CT scan, your husband had blood clots in his lungs and one we can't even locate anymore.... but his brain activity is on 0. His brain is swollen and now he is dead....', the doctor's voice trailed off.

All I could do was stand still because that is what my world had done-- stood still.

I was listening to this doctor tell me that "even if there was a way to decrease the swelling and he pulls through, the quality of life that he will have is little to none. Is that what you want for him?", he asked. He went on, "Mrs. Huff, I don't know how to tell you this but just being upfront and honest with you. We have tried all we could to decrease the swelling the in your husband's brain but the meds that we tried did not work. We were too late."

Evidently the look on my face startled everyone in the room because before I felt my knees buckle, I felt someone grab my arm and hold me before I hit the floor.

After I barely gathered my thoughts, I asked abruptly." so what you're telling me is....my husband is basically dead and there is nothing else that can be done...that's what you're saying to me?"

"Yes ma'am... all of what you see happening right here is artificial, meaning if we unplug this ventilator right now, in a matter of seconds, your husband's heart will stop beating".

This time for sure--I knew that if it hadn't happened before, surely my whole soul was sucked out of me this time! There was nothing left in me! Huff was really just lying there, with just an ounce of listening skills left. I heard the doctor say, " I'm sorry Mrs. Huff, but medically your husband has passed on, he is no longer here with us".

I saw the nurse walk towards me to tell me that I can wait to unplug the machines and to take my time. I found myself walking towards the head of Huff's bed and I just laid down on his chest. I could not even cry.

It was in that moment that I knew that everything else that I had to say needed to be said to him.

I just began kissing his face and loving on him, tears, and all. I told Huff how he had made me the happiest wife on the face of the planet, he was and still remains the best dad in the world to us, I thanked him for spoiling me and for giving me everything that I never had in any relationship, friendship, or marriage and that was genuine Agape love!

Even though I heard what the doctor said, I refused to speak death over him! I continued to speak life to him and tell him that all of the work that he and I did together and separately would not be in vain and that I would not abort the mission! I told him that I refused to let him go and to please not make me have to be the one to pull the plug because his life was in my hands.

I immediately walked over to the bay window in Huff's room and looked up to the sky, talking to God silently because I needed for Him to give me some kind of direction on what to do.

Without any signs, I automatically felt a strong sense of peace come over me and I knew that Huff was right there ready to walk through Heavens gates, but I just did not want to be the one to let his hand and heart go. I asked God for one more request before he allowed Huff to take his rest…

I instructed the doctor and the nurses to go ahead and leave him on the insulin, saline and medicine drip but take him off of the ventilator because even though his pulse was faint, I had asked God for one last thing before his heart stopped beating fully. Medically, Huff was already gone but knowing that he could still hear me until his heart stopped was the inkling of strength to say what I needed to say and trust that God would honor my request....and He did.

The very last words I said to Huff were: "If you love me like I know you love me; you won't stop breathing when they take you off of this machine. I asked God before he took you with him, to allow me to hear you breathe one more time, so you have to do that for me. I can hear this machine beeping and pushing air through you.... but I need to hear your breath! You have to be the one to pass the baton to me, not the other way around".

In strong faith, I asked for the nurse to unplug the machine because I asked for something to happen and I knew it would. She reminded me that in a matter of seconds, once she unplugged the ventilator, Huff's heart would stop working all together. I knew what she said, but I also knew what I asked my Daddy for!

As the nurse unplugged the machine, I kissed him and wiped my tears on his eyes and continued to just hold on to what I had left of him. I put my ear to his mouth to hear him breathe that one last time. The moment I leaned in and put my left hand over his heart, I heard Huff exhale short and quick...."Huhhhhh."

I looked up at the clock and it read, 4:36 pm. Immediately, I turned to him and said, "You did it bae, you did it just for me. I'll take it from here boo. I love you." I kissed him and just kept my lips on his lips.

Seconds later, the nurse walked in and said, "Mrs. Huff… his heart just stopped." I asked her what time it was, and she confirmed that it was indeed, "4:36 pm" when he passed the baton and won the race.

I know there is more work to be done. My husband left here prematurely at the age of 39. We were building a legacy, multiple businesses and manifesting the things that we wanted in life. Things were starting to look up for us and then I lost my best friend.

Listen, I don't know who needed to read my story, but whomever you are, whatever you are going through or have been through in your life or in this season, just know that there is still work to be done, you still have purpose in life, and no matter how much rain comes your way ...you have to become storm proof!

I (you) may bend, and I (you) may even break just a little bit, but know that my (your) broken heart (your crayon) WILL STILL COLOR.

Coach Promises R. Huff

(In loving memory of my late husband Coach William R. Huff) #HuffTuff

About Promises

Coach Promises R. Huff is an International Best-Selling Author, and Certified Life and Re-Entry Coach originally from Raeford, NC and now, currently resides in Greensboro, NC. She is a proud HBCU Alumni of Fayetteville State University (Fayetteville, NC). She has held many licenses and certifications, including that of Certified Daycare Management, Licensed Cosmetologist in three (3) different states, Licensed Paraprofessional, and now a Certified Life Coach of ICU Coaching Academy.

In addition to wearing all her hats in the corporate world, she found her greatest joy in being married to her high school soulmate, the late Coach William R. Huff, and mother to their four (4) beautiful, handsome, intelligent, and talented children. It cannot go unnoticed that she is also a dog owner.

With experience from the law enforcement industry, she has developed, nurtured, and heightened her passion and vision to new levels. They have been the motivation behind her desire to assist individuals and families to identify, establish, persistently pursue, and accomplish their goals and visions. She is taking it a step further, as she is striving to instruct, guide, and mentally rehabilitate individuals to adapt and take advantage of their second chance in life through the Re-Entry Program specifically designed for that population.

Promises is a devoted Christian and member of New Direction Christian Church. She is a member and volunteer in the communities representing Chi Sigma Delta Sorority Incorporated (since Summer 2019) and Krimson Kourts Incorporated (Kappa Sweet since 1999), and BSW (Beautiful Spirited Women) since 2018.

Chapter 23

A Mother's Heartbreak

BY DENISE GRANBERRY

As I am writing this, my heart is broken. We haven't had the chance to talk to my son, who is at a psychiatric hospital at this time. I'm so worried about him. God has been healing my heart as I have been praying and asking God to help me find out what is going on with him. I finally mustered up the courage to talk with my son, so I called him on Christmas Day. I didn't get to talk to him, so I called him again on the day after Christmas, but we didn't get a response until today, December 29th. His social worker called, and my daughter and I had a conversation on speaker phone with her. She had news about my son, and told us that he hadn't been feeling well, so he was tested for COVID19. She told us the test came back negative! The social worker went on to say that my son had been given some medicine for his ailment. At that point, the social worker went on to tell us that my son, Chris, has been causing trouble at the hospital with his behavior. He's been stripping down to nakedness and trying to jump on staff members. This behavior forced the staff to lock him down. My daughter asked about the medicine and any side effects it would have on my son, since he's taking psych meds. She went on to tell the social worker of an incident that happened when he was home. He had taken some over the counter medicine in combination with his psychiatric medications and had a reaction. The social worker said that she hadn't thought about that possibility, and that could be what happened.

My daughter went on to suggest another issue may be causing a problem as well. She said, "Well, you know what else could be wrong? My brother did not get to speak with us on Christmas". That seemed to get the social worker's attention, and she replied, "well, you know, you could be right about that because the holidays are hard".

Okay, that's what I'm talking about. When is it going to stop? When is going to stop and when are they going to stop treating people with mental health the wrong way? People with mental health issues are treated like they don't have feelings, or they are treated as if they don't know what's going on, as if they are unaware. These patients know that it is the holiday season, and it's a time for family gatherings. They expect to be able to talk to their family members. I know some people are not there for their children who have gone through things like this.

I had to take a deep breath and choose to trust God through the process. That's all I've got-- my faith in trusting God that's it. I wouldn't wish this pain on anybody. I just want to bring awareness to the issues of mental health. Get my son and other sons help. They need help so badly, it's a heartbreaking situation every day. God brings me through it, each and every day. And I'm thankful for that.

The problem is mental health. It's mental health in the African American community, and what I've gone through with my son. It's the systemic racism that me and my son endured while trying to get him help. You see, I saw the signs of my son having a mental illness at the age of ten when he was in elementary school, and I tried to get help. I tried to get help, first with family, by reaching out to my son's grandmother which is his father's mom. Now, my son's father had mental health issues: he had paranoid schizophrenia, and he was bipolar. And at first, I was in denial about it because as a Christian, you don't want to claim, mental illness; in the Christian world, it's like these are demons being dealt with, but it's mental health. So, you end up being in denial. Because you're depending and trusting on God to help you help your son get deliverance from something that his father has gone through. I fought hard, and I reached out to my son's grandmother, because she was the only one that I could reach out to that I knew that would help me with my son. I called her and asked her, because she helped me when my son was getting kicked out of schools. He was being belligerent in elementary and that's when it started.

When I reached out to her, she said, I need you to pray about it. Whatever you decide, and whatever God tells you to do, that's what we'll go with. So, I prayed about it and I prayed about it. It was so hard because I did not want to give up on my son. I did not want my son to feel I was giving up on him when he was screaming and crying out for help. There was nothing that the school system was doing, they were saying that my son was slow and that he needed medicine. At the time I did not have the education and I didn't want to put my son on medicine. So, I reached out to his great grandmother. I prayed about it and I was able to send my son to her. So, my son stayed with her. My son was acting out when he was with her, so he started going to see a therapist with her. After he stayed with her for like a year, he was still having signs of mental illness, so I went and got my son and brought him back here with me to North Carolina. When he was twelve years old, he started stealing from me and my fiancé. He was cutting up in school not doing this work.

At that point I was screaming and crying out for help again. They sent my son to this place here in North Carolina where it really didn't help at all. There we were again back to the drawing board, so I called his grandmother again, but by this time she's up in age, but she agreed to give it another try. By that time, he was kicked out of the school systems in North Carolina. His grandmother and I thought we could try it again and get him on the right track. So, I sent him back to his grandmother's house. It did not work like we hoped it would; he was belligerent and disrespectful while he was there, and his grandmother couldn't handle it, especially as she was getting older, you know. I told her to send him back to me, and we'll do what we have to do to get him the help that he needs. That is when my son's aunt intervened. She said she would try to help him. By that time, he was fifteen, almost sixteen.

He went to stay with his aunt, and he's cutting up doing drugs, driving her crazy. He's just doing all kinds of stuff. She called me one night and said she was washing her hands of the mess and that she couldn't do it. She sent my son back home to me.

As my son is approaching 16, and my son was cutting up on drugs. I am having a time with him. My son was using anything he could get his hands on to get high. The drugs, combined with his mental illness, made him violent, and it got so hectic that my son started putting his hands on me, and so I had to press charges on my son. Nobody wanted to help. When the police had to come to my house, they didn't know what to do and told me there wasn't anything they could do for me. One day, he put his hands on me again. In order for my son to get help from the system, I had to press charges on him at the ripe age of fifteen and a half. From there, he was sent to a group home.

Once he is in the group home, I do not know how they're treating him, praying to God that they're treating him right. They have got him on so many meds, but he has not been diagnosed yet. I wasn't able to get anyone to diagnose him in North Carolina. He acts belligerent at the group home and gets naked in front of them. He ends up getting kicked out of the group home because he was so disruptive there. He broke out one of the employee's car windows at the group home, so they had to file charges on him.

Once he turned 16, he was locked up in the county jail in Fayetteville, North Carolina. This is heartbreaking. This is so heartbreaking. So here I am again, back and forth to court because they are wanting him to do the time for vandalizing the vehicle at the group home he was at. Once he did the time, they have nowhere to place my son. I had to tell them that since my son hasn't had proper care and evaluation, I do not trust my son to come home because I'm scared. He's already jumped on me. He's already put his hands on me. We need to find out the right diagnosis and what's going on with him so we can get him on the proper meds, so that he can come home. That way I will know how to take care of him, because this is new to me too. I'm nearly breaking down not eating, not wanting to eat, because I'm going through all of this. So now he is locked up for nothing because they had no placement for him. One more heartbreak on top of a broken heart. I have become so broken, screaming, and crying at the injustice, and frustration of it all.

Finally, they offer a 'solution'. I have to sign over custody. I have to sign my rights over to the state of North Carolina, in order for them to get my son some help. This is also a broken system, and here goes my son, falling through the cracks. They got my son.

What I have learned about the system is that did not have placement. If they do have placement, they were not giving it to too many African American children, especially boys. Due to incorrect diagnosis, they put my son in a level one facility which he did not belong in. He belonged in a level five facility. In the level one, he was already doing so many dangerous things that got him into trouble. He was already stealing from me and my fiancé and was being put on probation. My son ended up running away and nobody contacted me from the state DSS to tell me that he had run away for almost a month. When they finally called, they asked me if I had seen my son. Now, mind you, at this point, I was upset, so I questioned them, asking, "Now, you guys are supposed to be helping me with my son... y'all are aware that my son has a mental illness, right?"

So, there I was on the search for my son in the neighborhood, and everywhere I could think of. Now everybody that I knew in the area told me that they saw my him. They told me he was asking them for money to get something to eat. I think he wanted to get drugs. A few days later, I get a knock on the door and it was a police officer.

He said, "Um, ma'am, Miss – Miss Granberry."

"Yes?"

"Um, we found your son".

When I asked where he was, the officer told me they had found him in an abandoned house behind mine. The police had brought him home to me, and he was waiting out on the front porch. Finally! I went out on the front porch to see with my own eyes, and there he was. I looked at him, and told him everything that had been in my heart to say:

"Son, I love you so much. We've got to get you the best help that we can, that's what I'm here for-- to get you help. You are going to go back 'til we see what's going on. You know I want you here, that's why we're trying to get you better. You know I'm trying to get you the help that you need".

He took a deep breath, and he went with the police officer. Now he's back in DSS custody. They finally found a placement for him-- a group home. It was a therapeutic group home, not somewhere that would help him but a therapeutic group home. They did not care if he was going to school during the day; all they did was dope him up with medicine. They didn't have a diagnosis for him. They didn't care to know what was going on with my son. This was court ordered. My son didn't want to go to school while he was at that facility. Every day was the same; they woke him up, he took his medicine, he went to a room that looked like a prison cell. He spent six months at the therapeutic group home. He was seventeen years old by then, almost eighteen. In those six months my son doubled in size because of the medicine they gave him, not to mention he was so doped up, he was like a zombie. I got custody back when my son turned eighteen. There wasn't anything else the state could do for my him they said. They did not offer any training for him, they just told me that since he was eighteen, he couldn't be forced to take his medicine, and that he was an adult. It was like he turned eighteen, and they seemed to think he wasn't sick anymore, like he was healed. But that just wasn't the case.

June 4, 2018

My son came home on. He started the same behavior as before. He was belligerent and started taking drugs again. He stopped taking the medicine the doctor had given him.

September 12. 2018

My son murdered my fiancé. In front of my face for no reason at all, all because he was mentally ill. He could not handle his mental illness because he wasn't taking his meds. From July, all the way to September, we were calling the police for help- crying out for him, screaming out for him! Pleading for help for me and my fiancé, but the system failed all of us.

After going through that, I went into a deep depression. Two of the most important men in my life at the time-- gone. Just like that. I didn't even understand why when I did everything that I could. I exhausted the whole North Carolina system trying to get my son the help that he needed before a tragedy happened.

Now I have PTSD, after all that I've been through, and seeing the murder of my fiancé by my son. It was very painful, and it still is painful to this day. I just want to tell my story because I know that there's somebody getting ready to go through this, or somebody who has already gone through it; someone who has come through a trauma and they don't know what to do. They don't know where to turn. They don't know who to talk to, because if they tell people the story about their children being mentally ill, and their children doing anything tragic, nobody's going to believe them. Nobody's going to believe them unless somebody else tells their story and how real mental illness is.

I just want to tell my story and let everybody know that God has me here for a reason. It is God. It is my faith in God, it is my faith in Jesus. It is nobody but God that gets me up each and every day, and helps me to forgive my son, each and every day.

I realize that I did everything that I possibly could do to help my son through his mental illness, and that mental illness is real. It's okay to talk about mental illness, it, and that mental illness is not just a stigma. I know that a lot of people are going through this and I know that God is using me to help others. So, this is why I tell my story, so that others can stay strong and have courage to talk about mental illness, so others can be bold and to help others and the community. This is my story. And it is God who is helping me through it. I know my story is not like others. I know that it may be possibly confusing to many. I was totally broken through this ordeal. I love my child with everything in me. The ordeal broke me in places that I did not know I could be broken. I almost gave up so many times. But I am here to tell you that you can still color. You can break through with the help of God and color your life vibrantly. I am here to tell you that broken crayons still color.

About Denise

Denise Granberry is a full-time entrepreneur that specializes in the Barber and Beauty Services industry and success Barber and Beauty coaching. She has a bachelor's degree in theology with an additional specialization in Branding, Marketing and Advertising. A renaissance woman, Ms. Granberry offers multiple services and levels of expertise in various industries. Currently, she owns and operates Vickie Styling where she designs and sell customized salon capes, smocks, aprons, shears, razors, and much more. Her latest successful venture is Global KINGS & QUEENS Preneur, a lifestyle brand that was created to empower women and men in the beauty industry to encourage Abundance, Luxury, & Independence to aspiring entrepreneurs of all creeds. While offering merchandise to salon owners and stylists is one arm of the movement, Global KINGS & QUEENS Preneur also deliver powerful coaching services and events to assist and motivate women embarking on their entrepreneurial journey.

Being in the beauty industry for over two decades, Ms. Granberry has seen it all! She understands what it feels like to have big dreams, without the ability to bring them to fruition. Through trial and error, she eventually found her way. Now she uses her experiences to teach others to prevent them from travelling the arduous, expensive journey she once traversed. Through her role as an educator, she travels to Beauty Schools and Salons to mentor and teach the proper way to be successful in the Barber and Beauty industry and grow a brand. She has a strong passion for making a difference and positively influencing the lives of others by teaching them to tap into their passion. Through teaching, assisting, empowering, and industry activism, Ms. Granberry is living her passion, and creating strong relationships of trust with all of her associates along the way.

Her faith in God has sustained her and she doesn't limit herself to anything. She encourages everyone to do the same. It is her life's mission.

Chapter 24

Convicted Felon

BY LATISHA A. RANDLE

The First Time Offender Who Never Gave Up!

Life is a continuous journey to get to your destiny. So please, never dim your light for anyone, let your light shine bright. You matter, you are worthy, and you have a purpose. That is what I told myself, and I want to convey this message to you as well.

I grew up in a predominately white neighborhood. I remember witnessing racism firsthand as a small child. We were the second black family to purchase a home on my street. I had a neighbor whose confederate flag would blow back and forth with the wind. As a young child, I really did not know what racism was or the history behind it. I was an innocent little girl, who would skip up and down the street, free from any harm and life's trials and tribulations!

"Hi Mr. Patterson."

"Hi."

I remember speaking to him, but he would not speak back. I often thought he did not hear me, so I would say, 'Hi', more than a few times. I would wave and smile, but he never acknowledged me. Mr. Patterson 's wife would always make it her business to speak to me. I told my mother about this and she said, "Baby that's just how he is, he don't like black folks."

I was a bit confused, but I still spoke to him when I saw him sitting on the porch. One day my mother got a phone call and she heard Mr. Patterson's wife passed. I felt so sad for him, even though he did not like me because of the color of my skin. While my friends and I were walking to Wilson Farms, there he was sitting on the porch. Can you believe he said, "Hi" and waved at me first? I noticed the flag was gone. I guess he may have had a change of heart since his wife passed away. I understand more now than ever, that it's never too late to change for the better. Sometimes life's experiences will either make you or break you. You choose!

My mother and father were divorced, and my mom became the breadwinner. She worked multiple jobs just to make ends meet; that led to her never being home. I can say my mother did the best she could to raise me at that time in her life. My older siblings moved out, leaving me to care for two of my younger family members.

I was well developed as I grew into my early teenage years, as a fifteen-year-old with the body of an eighteen-year-old. I was so naive, and I wore my feelings on my sleeve. I was a teenager taking on the role of an adult, with responsibilities that I did not know how to handle. At the age of eighteen, I gave birth to a handsome, healthy baby boy. I was so thankful for my son. Although his father and I were not together, I gave my son his first name but not his last name. I was being plain ole stubborn. Then I moved out of my mother's house when he was four months old. My mother wanted me to stay home but I was hard-headed. I could hear her voice like it was yesterday.

"Tupper, stay home baby and finish school, save your money, and buy you a home."

She always wanted the best for me. I ignored her concern for my life, and I moved out. In case you're wondering how I got the name, "Tupper", my mother used to sell Tupperware. She went into labor with me at a Tupperware party, and "voila!" the name has stuck with me ever since.

Let me share with you the choices I made that brought me to this point in my life. I had a boyfriend and we moved in together. I was a cashier by day and sold drugs by night. I was living the life. So, I thought. After about a year we broke up. Our relationship was both mentally and physically unhealthy. The break-up did not last too long. We ended up right back together. Although I had an order of protection against him, he would still come over to my house.

One day, we got into a huge fight. He grabbed a knife and threatened to stab me. I was able to calm him down. Once he placed the knife on the counter, I grabbed it and ran to the front hallway, seizing the opportunity to get away to protect myself and my son. I ran to the front door thinking my grandmother was pulling up to my apartment. Eric made a comment that he would hurt my grandmother. At that moment, I blacked out and stabbed him in the back as he walked away. There were puddles of blood all over the floor. The police came and took me to jail. Eric wanted to press charges. So, there I was eighteen years old going to jail for what could have been attempted murder. I just wanted to protect myself; I thought, God, I don't want to serve time in prison. What will my son do without his mother? The charges were dropped because I had an order of protection against him already for domestic violence. The police arrested him while he was in the hospital.

We eventually got back together, and no one could believe it. Ultimately the relationship did not last too long after. But we remain friends to this day.

I had this saying back in the day: "Ex to the next!" Maybe because I witnessed how my mother interacted with men! If the negro failed to act right, she would definitely move forward. I am sure a lot of women and men can relate to this. As time went on, I got involved in another relationship, having no clue of what was ahead for me. My life changed forever again. Choices are so real!

I was a high school dropout with no vision, as I continued to hustle and work. When I was younger, I had dreams of becoming a police officer or a lawyer. Somewhere along the way, I lost myself and made choices that took me in the opposite direction. I continued to feed more of the bad in me than the good. This girl was in the streets. You could not tell me anything. I was getting money, smoking weed every day, drinking and partying. I had no problem being violent if I needed to, but deep down inside, I knew I wanted more out of life.

I was broken.

My mother worked as a Patient Care Assistant and she encouraged me to enroll in the training program. I completed my application and attended the two-week training. I aced my exam and my skills test. I was on the move. I got wind of an opportunity to become a HHA (Home Health Aide). It is sort of like a PCA, but you have more skills. For example, I was skilled to take a person's blood pressure. It was like I was living a double life. A PCA/HHA during the day and a beast at night. I would get up in the morning and get dressed in my professional all white nursing scrubs, as if I were already a Registered Nurse, which was my ultimate goal. I knew I couldn't hustle or be with a hustler all my life. At that point, I knew I needed to get my general equivalency diploma (GED). After completing my HHA, I got clients who loved me. I was a very respectful young lady. My mother always taught me to respect my elders. I remember one of my clients, staring at me and saying, "You dress so professional, a lot of these girls come here, wearing pants with their ass hanging out and low-cut shirts, I could see all their cleavage." But you, you dress so nice and professional!"

"Thank you," I replied with a smile.

She had no clue I was just like those girls. I wore low cut shirts showing my cleavage and tight ass pants. My mother always told me there was a time and a place for everything. Although I was young, I still knew how to be professional. I could remember daydreaming about my life and the life I wanted for my son. And it all changed in the blink of an eye!!

One day, I was downstairs at my neighbor's house, braiding my son's hair. It was so long and thick, people would mistake him for a little girl. I had a strange feeling in the pit of my stomach while sitting on the couch. It was like I heard and saw someone running across the grass. I looked out the window and saw nothing. Soon after that, I went upstairs. Always follow your gut feeling.

BOOM! this loud noise came from downstairs and I heard a stampede of footsteps running up the stairs. SWAT came with the battering ram.

"Damn! My house is getting raided!", I thought to myself.

One of the officers looked at my homegirl (who I thought was my friend), and said "What are you doing here? Didn't I tell you to stay from over here?"

With her hands up in the air planted on the wall, "She replied "Sorry officer, sorry".

"Wow ", I thought, she was a snitch!! I was furious but there was nothing I could do. My son went with my downstairs neighbor and I was hauled off to jail.

I got out the next day, not knowing what was ahead of me. Needless to say, I did not have a paid lawyer. I had a "Public Pretender". They told my mom that I was looking at fifteen years in prison. I was devastated!

"Fifteen years," I thought.

I was in total disbelief. Again, my life did a whole 360, I was back at the same point. I was facing a possible fifteen-year jail term for my self-destructive choices, possibly leaving my son without a mother to take care of him. I felt hopeless, sad, angry, and hurt. The judge slapped me with a felony for possession of crack cocaine. I believe it was a draconian decision. Since I was a 'first time offender', I was sentenced to five years' probation. and granted a "Certificate of Relief from Disabilities. In a nutshell, it is a document that gave me a second chance at life. Having a felony is a true defamation of character.

I had to report to my probation officer every week. She went over the guidelines. Informing me, I could get off early for good behavior. Now it was time to get my life on the right track. No more drug selling or weed smoking. I would get drug tested randomly. I hated it. I told myself I did not belong here, reporting my life to this lady. Gave me such a feeling of disgust. This is not my life I thought. I felt my life was ruined. I explained my future plans to become a nurse. She looked me straight in the eyes and said, with a smirk, "You can't become a nurse. You have charges for drug possession and in that field, they handle narcotics."

My heart dropped. I was devastated. I left her office with my head down. I cried all the way home, and for many years thereafter. Damn near every day! My dream of becoming a nurse was shattered. Later I discovered I could have attended a nursing program. But my probation officer failed to educate me. No blame, I should have done my own research!

My life got worse. I could remember filling out my first application after my case was over. I noticed the question, 'Have you ever been convicted of a felony?' As I gazed at the question, feeling sick to my stomach. I have to check yes, "oh my God!" What does this mean for my life? Why do they have this question on a job application? I am a good person, I just made some mistakes in my life, is what I thought. I no longer could check 'NO'. I have to tell these people about my secret life. I did not get a call back from that company and many others to come. I could not find a job. I felt stuck. I was broke and broken.

I held onto hope, telling myself somewhere over the rainbow dreams do come true. I worked menial jobs and received housing assistance. I also received social services. I felt so ashamed going back and forth to appointments with those people. Some of the workers were just plain nasty and racist. I would cry because I knew that if I cussed their asses out, it was a possibility I could go to jail.

I started a new life. My son's father and I decided to get back together, and we eventually got married. I was determined not to fail. I enrolled at Erie Community College, where I received an associate degree in Liberal Arts and Science, Humanities, and Social Science. Then I transferred to Buffalo State College graduating with my bachelor's degree in Sociology. Shortly after that, I enrolled in a master's program in adult education. Due to unforeseen circumstances, I had to quit the program. During these life events I continued to mentor and work with youth. I really love it. So much so that the girls started calling me "Martin Luther Queen", as a joke. I showed gratitude and explained to them why I felt honored. Fifteen years later, God blessed me with my healthy beautiful Princess. I was so thankful. I had my boy and now my girl.

I had been through so many trials and tribulations; I never saw it coming. I guess that is the beauty of life: I have made so many bad choices, and I have made so many good ones, never giving up on myself!

So, in the present day, I have a career at a great company, where I am a caseworker for youth in foster care. I also have a part-time job working with at-risk young women. Ironically, I applied for these two jobs years ago, but I never heard back from either one; clearly, you know why. God is a way maker, though. I turned my pain into purpose. I knew that I did not want my children going down the same path I did. I wanted better for them. I needed to break the generational curse.

I have been mentoring youth in my city for about fifteen years. I am in the process of starting a mentoring program for young men and women. This program will educate on topics like the prison system; judicial system, how to overcome obstacles in life, and tapping into their purpose. In addition, I started a T-shirt company, and I am a Life Coach. I want to let people know to never give up on their goals and dreams. You can create your own destiny, no matter what people may say. Understand that God put you here for a reason! I love people and I love helping people. It makes my heart and soul smile to contribute to this world. So, although I am a broken crayon, I still color.

Life is a continuous journey. Needless to say, I still did not give up. I failed in so many areas of my life, from professional business ventures to personal issues. But no need to play the victim. You must define yourself for yourself and keep pressing forward. Ask God for forgiveness, forgive others, and ultimately forgive yourself. An angel sent from God told me that. Knowing who you are and learning to grow from all the mess you create in your life is a major key. I have cried so many tears looking at my life, and the people who contributed, good and bad, were all lessons learned. No more guilt or shame. I realize I am not able to change my past, but I can change my future.

So please never dim your light for anyone. Just like a diamond has to experience pressure to become that diamond, so do we. Let your light shine bright like the diamond you are. Life is full of ups and downs, dark days, and sunny days. Always know this: you matter, you are worthy, and you have purpose! I discovered my purpose and passion. I will continue to speak life to others and meet people where they are. Just like Mr. Patterson, it is never too late to change, as long as you have breath in your body! You do not have to wait until tragedy takes place. Remember it is the dash that counts!!!! This Broken Crayon Still Colors…

About Latisha

Latisha Ann Randle is a native of Buffalo, New York. Who loves to shine bright like the diamond she is!!! And she wants everyone to shine bright right along with her. She is a genuine people person. Latisha is a mother, wife, daughter, sister, auntie of a host of nieces and nephews and friend. Recently she became a certified life coach through ICU Academy. She is super excited about this journey. To GOD BE THE GLORY!

Latisha is a newbie in the writing world. But this is only the beginning for her writing career. Broken Crayons Still Color gave her the opportunity to write about her pain. And to share with the world, in hopes to touch lives is a positive way. Latisha wants people to know that a couple major keys in life are to 'Love you first' & Never Give up!"

Latisha attended Erie Community College and graduated with an Associate degree, in addition to obtaining a bachelor's degree in Sociology from SUNY Buffalo state college. Latisha has received a number of certificates.

Latisha is a mentor and a motivational speaker, who currently mentor youth, while teaching independent living skills. Latisha loves discussing topics on systemic racism and social injustice. And different approaches to curtail recidivism, she has a heart of gold and true passion for humanity.

Fun Fact: Beyonce and Jay-z are her All-time favorite music artist, next to Meek Mill! Latisha loves rap music. But it is a must that the music has substance.

Latisha loves to dance to Hip- Hop, Reggae and Salsa...

Chapter 25

Inspired by my Life Experience

BY TERRENCIA M. ADAMS

Have you ever thought of your life as being a roller coaster? You are faced with obstacles such as heartache, pain, and many other challenges. It may appear as if no one cares about you or your situation at times. When we hit unexpected bumps in the road and see no way out, our minds may suddenly be filled with negative thoughts, a loss of hope, full of doubt and fear. We never stop to think and ask ourselves, where is all this negative energy coming from? It is normal to have pessimistic thoughts when bad things happen; however, we have control over our minds and this type of behavior can be avoided. We have control over how we think, how we feel, and what we allow to affect us. Challenging times will come in our lives but understand that trouble does not last.

Growing up in a single parent home was not easy. My mom of course was the breadwinner while my now deceased brother acted as the man of the house. It was sometimes difficult to make ends meet, but my mom did the best she could to raise both my brother and me. I have other siblings which include a twin brother and an older sister. They lived with other relatives during our childhood because my grandmother knew my mom could not take care of four children on her own, especially that we all were only a few years apart in age. Although my siblings and I did not grow up

194

in the same home, we got along very well with each other. We did not get to spend much time together; however, the time spent was well worth it.

My mom found companionship and things started to turn around for the better for both me and my brother. My mom's boyfriend took the role of being a father figure. We were able to experience family living. My stepdad was a great provider for us as a family. He made certain we had what we needed and some of what we wanted. As we got older my mom and stepdad separated for whatever reason and things began to get a little unsteady. Both my brother and I were at the age where we understood more about life and growing up. My grandparents played a major role in our lives during that time. Of course, my mom was still there doing the best that she could. We were going to school and working all at the same time. At some point, my brother and I started living with our grandparents who had other family members living with them as well. In total there were about ten of us living in a three-bedroom home in a very nice neighborhood. Of course, that was a lot of people, but we made it work the best we knew how.

I started working my first fast-food job when I was in high school. My grandmother was my transportation to and from work since my mother did not drive. I was responsible for paying fifty dollars every pay period to my grandmother. This enabled me to help with a utility bill and taught me responsibility. To me, that was a lot of money to pay back then, since I was not making much from the start. Nonetheless, I graduated high school, started working in retail, finally purchasing my very own vehicle.

I wanted to go to college however, I had no guidance from family of where to start since I was the first to pursue a college career. I decided to go to our community college and seek help on getting signed up for classes. I was able to start my college courses with the help of the advisors from the school. While in college I became pregnant. I continued to go to school until about 6 months into the pregnancy. I felt that my mom would have understood my pregnancy at the age of 19 because she had her children at an early age and not being married; however, my grandmother who had a Pentecostal Christian background was not so happy about it. She believed that you should have no sexual relationship unless you were married. Yes, I grew up with that same background, so I knew better.

I never looked at my pregnancy as a mistake, instead I prayed to God for forgiveness and looked forward to being the best mother that I could possibly be. My boyfriend and I were young, inexperienced as parents and not making much money as we prepared to step into a huge responsibility. Our first decision was to find an apartment for us to be able to live together and make ready for our new baby boy. Grandma did not believe in shacking up together either; however, I was about old enough to make my own decisions and as long as I was not living under grandma's roof, I could do what was satisfying to me.

Preparing for our new baby boy we had a great support system from both sides of the family; however, we were still solely responsible for our baby.

Our beautiful, healthy baby boy was born. We named him Benjamin. I was overjoyed by becoming a new mother although I had a lot to learn. Getting the baby home was when reality sunk in for me. Sleepless nights, breast feeding, and nurturing this innocent baby was a lot of work. It was very time consuming and required a lot of energy and attention. Although my mother had all her children at an early age, I never saw myself being a mother at the age of 20 years old, not married with no career. This was not how I was raised, and most definitely not the lifestyle that I had imagined for myself. In fact, I was taught to do the opposite of my mother's life decisions. I envisioned myself to be married with a career and maybe one child. Obviously, that wasn't the case.

God had another plan. Life with my sweet little baby boy was great yet challenging at times. This baby brought so much happiness into my life; he was the motivator that kept me going. Although I knew I had to get back to work sooner than later, leaving my baby with family was helpful but not what I wanted to do. Please understand, I was grateful for the help that I had however, I was not satisfied with the little time that I was sacrificing for my sweet little baby boy. I felt like I was not committing enough time for him and being the best mother that I could possibly be. Work was very important for the reason that it was the way of providing for my household, yet it was taking up so much of my mother time. After I came to the realization that this was going to be my life for the moment, I had to put my game face on, come up with a plan and foresee my life turning for the better. After getting accustomed and emotionally attached to the baby, I started having mixed emotions about going back to work and school right away. I commenced praying and asked God for guidance with my life especially after feeling guilty for having a baby out of wedlock.

I had goals, and I refused to repeat the way I grew up, so I resumed working and started the process of going back to school. Since college was taking a lot more time than I wanted it to, I decided to go to a trade school to become a licensed Nail Technician. Thinking back on the time when I made the decision to go to Nail Technology school, I am reminded of how a family member who I still to this day admire so much, condemned my dream of going to school to be a Nail Technician. In her words "Why would you choose to do something like that? You cannot make money doing that type of job. This type of work is not for you". After hearing this come from a person that I always went to for advice, not only tore me apart but crushed my heart to pieces. I waited a few days before signing the contract for the school because I really valued the opinion of my loved one. This very same situation reminds me of a saying quoted by Oprah Winfrey which states, "Often we don't even realize who we're meant to be because we're so busy trying to live out someone else's ideas. But other people and their opinions hold no power in defining our destiny". The very next business day I was at the school enrolling in the Nail Technology program without anyone knowing. Once I got started with the class, my heart was full of joy and peace. Although I was at peace with my decision, I knew that this was going to be a bit much for me; however, I had goals to meet, and I was going to do whatever it took for me not only to be the best mother but an educated mother with a great career. I was determined to complete the trade school and so, I completed the 6-month program in 4 1/2 months. I found it necessary not to tell anyone about this accomplishment until a few days before my graduation. A few family members shared in the joy with me on that day. It was a moment to remember.

I landed a commissioned based job in a salon right away after becoming certified, only to find out I was going to be making less money than what I had been making at the time. I was concerned about my pay decrease although I had the option of making better pay if I was able to maintain my clients on a consistent basis. I was determined not to get stuck or complacent in a job that was barely making ends meet.

My goal was to put forth effort to become a skilled Nail Technician, with a great clientele and pursue becoming my own boss. My clients were not just individuals I serviced; I gained a very close friendship with many of them. I am reminded of this one friend who started out as my client, she encouraged me to start as a booth renter in a salon and work my way up before opening my own personal salon. With a smile on my face, I can remember telling her I might just do that; however, I was concerned about how many clients would follow me to my new salon location. Of course, I began to pray and trust the process. I remained at the job to get the experience, building a clientele. I gave out flyers, did complimentary hand massages for the hair clients while they sat under the dryer, I even made time to call my past clients for them to rebook. After these efforts, I noticed more people booking me, and my take home pay increased as well. Subsequently, I was able to save extra money. I was getting closer to the day I could resign from my commissioned based job. I then had to research the next venture which included renting a booth at a salon. I knew booth rental came with paying a weekly rent and supplying my own product, so I was going to need some cushion money to get started just in case my current clients did not follow me. I had no idea how much capital was needed to become a booth renter. I basically stepped out on faith and maneuvered things the best way I knew how with the $1253.00 in savings I had accumulated. Exactly three years later to the day I decided to step out on my own to become a booth renter which was going to require me to be my own boss. It took me a little time getting used to being a booth renter. I was responsible for everything concerning my business except for the actual facility that I was renting space in. This was very motivating to me. Shortly thereafter, I became a certified educator with the number one nail company in the world. This was a huge deal for me. I was able to train, travel and educate people all over the world. I began to see things turning in my favor. I started making more money, getting more clients, and investing in more nail training. I also had the ability to create my own schedule which allotted me more time for family and the opportunity to get back in college. This brought great joy to me.

After enrolling back in school at a four-year college I was determined not to quit until I earned my Bachelor of Science Degree in Business Management. As I began my college courses, I realized that some family time was going to be lost again; however, I felt that it was essential to keep going unless I was going to fail at life once again. I became more inspired, and I started meeting people in accordance with where I wanted my life to be. My mom always taught me the motto "what you hang around is what you will become". I found this saying to be so true. Not only did I meet great people in the salon world, but I met great individuals in the college world as well.

Booth renting, traveling for the nail company and going to college was going just as planned; however, my companion and I were not seeing eye to eye. We separated when our son was about 2 years old. Even though we are not together, he has continued to be a great father in our son's life. In fact, his family continued to support in all ways necessary. I did not let this bump in the road steer me away from my dreams and goals. I remained focused. The truth is this situation forced me to fight harder for my accomplishments. I never realized up until then how much time I had committed to others, at my expense. I decided it was time to define who I was. Since I was working on my goals, I moved onto the next achievement.

While I was seeking a business degree, I collaborated with my professors at the college to get some ideas of where to start on opening my own business. I was directed to contact my local business centers for complementary assistance. I gathered a tremendous amount of research on owning my own business, so I knew it was time to utilize my resources. As a result, I was able to open my own salon.

Finding companionship was the least thing on my mind, because I was excited about being able to make ends meet on my own for me and my baby boy and being on the right path of accomplishing my goals. Not intentionally looking, I found my new companion named Troy. A man with a heart of gold and who did not get in the way of my dreams. He was able to pour into me and I into him. This was a Godsend. Troy was a long-distance truck driver when I meant him however, his past career was a licensed builder. How coincidental was that? My next business move was to own my own salon. Not only did I want Troy to know about my goals, but I was very interested in knowing his life objectives as well. After many conversations, we both realized that we had a lot in common. Even though I was already in the process of looking for a building, Troy began to encourage me to continue looking for a new home for my salon. He even agreed to help me with all the renovations. I inquired about the building that I had my eye on for a while. After looking at the building we saw that the place was going to need an astronomical amount of work including new paint, flooring, cabinets, walls, crown molding, base board, and the list goes on. I knew that the location would be ideal for my new salon but where in the world was, I going to get all that money to renovate the place? Having good credit got me the lease on the building with no deposit. Because of my negotiating skills the owner was willing to give me six months' rent free to fix up the place. Once I got the keys Troy and I began to renovate the building on the days I did not have to be in class. Sometimes we would be in there until one or two o'clock in the morning knowing we had to be at work early the next morning. Those times that Troy had to work late, my grandfather would come and help me paint. This meant so much to me. I thought we were never going to finish renovating because it was just so much work. However, I was solely committed and determined to finish before our six months of free rent was up. Right at the nick of time all renovations were completed for our new salon. It came out extremely beautiful. Wow! How the tables turned in my favor! I was no longer known as the booth renter I was now known as the owner. The hard work and dedication we put in really paid off. I never saw myself being a business owner. Just thinking back, had I allowed my loved one to make decisions for my life I am quite sure I would not have been in the position of owning my very own salon to this day. I am grateful that I followed my heart and did what I thought was best for me. This was the best decision I could have ever made.

Next, I began to market my salon on my social media platforms and through word of mouth. I worked at that salon for about 2 years by myself. I was thankful for cushion money. I was also thankful to have learned to never open a business that you cannot afford to operate on your own. This information was knowledge for me since I had no booth renters at the time, and I had to use the salon capital sometimes to keep the business functioning. Finally, the time came when I was able to build a great team of licensed technicians with little to no turnover. Business was great. My savings of $13,000 helped cover the cost of the renovations. However, my companion saved me thousands of dollars on the repairs since he was able to do most of the labor. Wow! Was this exciting to me or what! I now had over $6,000 left from my savings to use as capital to operate the business.

I frequently met with my local small business office for direction and advice, so I was able to maintain a profitable business. The resources came in handy and guided me in running a successful business.

After a few years of dating, Troy and I was expecting our first child together. We were blessed with a beautiful baby girl by the name of Taylor. Life was not as hard as the first pregnancy since, I was a lot more experienced as a mother, I made more money, and I was yet blessed to have a great support system from my family as well as Troy's family. My aunt Nancy took the role of being our baby-sitter while Troy and I continued to make ends meet. Aunt Nancy not only was a great babysitter, but she made certain that my family dinner was prepared on our long nights of work.

Although my mother was not able to take care of us growing up, she always made sure to sacrifice time to spend with her grandchildren. Since traveling with the nail company required overnight stays, and Troy worked long hours, my mom made certain that she was there to stay with her grandchildren and boy did they love spending time with her!

After experiencing the unexpected death of my mom, I felt a sense of emptiness and of course a loss for words. My mom did not have much but whatever she had she was willing to share. She was a very caring and lovable person. I am grateful that we are able to hold fond memories of my mom. She most definitely made up for lost time by spending it with her grandchildren.

The time had come for me to graduate with my Bachelor of Science Degree in Business Management. I was so ecstatic and honored to have my family there cheering me on and supporting me. The love was heartfelt and very memorable. It felt even better not to have had to find a job because I had already established entrepreneurship. The degree was accomplished in case I needed a backup plan.

My relationship with Troy was going stronger than ever. We continued to build each other up, sharing ideas and providing for our family. We also took time to find ways to enhance our careers. Troy decided to go back and get his builders license and become self-employed while I maintained the salon.

In 2012, Troy and I decided to get married. Taylor was two years old, and Benjamin was 11 years old. We are not only a married couple, but we are best of friends. Our good times most definitely outweighs the bad. Patience is a virtue. I am grateful to have waited on my Boaz.

I may not have had the best life growing up, but it was my experience. I do not regret my upbringing, yet I celebrate it. In fact, it made me into the woman I am today. I have learned over the years that life is what you make of it. I have decided that my past will not deter my future; instead, I will be inspired by my early years of life.

About Terrencia

Terrencia M. Adams received her Bachelor of Science Degree from Limestone College. Her other professional degrees include a Master of Business Administration and a Master of Arts, Management and Leadership, both earned from Webster University.

Terrencia is a successful entrepreneur of many talents. She is a Life Certified Business Coach and founder of Discovered Solutions Consulting and Coaching Academy. She has the gift of inspiring, encouraging, and motivating others to fulfill their life dreams and goals. She is a Licensed Nail Care Specialist and the current owner of Face360 Hair and Nail Studio (LLC). Prior to this, she was a Certified Trained OPI Educator. She is also the proud owner of Carolina Posh Wedding and Event Planning (LLC). Terrencia is well known for her excellence in the nail care industry and her creative niche in the event planning sector. She is often praised for her ability to help others succeed and grow in their career path.

Terrencia was born and raised in Columbia SC. She is a loving and devoted wife and a mother of two beautiful children. During her free time, she focusses on giving back to her community, shopping and traveling. There is nothing more gratifying than for her to see others strive and accomplish their goals. Therefore, Terrencia is committed to being a great role model and remain persistent on empowering others.

Chapter 26

Healing From An Unspoken Abortion

BY JAYRESA SASS

I was a pregnant fifteen-year-old, and I didn't know what to do. I was only given one option at the time and forced to have an abortion. Traumatized afterwards, I shoved it down and locked it away in the deep recesses of my soul. Years later, after two children, and obtaining my Certification as a Life Coach, I realized how much healing I needed. I was still trapped at age fifteen and broken.

Loss of Innocence

I was only fifteen years old when I fell in love with a fellow classmate. He was that guy that I thought I would be with forever. Did you write your name + your boyfriend's name everywhere, followed with the words," together forever"? I know I'm not the only one. OMG! He became the center of my being and my reason for living. It was the fall of eleventh grade that I freely gave myself away. I was never the same after. Then the unspeakable happened. I realized that I could possibly be pregnant. At first, I was not too worried "my period is probably just late," I thought, "I couldn't possibly be pregnant." My feelings were scattered everywhere, fear racing through my mind, what the hell was I going to do? What will I do with a baby? How was I going to feed this baby, dress it? At that point,

I knew I had to figure out my consequences. Most importantly how was I going to tell my mother? When I told my boyfriend, he looked at me and asked, "What are we going to do?" Hearing his response at that time meant the world to me. Now you and I both know most boys that age would say, "What are you going to do?" My boyfriend was willing to be by my side.

Now I Know

I immediately took several tests, and they all read "positive." Still in disbelief, within a week I was sitting at a local clinic waiting for the results of a pregnancy test.

"Yes, you are pregnant", my fears were confirmed. "Would you like to talk with one of our counselors?"

I don't remember much of anything else that was said after that except for these few words, "No one needs to know. I can help you with your problem." Those words resounded in my spirit: "No one needs to know. I can help you with your problem."

My boyfriend and I kept the pregnancy a secret between ourselves. I was so scared, and I was looking for quick relief, an escape from the consequences of my behavior. My desire was to be able to finish high school and continue to college.

The Quick "Fix"

It did not help that I no longer had the support of my mother. She had recently told me, I had to get rid of the baby and it better be gone when she returned from vacation. I wept and cried to my boyfriend. My mother simply wanted what she thought was best for me — for me to be able to go to college without having to go through a pregnancy as a 15-year-old. I felt alone and very scared. Part of me was excited to have a little being growing inside my tummy. The other part of me was very scared to face the consequences of this unexpected surprise. There seemed to be no other alternatives. Left with no instructions or assurance from my mother I had to figure it out. We looked up abortion clinics because at the time I knew I had to get rid of the baby. I had a good life. I was a very smart and talented teenager. Eventually I found a clinic downtown in Brooklyn, only to discover that because sex is not legal until sixteen, neither is abortion. To go through with the abortion, I had to convince a counselor, I was mature enough to know what I was doing, which I did.

So Ashamed

We made an appointment in enough time before my mother returned from vacation. I missed my appointment at the abortion clinic. I do not know how or why. Maybe I was scared, or maybe I just knew deep in my heart that I did not want to go through with it. I never talked about it. I just continued with my pregnancy knowing that I would either keep the baby or abort it.

I finally built up the courage to go and it was one of the most devastating things I ever experienced. I felt like I was walking down death row watching the Nuns lined up alongside the stairs as I walked up to the clinic. Chanting while holding their crosses.

"God will never bless you. You are going to hell. Only evil people kill babies."

What would I do especially after hearing all of that? Is it true that God would never bless me with another baby? What would I do?

It's Done

My boyfriend was so supportive during the process. I returned home, and so did my mom. Would you believe she said nothing? She did not ask anything at all. I had to return to school, and once again I faced another challenge. I had to explain to my peers why my white pants were full of blood. I could feel golf ball sized drops of blood down my legs. Not sure of what to do, I had to figure out what was happening to me all alone. The only response I received from my mom was, "Call the doctor and ask them if that is normal." ... (Huh?)

The relationship with my boyfriend changed and led to a life I never thought I would survive. I was being abused. I blamed my mother for every situation I encountered with my boyfriend because she forced me to get rid of his child. Some of those nights of enduring his abuse I knew he still held a grudge towards my mother also for making me have that abortion. He would intentionally beat me while she listened on the phone. This went on for the next 5 years.

It Was Not Her Fault

In the years to follow I would blame my mother for the pain I was feeling and the abuse I endured. Then I got a chance to hear her story. She too was a teen mom. She had to endure the un-filtered words of the community and her friends. Although we still have not talked about it, I forgave her and most importantly myself. As a mother I understand that raising children alone is hard. You must have all the answers on demand, along with the band aids, tissues, food, and the list continues. As children we never think that our parents encountered painful things too, experiences they have not healed from themselves. So why is it that we expect our parents to have it all together?

Only with time would I learn and accept that I, alone, was the one who had to live with the consequences of my own choices. No one could have made me get an abortion if I did not want one. I have learned from the advice other people gave me, but I must continue to decide what is best for me. I freely gave away that part of myself. If I had taken the right safety measures, I could have prevented the pregnancy.

I Was Still Blessed

Believe it or not, there is hope during a difficult situation. Looking back on that time, I lost my identity in who I was with God and placed it in the value of men loving me. I was striving not to be alone and found myself pregnant and ended up being forced to having an abortion, something I vowed I would never do. I was broken and realized that no counseling was done. I commonly believed that I committed, "the unforgivable sin". I stayed away from the Church most of my adult life after an abortion as a teenager. The good news, God forgives abortion, and I have no worries and am blessed with two beautiful children. And ultimately, what I experienced may have left me feeling broken, but it did not happen to me-- It happened for me.

About Jayresa

Jayresa is a Native Thriving Woman of Brooklyn, New York. She graduated from Mercy College with a degree in Liberal Arts/ Psychology. Although she obtained her degree at age 34, the long journey allowed her to become a scientist of her own life. Her curiosity of becoming this scientist began when she noticed significant behavioral similarities in the people, she was providing support for. Never knowing her own story until age 34, she learned she lost both of her parents to incarceration at 10 months old. She then discovered that her childhood trauma led to all the traumatic series of life events she experienced that disrupted her sense of safety. These traumatic experiences included domestic violence in relationships, emotional, physical, and verbally abusive behaviors, intrusive medical procedures, neglect towards oneself and children, unstable and unsafe environments. Not to mention going through a divorce at the age of 32.

Eager to heal and with God's order she left NYC with her 2 children, moved to Norcross, GA and never looked back. She Is excited to share her empowering story and experiences of how she turned her life around to help other women do the same. She birthed, She is Not Her Trauma during the most traumatic time for the world, Covid-19. During that time, she became a certified Trauma/ Spirituality Coach eager to teach women how to strengthen their emotional and spiritual mindsets through restorative healing avenues of support and engagement to embrace their TRUTH. Embrace their TRAUMA. Embrace their TRANSFORMATION. Today her mission is to change the narrative in women during these difficult moments in time by hosting several interviews, masterclasses, and workshops on how to recognize and insert themselves in the healing process from trauma to defining freedom and success.

While Striving for excellence in her field Jayresa has been awarded several awards for making a difference in the community and giving back to those in need.

Chapter 27

My Crooked Nose Moment

BY TAMARA MILLS

I remember the heartbreak that actually ended up saving my life.

I was in my mid 20s when I met him. At that time in my life, I had not had any real successful relationship, and I was over giving my heart and time to someone just to feel played and misused in the end. I have always been a giver and a fixer. I am that friend you can call to share whatever it is you are going through, and I will be the ear, shoulder, and hand you need to stay encouraged. This is who I am; I want to see people living their best life and help in any way that I can. I understand-- we are human and far from perfect. We mess up things at times and should not be written off because of it. We all need help and I do not mind being the help someone may need. Yet, these are the same things that can easily be used against you in a relationship if you are not wise about how you deal with people.

I had just gotten out of a relationship that was going nowhere fast and made up my mind I did not want to be in any serious relationship because I was tired of all the games. Did this mean I was going to take time for myself and get some much-needed healing, so I did not keep attracting the wrong guys? Of course not. I fed into the hype that this is just how relationships go and thought I was big and bad enough to be out in the dating world and do my thing while keeping my emotions out of it.

Well, the world lied to me and I lied to myself, not to mention this went against who I was, because my nature is to care about people. Oh, all the things we would have done differently had we only known better!

I started dating two guys at the same time. I was very upfront and honest about it. I let them both know that I was dating someone else. I remember after about a month of dating them both, one of the guys told me I was doing this because I was trying to keep from actually becoming seriously involved and I needed to pick who I wanted to date. Well, he was absolutely right, and him calling me out like that gave me food for thought and I chose, and it was not him, of course. No, I chose the one that I had said to a friend and I quote, "He is going to be the one that breaks my heart." Talk about a self-fulfilling prophecy.

We ended up dating for two years. At the time, it was my longest serious relationship. I felt we had so much in common, and we really had a good time when we were together. It was the times we were not together that were the issues. And let me tell you, it is just as important what someone does in your presence as what they do when you are not around. That is when you learn if someone really loves and respects you and your relationship, and this is true for any kind of relationship.

In the beginning it felt good, but there were quite a few moments that did not feel good which were more signs that this was not where I was supposed to be.

It's funny how we will overlook our intuition and all the signs God is showing us just to hold on to something that we think is love.

Towards the end of our first year together, he ended up reconnecting with an old childhood friend who stayed with his sister. He started hanging out with his friend a lot and I had even dropped him off on a few occasions to their house. Well, more signs started to show up and things were not adding up. I forget how I actually put it all together, but when you have a heavenly Father that loves you and wants the best for you, you will find out those things that are done in the dark against you. And I found out that he was cheating on me with his friend's sister. That should have been enough for me to be done right then and there with the relationship, right? Apparently, it was not.

There I was, being so understanding. It is ok to forgive, but not every situation needs to be returned to. For you to allow someone to do you wrong or keep doing you wrong is not healthy. Yes, people absolutely make mistakes and should not be written off because of it. Yet, in this relationship, there were so many signs prior to this that told me he was not what I deserved. See, the thing was mid- way in the first year of our dating I started praying about our relationship, asking if he was the one for me because of all the signs I was seeing. I should have been praying from the beginning but that would be the last time I made that mistake. And even though I was in love and enjoyed the times we had spent together, there were many shady actions outside of our time together that made me question a lot of things. Still, I put up with it because I wanted to be loved and be with someone I thought loved me. Never forget love is an action word. It's not what a person says but what a person does consistently that shows if they really love you.

I remember every time I would pray asking God if he was the person for me, it would never fail that right afterwards something bad would happen like him blowing me off or going MIA. I knew God was telling me he was not the man for me, but at that time I was so in love and headstrong about what I wanted that I felt that God was wrong and what I felt was right. Oh yes, even then I realized I was thinking I knew better than God, so we already know how that was going to turn out. So yeah, I took him back and when I look back now, I just shake my head. In retrospect, all of the signs that God showed me was confirmation that it was not the relationship for me. He was also showing me that I was broken and needed healing. Yet, I was too caught up in holding on to what I thought I wanted that I could not see the truth.

We are so capable of making all kinds of excuses and reasons to be with someone when there are so many signs that we should not. I made excuses for his cheating. My excuses for him were his sob story about his child's mother treating him so wrong. She cheated on him and would not let him see his son, and blah, blah, blah. You know there are always three sides to a story. His story, her story, and what really happened. I would find out later on from his own mouth that he cheated on her multiple times.

Still, after all the signs, and the pain of betrayal when I found out he had been cheating on me for months, I let him come back.

I remember months before the big break up, I had a particularly unforgettable dream. See, I am a dreamer; it is one of the ways God will speak to me. So, in this dream, his child's mother and I had fought over him. He then left me to be with her. I remember waking up so mad at him and he thought it was funny. I had this dream four months before it happened for real.

He did not get his son the whole first year we dated. It was not until I actually talked to his child's mother for the first time that we started to go get his son every other weekend. She gave me her sob story of him not wanting to get their son since she was with someone else which, of course, was opposite of what he had told me. I asked if she was okay with us getting him and she agreed, and we picked him up that very weekend. After that he started spending time with his son more consistently. You're welcome. Now, briefly about her. Even after what I did, she did not like me, was usually rude to me, and tried to cause unnecessary drama even though I had never done anything to her except date her son's father. Anyway, he usually would go to the basketball court on Sundays. This one Sunday, he had his son with him, and I was watching them play while waiting to go pick up my son from his dad. So, she pulls up to get her son. I walked to her car hoping to talk to her about us being civil with each other since we are both grown women. What was I thinking? She was extremely rude, disrespectful, and just downright hateful.

What I had not known at the time was that her guy had left her and now she wanted her child's father back despite their unhealthy track record. And can I tell you I walked away from her car three times. Three times I walked away, but hey, I am just as human as the rest of us. So, each time I walked away she would say something nasty, and disrespectful, and I would go back to show her I was not the one. One thing led to another, one word led to another, and before I knew it, I was almost in the car with her through her window, fighting with her.

Oh man. When I tell you, she had brought the worst out of me. I like to help people. Yet, here I was a helper to the soul, doing my best to hurt someone who essentially was broken herself. So, my ex pulled me out of the car and told me to leave because she was going to call the police on me. Now had I not had to go get my son, I was going to wait for the cops to come, but God in His infinite wisdom saved me from myself by having me go get my son.

So, in her brokenness and her campaign to get back the loser we shared in common, she filed an injunction against me. To file an injunction, you need to have had two incidents, so she lied and made up a second reason so she could file one. And while I was upset and dealing with the upcoming court date, my ex broke up with me and told me it was because he needed to get himself together so he could be the man I deserved. Yes, it did hurt my heart, but I was still understanding, and we were still talking to each other.

So, we had all that going on, and I still had to go to court because of his child's mother's lies, which we both knew she was lying. I asked if he would come with me because he could let them know it was not true. He let me know he did not want to get involved because he did not want her to stop him from seeing his son. Did I understand? Sure, I did. Did it hurt? Of course, because once again he was not there for me when I needed him. Just more signs of the winner I had fallen for.

I ended up getting my pastor at the time, Rev Hollingsworth, to come with me. To this day, I am so thankful for him standing by my side in one of the most pivotal moments of my life. He was a much-needed rock in such a turbulent time of my life. I will always be thankful to Rev. Hollingsworth for being there for me, as a mighty man of God! So, I will never forget the moment my heart shattered into a thousand pieces; more pieces than I thought possible. While in the lobby of the courthouse with my pastor, I turned around only to see them walking in together, my ex and his child's mother.

I am pretty sure my pastor heard my heart shatter. The hurt and pain was so strong I felt like I was suffocating. All breath had left me. My brokenness hit a new level I did not know was possible. There was the guy that I was still in love with, walking in with the woman that he knew was lying on me. The same woman he talked so bad about for two years claiming he hated. The pain was overwhelming as tears escaped my eyes and if Rev Hollingsworth had not been there to be a rock to lean on, I do not know what I would have done. In that moment, the pain of the past years had culminated and the dam broke. Yet, I refused to let her see that her ploy had worked. With the assurance and comfort of my pastor, I stood strong and held it together.

Only she and I were allowed in the courtroom and with God on my side, the judge saw through the lies and threw out her case. My ex ended up calling me, I assumed right after she had dropped him off after court. I guess he thought he could put a bandage on a gaping wound. But at that point, I was done. I was devastated. And I did something I never ever did before after a heartbreak. I took time for myself to find sanity, direction, and healing from all the madness. I took time to see about me for once.

I went and I stayed with my parents for a month. They never cared for my ex and even tried to warn me, but just like I did not heed the warnings from God, I overlooked theirs as well. Still, they were there for me after the heartbreak and opened their home to my son and me for as long as I needed. I will always be grateful for my mom and dad; they were my rock whenever I needed them. It was December, close to Christmas time because my brother Rafeal, who is also one of my best friends, came to visit. I stayed that entire month looking for guidance on my next step to recovery from a broken soul.

My utter brokenness was the final straw I needed to start me on my journey to wholeness. That month became the turning point that would save my life and spur me on in truly walking in my purpose. It started me on a much-needed journey to a closer walk with God.

See, I was raised in the church. I always believed in God and even said I was not dating anybody unless they believed in God too. But what I had just learned was believing in God and trying to walk with God are two vastly different things. I had believed in God, but I was not trying to walk with God. I tried to be the best person I could be and not do wrong. I even was encouraging others and being there for those who would confide in me. Yet, I really was not trying to walk with God. I wanted the benefits without the participation and that became truly clear in that time of my life. I understand now, the gift is within each of us, and we are able to impact others' lives, but that impact is limited because we are blinded by our own brokenness.

While I stayed at my parents' house, many nights I was tormented by dark dreams attacking my mind. One night I had a dream in which I was pregnant, and demons were chasing me trying to destroy my baby. I did not stop going until I came to a house where angels were, and the angels protected me and my baby. I didn't quite understand the meaning of the dream right away. I came to realize it did not mean that I would be physically pregnant with a child, but it was me being pregnant with purpose. God has placed within all of us a powerful purpose for this life.

God was showing me that even though the enemy was trying to destroy my purpose by keeping me broken, God was with me and I had protection as long as I kept going. With everything I went through, my purpose and I could not be destroyed unless I allowed it. Even when I could not see it, God was with me urging me forward so I could walk forward in who I was always meant to be!

Part of that divine support was being able to be surrounded by people who genuinely loved me and wanted to see me at my best. Despite feeling like the ultimate fool and idiot for how I let my ex play with my heart, my family loved me and helped me to move out of that space of hopelessness and brokenness. Having Rafeal around was such a saving grace to me. He is a year younger than me but had been on a serious walk with God longer than I had, and he would teach me about fasting. Rafeal helped me do my first fast as I sought guidance on whether to stay in Georgia with my parents or move back to my hometown in Florida. Although I never felt I got a clear answer, I now realized I was fasting to draw myself closer to God and start reconnecting in a relationship I had taken for granted for so long.

In that place of torment, hurt and pain, I was still able to encourage my friends who called me to check up on me. At a time when I felt like I was an utter mess, they were still looking to me to speak life and pray with them. It goes to show, God can always use a heart that is willing no matter how broken you may feel. Yes, broken crayons still color too. The biggest revelation for me was that I was broken long before I got into that relationship.

That brokenness was one of the reasons why I kept attracting the wrong kind of guy. I thought I had it all together. I thought I was self-confident, pretty, smart, funny, a cool chick, and on top of all that, being a single mother raising her child while doing her thang. I was able to encourage my loved ones. How could I have known that I was only exuding a fraction of the shine that had gotten buried within me?

Long before I ever had my son and long before I had met my ex, Rafeal had me talk to his friend who operates in the prophetic. I spoke to her over the phone, never having met her before, and she told me things that let me know she truly heard from God. She told me that I had gone through things from my past that had blown out the light behind my eyes. Yes, I seem happy, but it is not true happiness. I did not take from that situation what I was supposed to, and God was sad about that. Catch that, not that I went through the situation, but that I did not learn from it what I was supposed to. So, since I did not gain from it what I should have, I was now like a crooked nose--a nose that got broken but did not heal properly. Guess what you do to a bone that breaks but does not heal correctly? You break it again, so it can heal properly. Sounds painful and it was, but I remember her laughing her joyful laugh when she told me this part. She was filled with joy because she saw how beautiful, happy, and powerful I was going to be once I healed properly.

This is why I allowed myself to endure all that I did and unfortunately, later on even more with my ex. Spoiler alert: I moved back to Florida and would end up spending another five years off and on dealing with him and his child's mother, before I finally walked away for good. Don't shake your head-- that heartbreak started me on my road to healing and wholeness!

I knew that heartbreak was my crooked nose moment. Yes, I took years afterwards to fully receive the wholeness that was always mine.

It is one of the greatest feelings to know there are paths you will never have to walk again and greater paths available to you because you chose to truly love and heal yourself and refuse to stay broken. When I finally walked completely away from my ex, I took three years off from relationships, drew even closer to God and my family, and took time for my healing. I had continued to grow while I was still dealing with my ex and had even started with my siblings a prayer/Bible study line that is still active today! Yet, when I finally shook off the last lingering attachment to the broken version of myself, so many more doors and opportunities to walk in purpose opened up!

Today, I am still growing and embracing my greatness which I never would have found had I stayed broken. I met, dated, and married my husband. I finally found out what it meant to have someone who truly loves you! Together we push each other to be our best selves, grow, and walk-in purpose. We are raising our family, loving them, and doing our best to show them the power of God, love, and their own greatness. I have led a women's study group on drawing closer to God. For a year, I wrote a daily word, 5 days a week, encouraging others in their daily and spiritual lives. Our bible study line encouraged and taught many as well as covered countless in prayer. And there is so much more still to come. Remember, yes, you can color while broken, but the picture comes together so much easier and reaches so many more people when you color as the whole crayon you were always meant to be!

About Tamara

Tamara Mills is a mighty woman of God, loving wife, and mother to eight full of personality children. Her passion is helping others to walk in their purpose and live an enjoyable, impactful life. She is a life coach, as well as a spiritual inspirational leader. She has helped many people grow in their own personal walk with God and she looks to help countless more.

Having to navigate her own personal battles to move forward in her own purpose, she truly understands and empathizes with the battle's individuals face in their everyday life. She understands that everyone's journey is unique. Yet, we are able to learn from each other and grow together when we can get past feeling condemned and stuck from our past mistakes and instead realize the transformational power of love and God in each of us. She utilizes this insight to help others see the greatness already in them so they can bring it forth and start living their best lives!

She is currently working on a new entrepreneurial project that she hopes will be an invaluable resource to one's process of growth in each aspect of one's life: physical, spiritual, and mental. Look for that project to launch later this year. In her downtime, you will find her spending much appreciated time with her family laughing and loving each other!

Chapter 28

Being Me on Purpose

BY IRIS CARR

What's in a name, you ask? My name is Iris. It has been said that Iris is Greek for "rainbow", Christianity teaches this as the symbol of God's promise. The meanings of the flower are faith, wisdom, peace of mind, friendship, and hope. The irony is that it took so long to uncover those hidden treasures God had placed in me.

It has taken time. Through my mistakes, and experiences arising from ignorance, I grew to love and enjoy me. My name is Iris, just like the beautifully regal flower. I am learning and discovering more about that hidden part of my identity, "Iris", every day; as this journey of self-discovery unfolds, I'm determined not to allow others to define me. You see, for much of my life, I didn't have a clear revelation of who I am. I've come to embrace the true Iris, and the beauty within. I can speak words of life and belief into my world by learning and encouraging this unique woman, Iris. It is okay that I may not look, talk, or act like others because we are all made different in the image of the Creator.

Fear of rejection had kept me from using my God given gifts and talents. I feared stepping out and walking into my purpose, because I did not want to be noticed. I was afraid I would be belittled and scorned. I was silent and made sure I was considered "that quiet girl" by others. Dealing with low self-esteem, shame, embarrassment, lack of confidence, and lack of faith, I suffered. I did not know how to stand up for myself in what I wanted or deserved. I hid in groups among my peers in college, work, and friends. Even though I grew up in the church and was active within my congregation, I didn't think I was qualified to do or become what was possible. When I wasn't in my comfort zone at home with my family or at church, I put on an act in front of others. I portrayed myself as the situation demanded by others. Overall, I was a respectable young lady that stayed out of trouble. I was humble and wanted to thrive.

I believed I had more potential than I was given credit for, but because of negativity around my family and in my head, no one invested in me or gave me the opportunity for self-realization, leading to my silent desperation. Once I mustered the courage to venture out, it was hard for me to interact and communicate because of my lack of self-confidence.

I remember an especially painful blow to my senses of self-worth and self-esteem. One of my professors in college told me I was never going to graduate or become a Social Worker. As she spoke those words, I was speechless. I already felt unworthy, and her stinging words opened the floodgates of negativity. I succumbed to inner condemnation. "You're not worth it", "you're not smart", "see, she even saw who you really are, mindless", the voices in my head pelted me like a hailstorm. My professor seemed to confirm my suspicion-- there was no hope for me. As I listened to these negative thoughts, I distanced myself from my education and my peers because I feared failure, making mistakes, or saying the wrong words. Thoughts of humiliation overwhelmed me. I was muzzled. All because I allowed a person to dictate who I was-- and it changed my life. I gave up my dreams. I stopped believing in myself. I grew negative in my mind and environment. My sense of self-worth was so nonexistent, I felt like no one wanted me. As a result, I settled for less in life, accepting whatever opportunity came my way, whether it was a relationship or job. I thought to myself, "why dream something that you are not worthy of having anyway?" I felt like I was not qualified to make my dreams happen. Even when I messed up, I felt like I could not start over because I was too old, and it was impossible to finish college with small children with no support.

After giving up on my dreams I was miserable with my life. I felt like I was in prison for many years. I wanted out and wanted to be free. I asked myself how I was going to break this deep bondage? I did not know how, but I trusted in God and stepped out of fear. I had to have faith and find myself, who God created me to be on purpose! When I started to break the chains of fear, I was able to live my life on purpose. I am fearfully and wonderfully made. God has a plan for my life to prosper and to give me hope!

I could look beautiful on the outside but be hurt, weak, and torn on the inside. I was a victim of myself. I failed, and I know I will fall again, but I must get back up, dust myself off, and keep loving myself. The beauty of it all has been discovering who I am and speaking life over myself. The more I have accepted my failures and realized I was not faultless I have learned to love myself.

I have realized there is more to me than meets the eye. I have only just begun. I did not think I could attend college. I did not believe in myself, but as I made small steps, the more I have believed in myself. The more I have grown to love myself, the more confident I have become. My eyes have been opened to my true identity—the genuine Iris. I have come to appreciate my care, gifts, and talents help me walk into my purpose. If I allow others to muzzle who I am, I am not living life to the fullest.

This is me sharing my story of low self-worth. Although I have been broken, and now I am on the road to healing and valuing myself, every day I tell myself:

BROKEN CRAYONS STILL COLOR!

About Iris

Iris Jane Carr is a single mother of three children. She is a worshipper and intercessor. Iris is a Certified Life Coach. She believes in inspiring others to reach their dreams and finding their God giving purpose. Iris is a co-author of "My Pink Stilettos" and "Broken Crayons Still Color". She is the founder of Impact Growth Academy, LLC, where individuals are empowered and are capable of sharpening their skills in the areas needed to enhance their lives and the lives of others in their communities. Iris is a Global Executive Member of Ladies of All Nations, changing the world through collaboration, cooperation, and education. Iris is a Bachelor Social Worker. She works with families and children at Department Human Service and Head Start.

Iris is a certified Life Coach and certified to teach parenting education that helps parents develop confidence and skills that are needed. She desires to be a modern-day example of the love of God in this generation.

Chapter 29

Broken and Resilient: The Blessings of the Two

BY LAKEISHA C. MUHAMMAD

"My divine Creator heals my broken wounds and renews my strength and restores my peace."

I recall when my children were small, and I used to tell them to stop breaking those damn crayons. It would be at that moment I was reminded that all kids break something. It would be okay, I'd tell myself. Calming down, and realizing my attitude, I had to apologize for yelling, then I would start to throw the crayons in the trash. When they noticed me doing so, they asked, why are you throwing my crayons in the trash Mommy?" I replied, "Because you broke them. What are you going to do with broken crayons?"

I would always do this because I hated broken crayons all over the place. I would just buy new ones without complaining. Yet, knowing that those brand-new crayons would end up broken again. Eventually, I stopped buying crayons and started buying markers and colored pencils. Yes, colored pencils can break too, but not as fast as old crayons.

I do not want to bore you with my kids' stories so let me share the adult revelation I learned later in life about brokenness. My friend used to say to me, "Girl, why are you putting those broken crayons in a sandwich bag? Throw them away." I turned to her and I said these exact words, "Why would I throw away broken crayons when they could still be used to color?"

I changed my mindset, and it was refreshing to see things in a different light. I cannot tell it all here, but what I will share with those of you reading this is that I have been broken many times in my life: in my family relationships, old friendships, intimate relationships, spiritual relationships, and in my marriage. Sometimes the brokenness was unbearable and suffocating. God knows the brokenness you experience in a marriage can and will leave you depleted at times; marriage was not a dream idea to dream again after way too many heartbreaks.

I guess God had another plan for me to meet a man I never dreamed of. And when we did meet in the physical, we both had this strange, familiar feeling as if we already knew each other. Neither one of us had ever experienced that with anyone else.

I recall telling a close spiritual friend of mine at that time, "Girl it was weird!" She said to me, "Keisha, it's not weird, it's God!" I was not in a spiritual position then so of course, I laughed about it and made jokes. She broke it down how there are people aligned in the spirit before we meet them in the physical assigned to our lives for different reasons. She told me that he was the piece to my soul puzzle and what God was going to start doing in my life and his. Our souls were familiar with each other, but the time had come for us to cross paths.

Again, I still thought it was all weird and I even thought it was the devil! After all was said, time continued to unfold, and things started shifting and changing in my life. I recall some years later, I listened to another message on "Soulmates" and Pow! It was right in this message where I got revelation and it hit me deep in my core. Your soulmate is set up in the spirit and sometimes you both get lost on a journey before you find each other. I believe God was giving me insight in the midst of my uncertainty.

At that time, I questioned everything because we were in such different places in our lives. Now I know we are connected for a divine purpose. Even with all the brokenness we experienced together, I do not regret anything that has happened for us.

We are actually better individuals today because of it all. No one is perfect but there will be and there is someone perfect to fit in your life for you! Some marriages stay together and survive it all and some do not, but I encourage women and men that you must always do what makes you happy and gives you peace. Never stay in an unhealthy and unhappy marriage that is not presenting any action of change. We did separate many times to examine ourselves because we are the two people making the marriage work or not. We kept facing the same test until we both finally figured things out. I digress...I do not know which couple, or single person needed this part of my story, but I hope it encourages you. I hope you and your marriage and relationships will be restored with healing, love, joy, and peace.

It has been a journey that I cannot imagine myself ever being on. There were times when we were not good at loving, or liking each other, ready to head to divorce court every year. It is those moments when I found myself questioning the purpose, my own thoughts and whether I made the right decision or was this meant to be. When in those times of doubt, I would pray and ask for clarity. I promise you my prayers were answered. When we will come into a positive space together. That became a starting place for us to heal together.

I admit that I have injured people with my words. They say words have power. So be mindful of what you say, guarding your thoughts, and being led with action. Never put yourself in victim status, only victorious status. When someone hurts you or lies to you, never accepting accountability, with no apologies offered for the offense, it makes it hard to control your emotions. when I look back at my brokenness, I know how I was functioning through it all.

My divine Creator was my keeper, my shelter, my protector. I believe my strong female ancestors walk with me every day, even if I did not seek or feel their presence. I used to pray that "Ceily prayer", for real. "Go get them right now, before I do." I am not going to sugarcoat how I felt. The Spirit be like, "Lakeisha, please calm down before you end up in some trouble with the law." I didn't even care. Okay, wait – yes, I did. I love my physical freedom way too much, and I have loved ones already in prison.

I confronted the brokenness for my absence, but y'all feel me: brokenness does not look the same for everyone. My brokenness was in the form of loss, death, homelessness, abuse, trauma, abandonment, dysfunction, lustful encounters with the men, and more; however, I am a person who does not like to stay too long dwelling on past issues or old feelings and emotions. Once I have processed it all, I move on. Now I say thank you for it all.

What happened to me was for me. Why? I get to share parts of my story in books like these. I get so encouraged by another someone says, "Hey, life happens, but baby-- you lived to tell!" Now you get to choose how you want your story to end. How do you want the next chapter to be read? Do you want to stay broken or move forward? You may ask me how did I got here? It is not easy. You are correct. It was not easy, and bitterness did seep through, but when I was able to identify that toxic seed, I had to pluck it from the root.

I can tell you that when you challenge yourself to do what is hard for you to do, it gets better, you start to feel better. Your health improves, you have more peace, more joy, and more happiness. All you must do is make a choice. See what and who you need to support you during the process. I got to where I am in my life today with interventions and supportive people who could relate and understand my pain. That helped me to see how full of purpose I am.

There are people who need to hear my story to understand the glory. There are people attached to your story. There are people attached to your purpose. There are people attached to your pain. There are people attached to your healing if we just take time to pay attention to that revelation. I chose healing and I continue today to heal. I believe there are different levels of healing you will go through as you continue in different stages of your life. Life is a journey that will always reveal many things. You will make more mistakes, learn more lessons, have more losses, more wins, experiencing changes and growth along the way. You will encounter more people who will be just like spring, summer, fall and winter as they pass through your life. Many people come and go like the seasons.

Just like the seasons of the year, and the weather they bring, the people you encounter will either be fair or foul. You just have to know who to keep, who to watch, or who to let go of. Once I stopped allowing myself to be devalued and broken by people who were broken themselves, things became clearer, and life started changing for me. I gave them too much power over my mind, heart, emotions, and spirit. I am a student of life, even in my 40s.

Oh, the blessing and grace to not look like what you have been through, or what you may still be going through, as long as divine grace sees fit. I am going to keep coloring brightness in my life as someone has learned to smile and appreciate the sunshine through my story. It is a part of my resilience I know that. It is okay if I am not strong all the time. And it is okay to need a shoulder to lean on. My best friend always says to me, "my back is strong. I can handle the weight of your precious light." I felt such a great sense of relief when I heard those words, to know that I truly had someone who had my back no matter what. A friend who would always be there when I needed them to be. Do you have that one "ride or die" friend in your life? If you do, honor them and be thankful for the blessing of their presence in your life. Some people say, "I would rather die for you", "I got you", "I'll be there", but when you need them the most they walk away, nowhere to be found.

It is a blessing when people show up in your life and their good hearts are revealed through tests, trials, and adversities. Those people who never switch up, and if they do fall short, they are still open and honest about it granting the sincerest apologies. Keep them around.

I appreciate you for rocking with me in my chapter, listening to my story. I would like to leave you with some helpful quotes and affirmations, personal tools from my self-care box that have helped me throughout my life. I hope they will help you as well.

It's not what happens to you but what happens for you.

Do not look at your adversity from a victim mindset but a victorious one, take the lessons learned from them, then apply them.

Celebrate where you are in life today.

Embrace your journey and enjoy the journey.

Do not give yourself a due date on your healing, take it one day at a time, on rough days breathe through it to acknowledge your feelings in the moment.

No one can heal you and no one can rush you to seek professional help. If you know that you need it, do not suffer in silence.

Prayer, meditation, affirming positive words ready to target the negative words you are either thinking or speaking. It is part of the positive mental attitude (PMA) system.

Write healing messages to yourself and stick them somewhere so you can go back and read as many times as you need every time you overcome an obstacle:

I believe there is healing in writing and journaling.
I have an abundance of wisdom.
I Am Peace.
I Am Healed.
I Am not Broken.
I will Smile. My energy is contagious, so let me spread it!
I Am an Overcomer.
I Am Loved.
I Own my Powers.
I Am Resilient.
Love and Light...Healers!

About Lakeisha

Lakeisha is a mother, wife, coach, author, speaker, and advocate in the CBD industry. Lakeisha is the author of, *The Jewelry Box,* and *I am dominating all of my internal Sh t*. She has also co-authored, "*Step into Your Power.*" She is a fierce fighter of adverse mindsets and environments as a leader. She is very passionate about empowering women for purpose.

Lakeisha is the founder of CoachingINC. She is a true motivator, continuing to empower and inspire people through coaching and sharing her own personal story in the spaces it is needed. She is a voice in the rooms God opens up to her to bless the lives and empower others. She believes in the foundation of building trusting relationships through transparency, love, and respect of persons.

As a coach she serves her clients through empowerment with the tools they need for personal growth, mind, emotion, and spirit. She supports her clients with goal setting, self-development skills, action planning, action steps, and guides them towards executing their goals.

https://www.facebook.com/coachingINC2020
www.instagram.com/lakeisha_muhammad
www.lakaeishacmuhammad.com
https://linktr.ee/lakeisha_muhammad
ladymuhammad18@gmail.com

Chapter 30

Not Everyone is Meant for You

BY PALESA MBOWENI

Let me talk and write about me today! I am a woman from Africa, my home is Johannesburg in Krugersdorp.

I am a mother, student, career woman, professional employee, philanthropist, and entrepreneur owning a business. Many do not know how many times I was broken in order to succeed in those titles. **The painful thing is that I am still on the receiving end of frequent envious remarks and acts from many around me, for what I have achieved so far.**

I love myself and I am proud of myself, for that, I don't need anyone's permission. I fought many battles, I cried many drops of tears, I have been broken, betrayed, mocked, called all sorts of names, accused, abandoned, and rejected, **but I am still** smiling, standing, walking proud, laughing loudly, loving, without unreservedly. I know I am beautiful inside and outside. My circumstances have taught me to stay 'humbled', as it is written in the Word of God in James 4:10.

I drew my strength from the life experiences I went through after I gave my power to people. I thought I was strong, energetic, confident, and happy. But only until I was challenged by the closest, most dear to me, loved ones. People will always expect more from me than what they can give in return. Some were helping me to add to their list of what they did for me, boasting with others about it. They revealed that what they did for me was not from their heart... Please hear this, **if you are helping someone because you are expecting something in return, you are in 'business', not kindness anymore.**

I built friendships and relationships (friends, partners, business partners, etc.) along my journey, but I was hurt in different ways along the way and left broken. **But every painful event in life is there to teach a lesson and every lesson has the ability to change a person.**

I gave my power away to people the day I let everyone into my space - without having principles. I was a free spirit, an open book to everyone, sharing my heart and my pain with anyone and everyone.

My character was too welcoming, lacking the discernment to identify people who were good or bad for me. This opened the door for people to take advantage of me. I was unable to see that the same person with whom I am sharing my heart, would be the quickest to break it. I would realize this only after it was too late - after everything was exposed. **God was fighting my battle for me though, and at the same time, He was also preparing my heart for forgiveness.** Unknowingly, the Word of God from Exodus 14:14 was manifesting in my life.

My forgiving nature meant that I would repeat the same patterns and mistakes. Opening up to the same people who would break my heart - over and over again. I would forgive too quickly and trust them too soon. This was me… it was who I was... but it was this repetitive cycle that brought me a lot of pain. While my spirit lacked discernment, I had a prayer warrior in my life. My biological mother was standing in the gap for me with prayers. She was praying for guidance, protection and for God to take all bad people out of my life. She used to warn me, but I never listened - she never gave up on me! Instead, she prayed for me and **today I am a living testimony to God's answered prayers.**

I thought I had it all. Good people, good connections, and a great time! A good, successful business and comfortable life. **Totally unaware that not everyone was happy for me.**

It was not easy to see who is happy and who is not happy for me, because I was too trusting. One of the things I had to overcome, was learning that some of my friends were flirting with and sleeping with my exes. Attempting to steal my joy, manipulating me, and gossiping about me because they wanted to be me... they wanted to destroy me. I had friends in my life who befriended me with an agenda. I was close to many known and successful people in both my social life and business. So, our friendship was based on them wanting to be connected to my contacts. Some wanted to have affairs, and some wanted to steal my business and to destroy friendships and relationships I had. If I had known, I would never have allowed them into my life. **Stay away from friends who are in your life because they want something from you.**

Ironically, those people were the first to say bad things about me. Then there were those who wanted me to **mentor** them, but they were only in it for their own gain. I even had **some friends** form groups, turning against me, building their friendship using my name. Nothing hurts quite as deeply as knowing that the person behind who caused you all your pain, is the same person you share everything with, trusting, loving, and relying on. **Trust means everything but once it's broken - sorry means nothing.**

This taught me that in life, you should not expect to receive the same amount of energy and effort as what you give to another person. I helped many people, being there for them emotionally, physically, and financially. They treated me poorly in return, not that I ever expected anything from them in return - only loyalty, honesty, and care. I wanted to be loved by them, but sadly I had to discover that **most people** lack love, making it difficult for them to give love to others. **Never expect loyalty from people who won't afford you honesty.**

I had friends who were judgmental and competitive, gossiping about others and very manipulative. Jealousy made them want what I had, but I was simply better than them at using what God blessed me with. People tend to forget that everyone has a unique gift and talent, you only need to apply it. **Do not be jealous, your day will come, it is just a matter of time.**

I experienced betrayal because in their eyes I did not deserve to be as happy or as successful... But jealousy is a disease planted in your heart. **Never hate jealous people, they are jealous because they think you are better than them and they are blind to their own blessings.**

I used to feel hurt when others mistreated me. I didn't understand my own uniqueness, **now I know how blessed and special I am.**

Also, when others are intimidated by what you have, and the favor you receive as a result, you become a threat. My success and the effect I had on people, in other words, my God-given talents and skills became a threat to others. And in response, they wanted to see me destroyed. **But everyone has a talent, a gift and time to shine and to learn from each other, and therefore one does not have to be jealous. Not everyone was aware that I was living the words in Psalms 90:17.**

It was a tough lesson to learn, and I often have to think about how I overcame my challenges. How did I face the fact that so many were spreading lies about me, set out to destroy me?

In life, some people will take advantage of the pain, they will talk about you behind your back, shame you, write you off. When I was diagnosed with depression, I was labelled a 'mad woman'. It broke my heart to hear that all this was said by the same people who called themselves "friends".

When days are dark friends are few...in life, some people will come to you during your pain not to support you, but rather to see if you survived. Others only reach out or see you, so that they can be the **first ones** to go and gossip about you.

In friendship, the two things I despise most are betrayal and disloyalty. I do not get along with those who do not know how to give a compliment or a word of encouragement, and who are not there for each other. Friends who displayed these qualities hurt me greatly, and I carried much anger towards them. **Remember, no matter what, do not laugh at someone's situation because you might be the one experiencing the same or worse someday - and then you might find you need to lean on the same person you laughed at.**

Another reason I found myself in this dark situation was fear, fear of losing friendships or the relationships I had. But where are they today? The truth is I lost them regardless. Fear is the biggest enemy in our lives, it can hold you prisoner and paralyze you. **Never cry about losing the person who hurt you, just smile and say, "thank you for giving me a chance to find someone better than you."**

I sacrificed myself, my children and my family for friends, relationships and for things that were not worth it. Spending quality time with them, holidays, finances, supporting them, were the things I lost due to the bad relationships in my life. Do not waste precious time - surround yourself with the right people. In life God will send some people to love you as you are, **family should be an important part of our lives no matter what happens.**

I lived for friends and other people - I have learned the hard way. People hated me without even knowing me, some being recruited to hate me and others because of false things said about me. Something that I found often happened, would be meeting a person for the first time and immediately they decide to work against you - an enemy for no apparent reason. This is especially painful because you can find no rhyme or reason for this person to hate you this much. **Don't let a stranger's opinion of you get to you.**

I almost lost my self-confidence and wanted to end my life many times, because of the pressure and expectations of some of the people in my life. This was a wake-up call for me! I learned **never to make a decision when I am sad, and also never to reply when I am angry.** I had a fear of walking on the streets, in malls or even to be around people - purely because of what was said and written about me! My children and family were tormented and affected by everything that was happening. I made sacrifices that I still think about, often regretting them, even today. Despite this, I have found lessons in the pain, and see it as part of my journey. I learned from it and moved on. **Take charge of your life. It is your breath and losing will cost you your life.**

I no longer have the patience for certain things, not because I've become arrogant, but because I have reached a point in my life where I don't want to waste time with what displeases me or hurts me. I have no patience for critics and demands of any nature. I have no patience for anyone who doesn't deserve my time. I encourage you to choose friends and partners wisely. I know it's not easy to keep things to yourself, but it is important to talk to the right people. **Invite God into your plans, make sure you pray for friendship and relationships before you get involved. Never share your plans. Rather keep the good news to yourself. It is best to show others the results of your plans and good news - because not everyone would be genuinely happy for you.**

I lost the will to please those who do not like me, to love those who do not love me and to smile at those who do not want to smile at me. I am no longer spending a single minute on those who lie or want to manipulate me. I decided not to coexist with pretense, hypocrisy, dishonesty, disloyalty, and cheap praise any longer. I do not tolerate selective erudition or academic arrogance. I don't respond to popular gossiping. I hate conflict and comparisons. I believe in a world of opposites and diversity and that's why I avoid people who are rigid and inflexible. Exaggerations pierced me and I have difficulty accepting those who do not like me. I let people go-ahead to talk. **I can't control what people say or think about me, but I can control what I do about it, either to focus on them or on myself.** "Keep talking about me behind my back and watch God keep blessing me in front of you."

When the people in my life revealed their true colors through their actions, they showed me that they were not for me, but for their own agenda. **What people think of me is none of my business. It is what I think of me that counts.**

People may judge you based on what they hear or in my case, read about you. Don't let this bother you. There is a time and a place for lessons to be learned from those in your life who hurt you - but you learn from it. After that, let them go. They are only meant to be in your life for a specific time and season - for you to learn from the experience. **Don't waste your time on revenge, those who hurt you will eventually face their own karma.** Life is surrounded by people who judge you day in and day out, they will talk about you when you succeed and laugh at you when you fail, you'll find those who will make you or break you. I found a secret here, is to **live a humble life that pleases God, not people, for He will lift you up in His perfect time.**

I am happy! I am a child of God and I received deliverance. This helped me to understand the purpose of forgiveness. It has taught me how to fight my battles. And revealed to me the benefits of being in His presence. I have been freed spiritually and physically - **God removed anyone from my life who was not supposed to be with me. There will always be people in your life who treat you wrongly, be sure to thank them for making you stronger.**

Today I live a life without competing with anyone. I am confident... and only compete with myself to achieve what I want to - without looking for any approval. **Do not force people to stay in your life.** I am so tired of people making excuses, if it's important for them to be in my life, they'll find a way no matter what.

I am not arrogant, but I choose to be a good friend to those who respect and love me despite all my mistakes, and those who don't judge me. If I focus on everything I've lost, **I might lose everything that I still have.** I have learned to defeat the devil and his plans, by not taking my eyes off God. This will make it impossible to be defeated by anything.

You may be at a stage in your life where you have goals, dreams, and plans, asking yourself how you will get there. But don't worry, God has ordained His word and His promises, and He will speak into your circumstances to see them fulfilled in your life, He is not done with you yet. You have to believe Him to walk with him. God's will, will not take us where the grace of God cannot sustain us. Always hold on to Jeremiah 29:11, remembering that God had plans for you before you were formed in your mother's womb **and His plans are to prosper you not to harm you and to give you a future and hope.**

Life never stops teaching us if we allow ourselves to learn. Always remember that your present situation is not the final destination, the best is yet to come!

I am proud today that I have a story to tell… One that can inspire and encourage others, illustrating how important it is to choose friends wisely, and how to heal from being hurt by those close to you.

How do you pick yourself up after a fall…? How does one carry on with the pain and hurt caused by relationships? After the many tears I have shed, after the disappointments, and hurt I've been through, I can share what I know guiding you on to carry on:

1. DON'T DWELL ON THE BAD: Replaying the incidents, thoughts and feelings won't change what has happened. Process and understand the situation, find the lessons you need to learn and move on while making sure not to find yourself in the same situation again.

2. LEAVE THE PAST BEHIND YOU: The past is meant for history books. Don't torture yourself with "What if's" and "If Only's". It is time to look forward to the future and focus on new beginnings.

3. FORGIVE: Forgive those who have done bad things to you for they too will have to answer for their actions one day. Forgive them for your own sanity, for your own closure so that you can move forward.

4. DON'T BLAME YOURSELF: It doesn't help to blame yourself for something you had no control over. Understand that things happened the way they did for a reason, accept it, and move on.

5. FIND YOUR SMILE: Learn to do the things that make you happy, relax, have fun, smile again! Don't be afraid to start again, set your goals and work towards achieving them day by day, because YOU CAN! YOU ARE ENOUGH. YOU ARE DIAMOND, KEEP SHINING…

About Palesa

A successful entrepreneur Palesa Mboweni, a CEO of Glimpse of Glamour and Woman of Power South Africa. She was born in Kagiso, Johannesburg in South Africa, a place that is surrounded by GOLD mines, and it is from these mines where she takes most of her glamour, inspiration, and drive to be succeed, multitalented professional, whose Glimpse of Glamour brand is a natural extension of who she is. Wine's industry is her new business venture. She started business and established her company in 2007 for events and project management, and today she upgraded to General Building and Civil Constructions.

Palesa is passionate about the youth, woman empowerment and senior citizens. She participates a lot in the programs and makes sure elders celebrate themselves and empowering youth and women. She symbolizes the crown of a strong Black Woman, a woman who is strong enough to make all her dreams come true without compromising her beliefs.

Palesa Mboweni, a mother of three, studied Electrical Engineering at Athlone College and Cape Technikon in Western Cape in South Africa. She is a graduate in Business Management and Entrepreneurship at University of Johannesburg. Palesa is accredited and certified with SETA on Coaching & Mentoring, Facilitator, Assessor, Moderator programs with ENJO Consulting and she is currently lecturing training with her accreditations she has obtained. She has studied Construction Management with NHBRC to enhance skills in her company. She is an Entrepreneur, Ambassador of Gender Base Violence, Cancer Pink Drive 2015 & Palesa Wines, Coach, Mentor, Motivational, online radio presenter & inspirational speaker & soon to be Author.

Awards &Achievements:

Young Businesswomen Award

Upcoming Entrepreneur Award

Nedbank Entrepreneur Award

Campaign & Awareness Brand Ambassadors

+27815175645 Palesammkn@gmail.com

Facebook: Palesa Shiluva N'waMboweni

Facebook: Palesatalksconnectingthedots

Instagram: @palesatalksconnectingthedots

Chapter 31

Love & Happiness Starts With You!

BY STACEY CHAPMAN RAGIN

You can, You must, You will Love Yourself!

JEREMIAH 29:11
"For I know the plans that I [a]have for you,' declares the Lord,
'plans for [b]prosperity and not for disaster, to give you a future and
a hope."

As I recall my childhood, we were never one of those families that gave a lot of hugs or other acts of affection; however, the love was there, and we knew it. My father had experienced a rough upbringing as a child. As a result, he set a goal to get away, using that brokenness to help him become the best father and provider that he could be. He joined the military at a fairly young age, so he did not get the opportunity to experience much affection before I came along. He became a dedicated leader in the army, so consequently, my sister and I sometimes felt like his little soldiers. It was not that bad though, we still felt like daddy's girls at times. My mother had also endured challenging times growing up, she overcame those circumstances to become a great mother and woman of God. She did her best to raise us with morals and Biblical principles, so she was firm too. Sadly, my parents divorced after almost twenty years of marriage. I was just in middle school, so that had a negative impact as well. My father left the state and remarried. My sister and I did not get to see him too often after that.

While still in middle school, I began to develop a real interest in boys, but never had an actual boyfriend. I observed other relationships and sometimes wondered if something was wrong with me. I had friends and the respect of my classmates as a smart and cool girl, but that was not enough for me. I wanted a boyfriend of my own. Deep down within, there was an empty void that I set out to fill, but not the right way.

After I made it to high school, I changed the game a bit. I decided to stop wearing boys' baggy clothes and dress more feminine. I stopped being so shy, but not to the point of throwing myself at the guys like some others. So, when I finally got noticed, it was a big deal to me. Unfortunately, I did fall prey to some wolves in sheep's clothes and that opened the door to a slow, destructive road. The sad thing is while I did suspect I was being taken advantage of; I chose to look past it because I was finally getting the attention I had always wanted.

1 PETER 5:7-9
"Having cast all your anxiety on Him because He cares about you. 8 Be of sober spirit, be on the alert. Your adversary, the devil, prowls around like a roaring lion, seeking someone to devour. 9 [a]So resist him, firm in your faith, knowing that the same experiences of suffering are being accomplished by your [b]brothers and sisters who are in the world."

At age 19, I married a charming man with one heck of a quick temper. He was handsome, intelligent, educated, but deceitfully clever. He appeared to be one of the most loving and compassionate men I'd met until we made the decision to commit to one another. Pointless arguments began to escalate and turn violent. Immediately after, he would put on a big apologetic show every time. Then came the emotional blackmail to make matters even worse. Only a few knew that he threatened to harm my family if I did not marry him. By that time, he had shown me just how dangerous he was and not just with me. So, I took him seriously and complied to protect my mother and sister. Marriage ceremonies are supposed to be joyous occasions, but I stood there wondering what I had gotten myself into. I kept my maiden name to help hide the fact that I'd gone through with it. I was so head gone that I even defended his actions by telling myself it was psychological and that he loved me but could not help himself. Does that sound familiar to anyone? My memory has a lot of blanks, but I cannot forget the feeling of having misdirected and unexplainable anger taken out on me by a man I loved. I continued to accept his lies and apologies for a couple of months until he seriously took it too far. At that point, I finally reached out to my mother. By the grace of God, I wised up and got away before it was too late. Thank God for a praying mother and friends!

After my divorce and a failed engagement, I went down a dreadful road of sex, drugs, and alcohol to numb my emotions of pain, betrayal, emptiness, and disappointment I had incurred year after year. I tried to pressure boyfriends into serious commitment and became frustrated because none of them seemed to love me as much as I "thought" I loved them.

After a couple more failed relationships, I was 31 and made the mistake of getting involved with a much younger man. Apparently, he could not handle being with a grown woman and lost his mind in a fatal attraction type of way. Seven years later, I am still dealing with this thorn in my side because despite the history of domestic altercations, we created a child together. Ladies beware of soul ties; they are a force to be reckoned with. A soul tie is established by control, manipulation, fear, intimidation, verbally abusive, mental abuse, and physical abuse It took me a couple of years to break each soul tie with my ex-husband and this particular ex that I just spoke of. It almost ruined my marriage to my wonderful husband of 4 years, because you actually take on the spirits and toxic behaviors of the individual you are tied to.

In 2016 I made a move from Tennessee to North Carolina to marry my best friend. We just knew it would be the beginning of a wonderful new chapter of life together. Boy, were we wrong! Four years of a beautiful friendship began to go down the drain because we rushed to make something happen before its time. I thought I would make a great wife but realized I did not know how to. He was my knight in shining armor after the hell I had just endured with my son's father. As newlyweds, nothing went the way we expected it to. I had high expectations, and they weren't being met, so I complained a lot. My husband felt unappreciated and started complaining too. Over the years we have taken each other through quite a bit, but that's most marriages. Because of my lack of maturity and self-love, my mind would go into dark places off and on. I would allow the devil to convince me that my husband did not want or love me simply because I was not getting the attention and affection that I wanted for the time being. We all deal with hurt differently. I can get over certain things quickly, but that is not the case for my husband; It takes him longer. It took God and the counsel of some great mentors to help me realize how immature and selfish I had been regarding my feelings in this area of our relationship. They helped me to realize I was wrong to rely on my him for love and happiness. I was actually being a little selfish and inconsiderate of what he was dealing with mentally and emotionally at the time. I am supposed to be content with God's love and self-love instead of seeking it from someone else. Basically, my entire life, self-confidence and self-esteem had been very low because I did not know how to love myself!

JOHN 15:9
"Just as the Father has loved Me, I also have loved you; remain in My love."

I thank God for showing me myself, mentally, emotionally, and physically in the mirror one day. A transformation took place after that. I thought all those years of struggling as a single mother, incomplete college degrees, battling two disabling auto-immune diseases, struggling spiritually as a woman of God, multiple toxic relationships with family included, promiscuity, drugs, and two abusive relationships had broken me and ruined my chances of being the successful woman and wonderful mother I had always dreamed of becoming. But God! He turned it around and used all of it for my good. I learned something valuable from all these experiences. God is always able to use our brokenness to create something beautiful. Many times, what we see as our biggest mistakes and failures can become what God uses the most.

ROMANS 8:28

"And we know that [a]God [b]causes all things to work together for good to those who love God, to those who are called according to His purpose."

Along with my son, I now have five beautiful daughters that I am purposing to do my best at teaching them how to be strong and successful women. I have a great business with Total Life Changes where I introduce people to great quality products that will help them achieve their health goals. I am a certified life coach and mentor. I am an advocate for domestic violence and breast cancer awareness. I have co-authored a book with Coach Stacy Bryant, that shares stories of overcoming violent relationships, as well as assisting and encouraging married and engaged women trusting God, using His Word to overcome the obstacles of marriage.

As you can see, I am passionate about helping, encouraging, and empowering women of all ages. I truly love the Lord and I'm an advocate for Him too. If it were not for Him, I would still be a mess caught up in mess. I have progressed in some way almost every year, but 2020 broke the mold. Not only did I learn how to love myself, but I learned how to forgive and love others. Unforgiveness will have you "stuck like Chuck" in more ways than one. Please forgive everyone so you can enjoy the feeling of freedom. And if you don't know God, get to know Him! I am proud to say that I broke barriers of fear and rejection and I see my purpose more clearly. I've mended relationships with family members and learned how to maintain the peace and love over time. I can now see my worth and not settle for less than I deserve. I've always had goals and dreams, but now I have visions that I'm writing down, making and creating plans of action to achieve them. I am still adjusting to this better version of me, but I love it.

No matter what you have gone through, do not ever feel as if God is punishing you. Yes, we suffer consequences for our actions, but it is not punishment. It is preparation because He does not call the equipped, He equips the called. I want to leave you with some of my favorite scriptures that help keep me intact, especially when things get a little shaky. The devil does not like love, happiness, prosperity, or anything good for that matter. His mission is to shut all of that down and that's why God's Word is so important to refer back to daily to remind us of who we are and whose we are. I pray for peace, blessings, and abundance over all who take the time to read this book. Like me, you can still color!

2 Timothy 1:7

"For God has not given us a spirit of [a]timidity, but of power and love and [b]discipline."

About Stacey

Stacey Chapman Ragin is a wife, mother, entrepreneur, author, certified life coach, mentor, and servant leader for her church that is dedicated to her passion of helping women of all ages to heal, grow mentally, spiritually, and overcome life's challenges. She is a 13-year Lupus warrior also passionate about inspiring others to improve their heath. Stacey is a health & wellness advocate and business owner with Total Life Changes. She is a survivor and advocate for domestic violence awareness and a spiritual influencer. She is a co-author in the book, "Her Story II", published in 2017. She has years of experience guiding women through enduring the challenges of marriage using Biblical and practical principles. She has also learned how to mend broken relationships with loved ones and maintain peace.

Chapter 32

Second Chance

BY LATOYA JACKSON

I was given a second chance at life.

As a young child, I knew I was different from my siblings and friends. I used to dream of imaginary friends. I had an imaginary friend I could not see, a boy I called Red Eye. When I was mad, happy, or hurt I would talk to him. It was like he was the only one who would listen to me. I did not come from a broken home where I did not have my parents. I just knew I was different. I had both my father and mother, we used to have so much fun when I was a kid growing up. My younger brother still asks me about my imaginary friend to this day.

I think back over my life and sometimes ask myself, "why?" I am not weird or crazy (maybe I am, in my own way), but I think a lot of my past. I was popular in school. My 7th grade teacher called my mom one day and told her I was not focusing on class. She mentioned to my mother, I had too many friends and could not do the work that was asked of me and the class. My mother and father were not having it. I remember my teacher giving me write offs to do. I had to write, "I am Going to Get My Work Done". Of course, I did the write offs.

That changed as I went on through grade school, I did the work, had lots of friends, and stayed focused in school. As I became older, I stopped talking to my imaginary friend Red Eye. I started dating my 8th grade year, to a guy that was in a grade higher than me. He was in high school, and a great athlete; he was a football and basketball player. I was in LOVE!!! We dated for almost 2 years, before we even had sex; nope, I was not having sex, I was too scared. All my friends thought I was having sex because I was popular in school and dating a handsome young guy. I had a lot of older guys trying to date me, I would tell them I had a boyfriend. As the older guys kept asking and approaching me, I gave in. I started to flirt back with them and started to hang out with older girls in high school that were not my age and even hanging out with girls out of school. It was fun at the time; I look back now and think of my high school memories. Eventually, I had sex with a guy 3 years older than me and it was not my boyfriend I had been dating since 8th grade. Afterwards, I could not believe I had sex with another guy. Yes, it was my first-time having sex and I was sixteen years old. I could not tell my boyfriend I cheated on him with someone else, but he found out anyway. I never saw him that mad at me, it was like a nightmare! Of course, he broke up with me.

We weren't dating each other anymore, but we remained friends and talked on the phone. I wanted it to work out, but he was playing hard to get! While my ex was busy playing hard to get, along came one of the guys that was cool in school and always had everyone laughing. He and my ex-boyfriend were mutual friends and hung out with the same friends.

This guy was slick! We had been friends, went to church together, and started hanging out in school together.

He would buy my lunch, walk me to class, take me home and even buy me dinner. He was a nice guy and very funny. He had a lot of friends as well. It was not anything serious between us at the time. His senior year he asked me to the prom, and I told him I would love to go to the prom with him. My ex-boyfriend at the time was mad at me for going to the prom with him. I reminded him he did not ask me!

Not long after that my ex-boyfriend became sick and was not able to attend the prom or his senior year graduation. It was heartbreaking! He did return to school the next year and he graduated. I was so proud of him! I went to his graduation and we actually took a picture together; I still have that picture right to this day.

After graduation my ex-boyfriend and I kind of stopped talking and drifted apart. So, that made me grow closer to my friend and we spent a lot of time together. He would come and take me to school, even though he and my ex-boyfriend had graduated school.

In my junior year my mother became sick; she in and out of the hospital a lot. I did not know why my mom was always in the hospital at the time. Later that year my mom had to have her foot amputated; I remember crying when I saw my mom when she came home from the hospital.

My sister had just told my parents she was pregnant, my sister was 8 months pregnant and ready to have the damn baby! My mom was so excited that my sister was having a baby.

My mom told me and my siblings she was ok and not to worry about her. She had a loving spirit and a heart of gold. She worked many jobs when I was a kid and a teenager. All my cousins and friends loved being around her. She would let me have house parties and even make finger foods for us. After my mom was sick, I stopped having the parties and I just stayed to myself a lot. Mom got sick again months later and was put back in the hospital, this time they amputated her leg, that really crushed me.

When I was a junior in high school, I stopped attending school and games. I did not want to be around anyone but my friend. I would skip school and go to his house. He made me feel loved, even though I should have been in school. You would think he would make me go as much as I thought he loved me. I loved skipping school with him. The school counselor called my parents and told them I had missed a lot of days. My dad was heated. I told them I had been skipping school, I would even get on the bus and go to school, and I would turn around and leave. I just did not want to be at school anymore. I finally stopped going once my mom came home from the hospital. That was the excuse I used to go to avoid school and stay home with my mom, or to be with my friend. I look back over my life and wish I had stayed in school and walked the stage with my friends. My friends did not stop being my friends because I dropped out of school, it was like they loved me even more. A few people ask me why I dropped out of school, but I would use the excuse of my mom's sickness. I regret leaving school, I think my life would be different if I had stayed. At the time, I thought it was okay to drop out, since I knew other people that had dropped out of school, including my two older siblings. My mom was the only one in my family that had graduated school. Even though we dropped out of school, I love my siblings with all my heart! We are not perfect. God kept us!

Time passed, and a couple of years later I got pregnant with my oldest son; I had been seeing my friend since school and even after I dropped out of school. I knew who the father was. I was already pregnant when I ran into my ex-boyfriend and we had a one-night stand. I do not know why I wanted this baby to be his child even with his mental issue. I still loved him and wanted to be his friend. I was telling them both they were the father I just wanted this baby to be his, even though I was in love with my friend and cared so much about him. I did not want my friend to know I was telling the other guy it was his baby as well. I told a friend my situation and she ran back and told my ex-boyfriend it wasn't his baby.

I hid my pregnancy from my family and siblings. I was telling the outside people, but I kept it from my family. I could not believe my parents and siblings had not found out yet.

My parents loved cooking and entertaining family and friends – that was a passion of theirs! They owned a restaurant in our hometown, and I worked at the restaurant with my parents. Looking back, I don't know how I hid my baby bump!

I remember like it was yesterday, when we got the phone call saying my mom was in a car accident while she was outside city limits, delivering plates. She had a stroke while she was driving and was hospitalized. I remember my dad coming to the restaurant and closing for the night. My mom stayed in the hospital for about 2 weeks. Ma Mae, my mom's mother was still living at the time of the accident. Ma Mae called every day to check on my mom. They would talk everyday just about two to three times a day. My mom loved her mother and I loved Ma Mae. Ma Mae would always get onto my mom about her health, telling mom to take care of herself and not to work so much since she became sick. My mom kept pushing and working even harder.

Only weeks later my granny (MaMae) was sick in the hospital, and she had her legs amputated. My granny was in the hospital for weeks, and she later passed away. That made my mom think about her own health; it bothered my mom, remembering how Ma Mae would tell her to take care of herself. At the funeral I still hid my pregnancy from my parents and family. Weeks had passed and I was at home laying on the floor in my bedroom, I was talking on the phone. I was wearing my granny's gown; it was special to me that I had something of MaMae's. My dad came walking by the door and stopped and scared me! I do not know how he noticed the baby bump, but he did—

"Latoya are you pregnant?!" He asked me, with madness in his voice. He called my mom to come to the room.

My mom said, "Toy! Are you pregnant, girl?"

Still trying to hide the truth, I said, "Naw, I'm not pregnant."

Dad was like, "Take her to the hospital!"

I was like, "For what?"

"Get your damn ass in the car and go to the hospital cause your damn ass is pregnant! Do not lie to me girl!" He growled.

He was mad! My mom drove me to the hospital in silence. She did not say anything to me on the way there. When we got there, she told them I needed to be checked to see if I was pregnant. The nurse came in and asked me she could check my blood and get a urine sample. I agreed. I was nervous as hell because I knew I was pregnant! My mom was not able to come in the room with me, she stayed in the waiting room and was ready to hear the results. When my mom finally came into the room, the nurse told us both I was pregnant, and the baby was due any day. According to the ultrasound results, I could have my baby within the next couple of weeks, if not sooner. My mother was so shocked and upset!

Not only had I hid my pregnancy that whole time, but I hadn't seen a doctor or anything!

My mom was upset at me because I did not tell them. Years before, my cousin lost her life trying to get rid of her baby herself. My mom said that is why she was angry; my sister had hidden her pregnancy as well. At that point, my mom called my dad and told him I was about ready to have the baby.

My dad said, "What the hell! This damn fool is about ready to have this baby?"

"Yes, in about 6 weeks," my mom answered.

When we got home, dad was so mad at me! He could not even look at me. A couple of days later, he told me he wasn't mad at me. He called me Munk. Munk is my family nickname. I knew he loved me; he was just upset that I hid my pregnancy and knowing what had happened to my cousin years before.

My big head son came weeks later. I had 3 ultrasounds that said it was a girl. I was devastated, in those few weeks after my family finding out I was going to have a baby, I had gifts and a baby shower, and everything was pink! I had a girl name picked out: Jazmine. My older brother and I came up with the name. While I was in labor my mom did not feel good, and I had been in labor for almost 24 hours. Remember, my mom had her legs amputated and had a few strokes. As soon as my mom left the nurse checked me again, to see why I had not given birth yet. My baby was breech and I had to have an emergency C-section. I was crying my eyes out! I had no one there with me and I did not want to call my friend or ex-boyfriend (the one I had told was the father). There was a lady standing in the hall of the hospital and she said she would go in the operation room with me. I did not know this woman from Adam! She held my hand while I was in surgery, the nurse came to me and said they had called my mom, and she was on her way back. The nurse told me they would take good care of me.

The doctor pulled my baby out and I heard the cry and the lady I did not know said, "Aww, he is so adorable!"

That's how I found out I had a baby boy. I had no name for my baby boy. Both my friend and ex-boyfriend came to the hospital minutes apart from each other. I was still in disbelief I did not have a girl. My friend knew it was his baby.

My ex-boyfriend said then and there, "That it is not my baby Latoya". I did not know what to say. He left, and I did not talk to him for a long time after that.

I stayed in the hospital for days with no baby name or boy clothes. Dad had stopped by the hospital to see me and the baby, that is how I got the name. He named my son after his grandfather and I got the middle name off of BET.

Months had gone by and I called my ex-boyfriend up, and he agreed to meet, so we could talk. I went to his house and we talked, and it made him even madder because I had the baby with me. We had the biggest fight! I left and from that day I went on with my life not thinking about how much I wanted him to be the father. I was hurt. It hurt me knowing I had hurt him, by telling him he was the father knowing deep down inside he was not the father. The love we had for each other.

So, I started dating my baby dad again, it was an up and down thing. He had started dating other women behind my back and I couldn't stand him cheating on me anymore. I was still staying at home, our son had just turned one year old, I found I was pregnant again with our second child. We both agreed that we were not ready to have another child. We were both living at home with our parents. I was 20 years old, and he was 21 years, and we talked about having an abortion. I scheduled the appointment to have the abortion. That day was the worst day of my life! I remember waking up with blood everywhere and I could not stand up or walk. I had to stay in recovery until I was able to stand and walk. There were girls of all ages in the recovery room crying, bleeding, and unable to walk. I felt terrible for weeks afterwards, and I was hurt because I had an abortion. I never thought I would have an abortion. It bothered me for a long time, thinking that was my baby girl.

We got our own place later that year, he continued to cheat so I started to cheat on him behind his back. We both worked the night shift and that is when I cheated, while he was at work.

I knew I was wrong, I wanted him to feel the hurt like I did. I had a lot of handsome men wanting to take me out.

He did not like it at all; he said, "Let's do this the right way!"

I said, "Yes, I want this to work too".

He said a friend told him, "You got you a beautiful woman who loves you and wants to make it work! She just gave you a taste of your own medicine".

We both gave each other the respect and love, then here comes baby number two. I moved back home for a few months, right after New Year's my mom had gotten burnt and was hospitalized for months in the burn unit. That took a toll on me! I worked while I was pregnant, and during those months we decided to move from our hometown. I had my second son on Valentine's day, after we had moved to the Nashville area.

I remember taking my baby son to see my mom in the hospital, I walked in the room and said, "Mom, here is the baby". She opened her eyes and looked up at us with a grin on her face. A couple months later my mom passed away. It hurt me to my soul!

I felt the love and comfort from my kid's father. He later asked me to marry him, I said YES! I had a ring on my finger, and it made me feel better and kept my mind off of my mother's death. We started planning our wedding and decided to marry the same weekend my mother passed away, which was Memorial Day weekend. It seemed like our love had grown stronger and made us come closer together. I did not see anything out of the norm, I was happy and in love! We married in 2002, one year after my mother's passing. I thought I had it all and the love! Months went by and everything was still going well; it had been almost two years and he had not cheated on me. Six months after we married, he cheated on me behind my back. It was with his friend's girlfriend. She had done my hair in the past. I ran into her at the store one day and she did not speak. I did not know she had slept with my husband. I came home and I said I saw Tee at the store, and she did not speak. He said do not worry about her speaking to you. I did not think anything else about it at the time. Weeks went by and I received a phone call saying my ex-boyfriend has passed away. I cried my eyes out. My husband was holding me, and telling me everything was ok, and he was in a better place. I went to my ex-boyfriend's funeral, not knowing my husband was mad cause I went. When I came home, I noticed he did not want to talk to me. Every time I asked him a question, he would give me a short answer. I was like okay; I will not say anything to him the rest of the night. I am in the bathroom combing my hair and the house phone rings. I answer the phone and it is his friend. He asked where my husband was and told him he was sleeping. I told him to hold on I would wake him up; that's when he said no—he called to talk to me.

I asked him what was going on. He said he had been wanting to tell me for a while that my husband had been cheating on me for a while, but when he slept with his girl, he crossed the line. I just got in the house from my ex-boyfriend's funeral, then I got this damn crazy ass phone call from his friend, saying my husband slept with his girlfriend. I was over it. I went and smacked his ass up out the bed.

I said, "You are still cheating on me dude!"

He said, "What in the hell are you talking about Latoya?!"

"Your friend just called me and said you slept with his girlfriend. Tell me the truth!" I demanded.

He walked out the door and did not tell me where he was going. We had only been married 6 months. I cried my eyes out! I thought I had put those days behind me. He came home about 30 minutes later and told me he was sorry. I told him I wanted a divorce! He hugged me so tight and would not let me go! He just kept saying he was sorry, and he loved me so much! He told me how it all happened, telling me that so many females wanted what I had. The next morning after he came home from work, he told me he wanted our marriage to work. I was still crying and upset.

Months went by, and I found out he had been cheating on me again. I waited until he came home, and I addressed the situation with him. I said I cannot keep letting you treat me this way!

I totally loved him and wanted our marriage to work because of our children He came to me weeks later and said he wanted us to move. I noticed every time he got caught up in some mess, he wanted to run or move further away. Of course, we moved; we moved into a brand-new house with three bedrooms, three baths, a bonus room, and two car garage. I was feeling good and enjoying the home with the boys and my husband. After being in the house almost a year, I started getting phone calls from women, telling me he was cheating on me with them. Right today I still do not know who the women were that called me on my home phone. They would call me from pay phones and even block their numbers. I saw a change in him when he noticed I was getting tired of his shit! I was working a mid-shift. I had to be at work at 5:00 PM in the evening, I got off work at 3:00 AM in the mornings. I would pick up the boys from their nanny early mornings. We both had the weekends off and that is when we spent most of our time together. It seemed like everything was coming together for us, we both seemed incredibly happy! The calls had stopped, I had not heard anything about him cheating on me or nothing! We would write each other notes every night before work and tell one another how much we loved each other and how much we loved the boys. I still have the last letter he wrote me saying how much he loved me. I found out I was sick with thyroid disease and I had gained a lot of weight over a few months. We both just thought it was happy weight, we both loved taking naps together. One day at work and I was not feeling well.

My supervisor told me to do something, and I refused to do it due to being sick that night at work, so I was told to go home because I was sick. I got a call a few days later saying I was being laid off. I became a stay-at-home mom and I loved it, but I kept getting sick and I did not know why. I went to have surgery and radiation treatment for my thyroid disease. I was not able to be around the boys or my husband for about a week. He would peek in on me and tell me he loved me! Everything seemed okay.

Months went by still all love! The letters did not stop! All love! I was happy and the boys were happy.

Then one day he asked me to get a part time job, I did not ask any questions, I agreed. Months before that, we decided to consolidate our bills into one payment. I thought well maybe this will be our extra funds. I went out and found a full-time job instead of a part time job. I had only been on the job for four days, when I came home that Friday after work, and he was sitting in the garage all dressed up with a fresh haircut. I asked why the boys did not get a haircut, that was really unusual. Normally, when he got a haircut, the boys did as well. He told me he would take them to get a haircut, but he wanted me to pick them up from the barber shop. I asked him why. He said he wanted to hang out, so I told him it was okay. I still did not see any signs of him leaving! I had to run to the bank and store and then I headed to pick them up. An hour went by, I pulled up to the barber shop and saw my boys sitting in the window, I walked in and asked, "Where is y'all dad?"

They both said they didn't know. I sat there an hour; the barber told me he just went to the store. I was like, "OK, we'll be back later."

When I got home, I opened the garage and walked in the house and went to our bedroom. I turned the light switch on, and I went to the closet. I don't know what led me to the closet-- I opened the closet door, and all his clothes and shoes were gone! My heart dropped; it was a feeling I cannot explain. I cried. My son said momma what is wrong, is daddy not coming back? I did not know what to say to them or myself! It was five days before our wedding anniversary. I drove around for three days looking for him. I called his parents and sister looking for him and they told me they had not heard from him. On the second day his sister called me and told me he was ok and for me not to worry, he was ok. I cried; the pain hurt so bad, it made me think of the years of cheating and lies! Even though I did not know what was going on, I just wanted him to come home so we could talk and work out whatever situation it was. That is how much I loved him! When I tell you, I was broken and lost, I was broken into many pieces. On the third day of riding around looking for him, my heart told me to go to his sister's house, and he was there. I walked in and I said what is going on?! He said to me, "What you mean? It is over between you and me". Just like that! I cried and asked him why he was doing this. After all the shit he put me through! He told me he wasn't coming back.

I asked, "What about the boys?"

He said, "I will be there for my boys". We argued, and he said he had to go to work, and he didn't have time to talk to me.

I got in my car and drove home crying my damn eyes out! I had not eaten in three days, I felt sick to my stomach, and my head was hurting out this world. It was like my whole world had fallen apart. I felt empty on the inside. He came over and told me we had to talk; I was ready to hear, "I'm sorry and I want our marriage to work". That was not the case! In his back pocket he had a large brown envelope folded up, he took it from his back pocket and handed it to me and said open it. I asked what it was. I opened the envelope and looked at it and my heart crumbled into pieces. I could not believe what I was reading and seeing in front of me. He had filed for divorce months before he left. I was so hurt and did not understand why! We had been telling each other every day how much we loved each other, and we wanted our marriage to work. I did not see this coming! I was so naive and in love I did not see this coming! Remind you this is my childhood friend, we went to church together, school together, high school sweethearts, father of my 2 boys, friend, and husband. It hurt, because we were abandoned, and he had filed for a divorce months before. Again, I remind you I dropped out of high school my junior year. He told me I would never amount to anything in life, I would never be anything, I would never have anything, and that he made me. Those words hurt me to my core! I cried. I mean I cried a river. All I could think about was my boys, my oldest son would always tell me, "Momma we are going to be okay!"

I turned to God and asked God to take away the pain and the feelings. We divorced a year later the right way, in court in front of a woman judge. She was not easy on his ass either! After our divorce I felt somewhat better, then four months after our divorce he remarried. That took everything in me!

"But" God said, "You are broken my daughter, and I need you to find yourself and heal from the inside out".

I moved back to my hometown and I felt the love from my family and friends. I had support there, and I was okay with the love coming from my family and friends. It was a different kind of love!

Then I met a guy in prison, a very handsome guy. I started traveling to see him in prison and my father did not approve of it! But I was 29 years old, and I felt like I could make my own decision. I was still broken looking for love! Six months later my father had a heart attack out on the lake fishing. It hurt me so bad I had a headache for two weeks. I was broken all over again! I Prayed and asked God to let my dad know that I did not travel that morning to go see my boyfriend in prison. I was the last one to talk with my father that morning before he passed away. God showed me signs: I saw my father in a white suit with angel wings smiling. God showed me that my father was not mad at me and he made it into heaven.

My father gained his wings! Fly high dad I love you! It took many years to realize this was not the life God had planned for me to live. I was still broken! I had not talked to my ex-husband in three years, when he called me out of the blue one day and asked if we could meet. I was shocked! I had not talked to this man in three years. I met him and he apologized. He said he got caught up in that relationship and did not know how to get out of it. I told him I forgave him. We became friends and started dating again, even though I was still dating the guy in prison. I did not want to hurt him; he was loving and caring. When I told him I was talking to my ex-husband again, things got ugly. He started verbally abusing me with hurtful words. I was like, "No God! This cannot be it!"

We talked, and he was like, "I cannot believe you are back dating him, after he abandoned you and the boys and married four months after y'all divorced!"

It made me think hard. My ex-husband asked me to remarry him and then here comes the lies and cheating again. He was still married to his wife at the time we were dating. I knew it was not right! He was not only seeing me, but he was also seeing women in our hometown. I told him I could not continue to see him anymore. He was mad and threw a drink at me. I was broken all over again! I told God to remove me from the relationship. After I stopped seeing my ex-husband, I heard he left his wife and he left her the same way he left me--abandonment! I could not do anything but think of the way he treated me, and she thought he was going to treat her better. I let the relationship go with my boyfriend in prison and my ex-husband. I felt much better! I was free. I was picking up the broken pieces and trying to piece them back together. I was mending my broken heart that was shattered into pieces. I went back and got my GED, went into the healthcare field, went to college, and started my business. Remember I was told I would never amount to anything in life, and I would not have anything! God has Blessed me with a new husband that loves me for me! All of me!

After being married 6 months I got really sick, I was sick in the hospital on the vent for days. My husband stood right by my side. I knew God was in the midst of it all. I was given a second chance at life! God has restored my trust and love for other people. God has replaced all the things that were taken from me. I'm so thankful this broken crayon can still color!

Thank you, God, for a second chance at life.

About Latoya

Latoya Jackson is an Entrepreneur, Caterer, Event Planner, Nail Tech, Life Coach, Co-Author, Leader of 2 Women Groups, and Mentor.

Latoya is a mother of 2 sons, called the Fuz Boys. She is a lovely wife. Latoya was born and raised in Springfield, Tn.

Latoya is the owner of Your Cost Catering & Events Décor. She loves catering to people with her beautiful decorations, food, and love! She is the founder of Women Of Peace (WOP) where helps women discover peace.

Latoya has a passion for catering to others and her purpose is to help others overcome fear and brokenness. Latoya loves to be around family, loves to shop, and make things beautiful.

Chapter 33

Victim to Victorious

BY MARLA CLARK

It seems like from birth the day I was born, the devil wanted me to believe I could not depend on or trust any black man. Let me just walk you through the start of my life.

On January 30th, 1974, my mother was scheduled to check in the hospital to have a c-section, but the weather took a turn for the worst, with a blizzard complicating my arrival. Desperately trying to get to the hospital, she thought she could drive herself to the hospital. My father, Mo, was nowhere to be found, because he was out supporting his addiction, but we will get back to that. Since the snow was so high and my mother could not shovel her way out, she called a taxicab.

After hours she finally made it to the hospital along with my grandmother. I made my debut at 6:17 AM January 31, 1974. Guess who showed up at 6:30? Of course, my father Mo. Despite his late arrival, he took one look and was in love.

That dramatic entrance into this world served as an introduction to what awaited me. I was a six-year-old kindergartener when I first had innocence ripped from my soul. In kindergarten, I went to school for a half a day then it was off to the babysitter afterwards. I loved my babysitter. She was the best cook and sweet as apple pie. One afternoon she was not feeling too well so her teenage son Mark watched all the kids as she went to the doctor. That is the day my life changed. All the kids were taking a nap and I was awakened because Mark was pulling my pants down.

I started to cry and screamed, "What are you doing? Why are you doing this to me"?

He responded, "Because you are the prettiest girl here".

He then proceeded to fondle my vagina. As the tears streamed down my face, he pulled out his penis and started to penetrate me. After he figured out, he would make a mess, my screaming woke up one of my friends, and he ejaculated all over me. I snatched my pants and ran to the bathroom crying.

He knocked on the door and I screamed, "I AM TELLING MY DADDY ON YOU!"

Mark interrupted, "If you tell him, he is going to kill me – "

I yelled louder at him because I knew my Daddy did not play about his baby. That was when he dropped the bomb on me, saying, "if he kills me, he's going to jail, and you will never see him again."

I was sobbing at that point, because I could not imagine my life without my father, My King.

Mark started screaming, "be quiet and do not tell anyone!"

At that moment, the little innocent girl was gone forever. As I laid there silently weeping, my friend Lora hugged me and told me it would be okay. She went on to say, "my dad does it to me all the time. The next time will not hurt as bad."

I began to cry more, not just for me but for her as well, knowing she lived with a monster. I cried myself to sleep, only to be awakened by my babysitter telling me my mother was there to pick me up. I ran to my mother and hugged her as tight as I could-- I finally felt safe again. As we rode home, I was so quiet it alarmed my mother. She began asking what was wrong and I replied nothing. I really wanted to tell her what happened, but I did not want my Dad to find out, so I stayed silent.

Once I arrived home my favorite uncle was already there. He lived with us, and he was like a brother to me. He took one look at me and asked me what was wrong. I had never lied to him before, but that day would be the first of many lies. I told him I was sad because I had a fight with a friend at the babysitter's house. He hugged me and assured me it would be okay. Friends fight and makeup he told me, then he hugged me as I cried in his arms. For the next week I played sick to avoid the babysitter.

By the age of ten, I began to develop at a rate much faster than my friends. When I began to develop breasts, I received more attention from the males around me, including some cousins in my family. They all began to say the one thing that made my flesh crawl which was, "you are the prettiest girl". Who would have known being called pretty by a boy or a man would be a massive trigger for me mentally?

I remember one horrible experience when I was spending the night over at a relative's house only to be awakened by my male cousin licking my vagina. When I asked him what he was doing he told me he was practicing, and he chose me because I was "pretty". Mentally I turned back into the helpless little six-year girl all over again and figured that this is what happens to girls and women. In my mind I determined that I would find a way to blackout in these encounters so I would not acknowledge the pain. At the age of eleven, I began to sneak into my Uncle's liquor, drinking to numb my pain.

During that time of my life, my parents were arguing a lot due to my father's gambling addiction. Many feel that a gambling addiction is not that bad, but you go through the very same things as having a parent on drugs. As I watched my father mistreat my mother, I began to resent men. I remember one time my father had been out gambling and lost all his money. When he got home, he jumped on my mother in a rage. While my sister tried to defend my mother, I froze. I was paralyzed with fear because I loved my Dad. After he jumped on my mom and sister, he called me over to him. Reluctantly I went and he grabbed me by my ankles like a little piggy and began to spank me, saying I am going to show all you mother f**kers who is the boss around here. In the heat of that moment, he broke my favorite blue headband and my heart.

You see, before this my father could do no wrong. He was always the light of my life because he never treated me bad until then. My father and I had date nights every Friday before he went to lose his money gambling. In those rare cases where he would win, he would buy me whatever I wanted and take me wherever I wanted to go. He would bring me a hot lunch to school and never miss a PTA meeting or parent teacher conference. He even went on every field trip with me. As you can see, he was not always that vicious. One night I was eavesdropping on my parents as they began to argue over him spending the money they had been saving for me to go to college. My Mother was distraught because he had gambled it all away. In that moment as a child, I determined college would not be available for me.

By the time I turned 12, my parents got a divorce and my mother, sister and I moved into our own townhouse. I remember the sense of relief, knowing that we could have some peace in our home. My mother had to work two jobs to make ends meet, so she was rarely at home. During that time, I began to act out, seeking attention from boys, searching for protection and love. In my heart I wanted to believe there were good guys out there that would treat me better than I saw my father treat my mother.

I sought out the popular guys and the street boys, which lead me to drinking and fighting. This was the basis of my middle and high school years. My senior year I was suspended so many times my counselor advised me I would not graduate unless I went to summer school. I felt like a complete failure, embarrassed because my friends were all graduating on time. I signed up for Job Corps. My mother was devastated; she didn't want me to go, but I was determined to get away from the embarrassment I felt I had caused for my family.

Entering Job Corps at 18 was a different world. I was independent and able to be me because no one there knew me. I could forget about college knowing we could not afford it. During my stay at Job Corps my addiction to alcohol became more intense because everyone around me was drinking, so it became acceptable. My first night on campus I hung out with a young lady by the name of Tee, and she asked if I wanted to drink with her. We went drinking with a group of people, later dubbing ourselves "the drunk buddies". Anytime one of us had a problem or were upset, our solution was to have drinks. We would drink MD 20/20 and mix it with beer along with Cisco. During this time, I dated different guys but nothing too serious because it would interfere with my drinking.

Then I met Baron. He was so nice to me and catered to my every need, but I felt smothered. I asked him if we could take a break because he was too clingy. It was the weekend, and he gave me until Sunday night to decide if we were going to keep seeing each other, otherwise he said he was leaving. I partied all weekend and looked for him Monday morning, but to my surprise he had left. I was so hurt but I knew I had done it to myself. The rest of my time in Job Corps I decided I would only be friends with the guys.

That was until I met O. He was like a breath of fresh air. We laughed, talked, played, and fell in love with each other. It was simply amazing. He encouraged me and supported my accomplishments. When I gained my GED, he was so happy. He encouraged me to take additional classes after I became a CNA. All was going well until he found out his ex-girlfriend was pregnant with his baby. He was a respectable guy with a good heart, so we broke up and he left Job Corps to take care of his first child. Once again, I was heartbroken.

After he left, I began to see different guys as a distraction but none of them compared to O. I began to see a guy by the name of James. He was not the type of guy I should have been seeing but it made time pass. As time progressed, O returned and was staying off campus. Of course, I broke up with James. O and I began to see each other again and I became pregnant with our child. At that moment, my life changed. James lied to O and told him I was pregnant by him out of jealousy. We broke up and I went home heartbroken once again. I stopped drinking instantly because I loved the child growing inside of me more than alcohol.

Having my beautiful daughter saved my life and helped me to change. I loved my beautiful daughter Key with every fiber of my being, and she became the light on my dark days. As Key started to get bigger, I became paranoid. I feared that she would be abused like I had been. At that point, I was 20 years old and every time she was with anyone besides my mother, I would check in between her legs when she returned. Every time a man would call her a "pretty girl" I would cringe.

I recall being at a park in Chicago with my first husband when a man commented that she was so pretty, and if she were older, she would be his girlfriend. At that moment, I blacked out and beat the man up. My husband grabbed me and put me in the car. After that situation, my marriage began to fail. I would blackout as if I were not there when he would try to make love to me. Once again, I started drinking and fighting. So many things happened in my first marriage that were traumatic for both of us. By now Key had turned 3 and I took her and relocated to Memphis, Tennessee.

I had been in Memphis for little over a year battling depression. My aunt was concerned about me and arranged for me to move in with her.

Eventually, I started to make plans to move back home with my mother in Illinois. At least that was the plan-- then I met my second husband, Mark.

Mark offered to get me an apartment and to take care of everything since I was not working. We moved in with each other and everything was going great until he became emotionally abusive, and rumors of cheating began to swirl around. I stayed, thinking I could save the relationship.

I became pregnant with my second child, Yaz. I was sick so much I had to quit my job, so we moved in with my mother in Illinois. Everything seemed great again until we moved into our own home and I became pregnant with our third child Jr. The cheating rumors started again, and I tried to hold on to hope of having a family where my kids had both parents in the home. After having my son, I became ill and had a seizure which caused me to go blind for 7 days. During this process I learned I had a tumor on my brain in an inoperable location. Once I finally healed, we started to repeat the same pattern of dysfunction. Exhausted with the rumors, I once again picked up and moved back to Memphis.

Moving back this time was met with all kinds of obstacles. Mark was the only one working and I went back to school to obtain my degree in the healthcare field. He became angry and resentful, and accusing me. He said I thought I was better than him. Then he started staying out late at night. Then he stopped paying all of the bills. I remember sitting in the bathroom, praying. I was at my wits end and began to pray and just like a movie God showed me what was going on. He was gambling and losing all his money, spending it on other women. All I could do was cry and think he is just like my father. We fought and argued for the next 3 months, when he finally left me for a younger woman who told him he did not have to pay bills. Not only did he leave, but he also told me no one would want me because I gained weight and had three little kids. I was totally devastated, knowing I was almost finished with school and would not graduate if I did not complete my clinicals. I became miserable. I did not want to do anything including bathe. I talked to the landlord and explained we would have to move because I could not pay the rent. Then my landlord, Mr. Sullivan told me we could stay here until we got on our feet if we pay the utilities. I was so overcome with gratitude; I began to cry uncontrollably.

God always shows up right on time. The next morning, I went to the human service office and applied for public assistance. I used that money to keep the utilities on until I gained a job after graduation. I was then able to take care of my family after two months while on public assistance.

During that time Mark stalked me and harassed me with little support for our kids because I would no longer become intimate with him. Sometimes Mark would get so angry and say he wished the tumor on my brain would bust. I asked for a divorce. He refused for many years until he moved away with another woman. So many things had happened to change me during that marriage. I became angry and bitter because I was a single mother.

I was so blinded by my anger I didn't realize how it was affecting my oldest daughter, Key. She began to shut down and rarely talked to me. That went on for almost a year, until I finally took her to counseling and during one of her sessions the counselor said to me, "you're here to listen, and no one can say anything."

As Key began to talk and I listened she said most kids grow up watching their dad or mom's boyfriend beat them up, but I watch my mom beat up my dad and stepdad. When my mom gets upset it scares me. At that point I cried and became devastated. Once again Key saved me from myself. That night I went home and fell face first to the ground and started praying and begging God to remove the anger and bitterness from my heart. The next morning, I made an appointment for counseling and started to change.

After counseling and numerous bad relationships, I decided to be single. During that time, I threw myself into helping women and children creating, "Bitter but Sweet". I also volunteered with nonprofits that work with youth. I became what I needed as a youth. While I was focused on helping others, God sent a man that has been there for me like no other man. His name is Pat, he has been everything to my children and me. We are currently 10 years into this relationship and the one thing I have learned is when you truly heal and give it to God, he will send you exactly what you need. Healing may be uncomfortable, but it is worth the end result.

Psalm 147:3 "He heals the brokenhearted and binds up their wounds."

About Marla

Marla Clark is a mother of 3 children and the Momanger of their careers which is her number 1 priority in life. She also holds a Degree in Communications and Business Management with a minor in Medical Business Management. Marla is the CEO of Bitter But Sweet, a self-help group to teach women how to live without becoming bitter after divorce or breakups based upon her own life issues. She also is a Certified life Coach and has recently opened a Coaching business, The Reinvention Elite Coaching. Marla is the Co-CEO of Romeo Franklin Productions and entertainment company surrounding our youth. She is the Director of Policy and Procedure with Beautiful Spirited women where volunteering is her life. She also volunteers her time supporting the youth at Heal the Hood Foundation. Marla feels that she wants to give back to the youth as much as possible and be that support system and voice she needed in her youth.

Marla Clark is a Brand and Marketing Strategist who partners with CEOs, executives, and solopreneurs to grow their personal and professional brands, human-to-human. After spending nearly, a decade working in PR and marketing for multiple startup companies, Marla knows what truly drives conversions and it is not mastering the marketing flavor of the week. It is how well you connect with the heart-beating people you are trying to help and communicate your understanding back to them.

Marla Clark understands that the Youth is the future and is willing to dedicate her life to making the future brighter by supporting One woman, one teenager with God's direction at a time. Marla's personal Motto: I am not a role model; I am a real-life model.

Chapter 34

From Dysfunction to Functional

BY RICARDO AMIR ALLEN

Sit with me as I share parts of my past and show you all just how well these broken crayons still can color. Remember these words as my testimony unfolds before your eyes:

"You can come back from ANYTHING, don't ever count yourself out."

From drug abuse, alcoholism, and trauma that have been passed down from one generation to the next, my family has suffered a lot of blows.

Sometimes trauma starts at an early age. My earliest memory of childhood trauma is that of being abused by a twelve-year-old when I was only four or five years old. At that age, I didn't understand what was happening. I thought it was normal, and that I was supposed to just 'go with the flow". I didn't have any idea what I was doing, or what I should have been feeling; now, looking back I know it never should have happened. I have spent my life in denial about the situation, telling myself it was okay, and telling others that I was "in control", not realizing there was something deeply disturbing about all of it. All too often when this type of thing happens, it's treated like it is normal when it is far from okay. It is traumatic and damages a child in ways I cannot even begin to put into words.

Imagine being seven years old, smoking weed with your older siblings. My mother suffered from drug addiction and my grandmother suffered from alcoholism. I watched as my mother almost died from a drug overdose when I was only eight or nine years old. How do you process these events at such a young age? The answer? You do not! You absorb and suppress it.

I was bullied for the birthmark on my face, ridiculed for being different. One may think all of this would make me a cold-hearted person, but honestly it made me love in a way I wished I had been loved. I have dealt with physical, mental, and emotional abuse at home and watched it too. I cannot sit here and lie, these kinds of situations can and will change the way you view yourself and for a while changed me. I hated what I saw when I looked in the mirror to the point that I avoided all mirrors and pictures of myself for a long time. The hate others poured into me I spewed onto myself even more. I became a cutter just to feel a different pain other than the familiar agony that I drowned in daily.

When I was 15, I tried to kill myself. I remember it was Martin Luther King Jr's birthday, and I overdosed on some pills. I ended up in a mental institution for a short time. I was prescribed Zoloft for depression which only made things worse, not better. You may be thinking that would break me, but it did not. I came back from that, still a fighter and a warrior but more importantly, still standing. I have taken so much from people and felt so low and disregarded. I missed out on regular childhood moments because I was truly forced to grow up faster than my friends and other kids my age.

In 2009, my god sister was murdered at the age of 14. The pain is indescribable when someone you love is snatched from you in a blink of an eye. She was the only sister I had, and a part of me died that day. I remember the hollow feeling in my soul when they pulled off with her body. We must cherish life as it comes because someone can be here today and gone tomorrow.

I became extremely withdrawn for a long time and chose to not engage with many people. A high level of trust was required before I would even mutter a word. I was so twisted and messed up. I did not realize it, until I got away from the dysfunction and got into a functioning environment. It took years for me to get out of that poisonous environment, to understand what trauma even meant, and how it was shaping me into someone I did not want to be. I was emotionless and I had no clue how to even communicate or express my feelings. There were many times when I lost hope, but the Higher Power always gave it right back to me.

I have had family members attempt to crush me and stop my dreams. The tongue is the most powerful weapon we have, and it is best to watch the words you speak onto yourself and others. I have been told I would not amount to anything, I was lazy, I did not want anything out of life-- the list went on and on. For a moment I believed it, but I did not allow those words to dictate my next move. Even if it took me longer to get there, I arrived.

These are some of the significant moments in my story and every single one of them led me to the next turning point in my life.

In 2011, I was kicked out of the nest and forced to fly on my own for good this time. I left Indiana and moved to Michigan with a significant other whose deceit overpowered any love I thought she had for me. It was pure hell. She even tried to stab me during an altercation. In the midst of the toxicity my grandmother passed away and I had no money and no way to get back home to attend her memorial. It hurt me to my core to not be there. Although the relationship was bitter-sweet she was still my grandmother and she loved us the best way she knew how.

After that, I fell into a deep dark depression. I was unhappy in my living situation and with losing my grandmother. It felt like nothing in my life had ever gone right. In my mind I was done with everything and everybody, even myself. I had given up. I stood on the back porch in tears talking to my best friend telling her I wanted to kill myself and I honestly meant every single word that came out of my mouth.

When I tell you, the tongue is powerful, it really is! The next thing that came out of my best friend's mouth was nothing but positivity that moved me like nothing I had ever felt before. She told me I was here for a reason and that I was worth it. She said I had a purpose on this Earth and to not allow my current emotions to overtake me or defeat me. She told me this too shall pass- and it did pass. Sometimes the pain we feel overpowers our ability to think straight and we just cannot see past that pain. It controls our thoughts and makes us expect the worst even when things may not be as bad as we think it is. We really do have the ability to control our thoughts. Although we cannot control every single situation that occurs, we can control how we choose to react to them. I am living proof a positive mind can and will change your life.

When I left Michigan on that Greyhound bus, I only had two shirts, two pairs of jeans and one pair of shoes to my name and my faith. I left with the intention to evolve and gain some stability. That was something my life lacked immensely.

I could not stay the same any longer. I could not continue to feel defeated, wanting my life to end before it really had begun. I could not be a quitter. I wanted more for myself. I was done feeling sorry for myself and allowing things to shake my confidence. I was done feeling defeated and beat down. I moved to West Virginia and it was the best decision I could have ever made. The culture shock was exactly what I needed. It was then and there I realized I had a choice, and that I did not have to become a product of my environment., The choice was mine, and mine alone to make. No one else could dictate it, I controlled the chapters to my story.

Although I felt broken, my crayon colored the same and just as vibrantly as any other crayon in the box, broken or not. The more I was around my best friend and her inner circle the more I wanted out of life. It is so true that you become who you hang around the most. These were extremely successful and positive people. They see the glass as half full, not half empty. Slowly but surely the negative mindset I had for such a long time started to dissolve. I felt differently, I thought differently, and I moved differently. You truly cannot tell just how toxic an environment is until you breathe fresher air. Did I magically change overnight? No, of course not. But over the course of time, day by day, I changed for the better.

During my time in West Virginia, I put myself through college and found a fulltime job making good money. I was even able to take care of my mom. I took the time to build myself up not just financially, but mentally and spiritually. My mindset changed and I too started to see the glass as half full too. I started believing that I deserved more. If I have anything to do with it, I am going to have it all. My faith is at an all-time high now, and I know God has bigger plans for me. I finally understand that I too have a purpose, and it was bigger than everything I had been through.

At the age of 32, I finally understood myself, realizing that for a long time I had suppressed the memories of my past abuse, never understanding how to address the trauma that I endured. Ultimately it led to a lot of mishaps in my life, but those mishaps were just steppingstones to a better me.

Although I watched my mother self-destruct for a while it never became my path. I chose to not indulge in that addiction based on the things I witnessed and encountered as a child. As an adult, I realize and empathize with my mother's struggle now. I understand that she was fighting her own demons and did the best that she could, being a single mother of four children. That could not be easy on any young black woman.

I never blamed her for any of it, while always taking things in stride. Her strength shined through it all and in the end, she rose above it and made the choice to get better and be better. This is where choice plays a major role.

I inherited my strength from my mother. The positive changes in my life were like broken crayons in a box. These colors started to fill up the empty spaces, coloring a beautiful picture. As you glimpse at what I have been through, please remember to hold on to my words.

"Don't ever count yourself out."

I am not in search of anyone's sympathy as I invite you all into my world. It has been invite-only for a long time. I want you to know there is hope, even when it is too dark to see anything in front of you. We must always be led by faith and never by sight. You do not need to see what lies ahead. You just really need to BELIEVE you will always get ahead even when you cannot see it in that moment. In some of my darkest childhood moments I understood this.

You see, so many of our trials are not punishment but preparation for the bigger battle that we may not fully understand at the moment. Trust me when it is time to go to war, we vividly understand exactly why we went through everything we did. I must give all the glory to God first, for he carried me through far more than I ever thought I could bear. Secondly, I am so grateful for my best friend. This woman came from God himself. When I counted myself out, she counted me back in. She saw the greatness in me before I knew how to believe in myself. All it takes is one person believing in you and seeing what you can be. When they say it only takes a mustard seed of faith, believe ME, this is really all it takes to change your life.

To anyone reading this if you have been searching for a sign you just found it. It's here in the words I write. You can do anything you put your mind to, but it all starts with how you view yourself. If no one believes in you, I am here to tell you, I do. I believe that no matter what your current situation is, you have the power to change the narrative. Anything is possible with faith and inspired action. You do not have to settle for mediocrity and dysfunction. Trauma is a death trap. We must let it go of the wounds of the past and heal. As my coach says all the time, "abundance is our birthright", so claim it rightfully. Anything is possible when you believe it is. Nothing is impossible unless you choose to not move your feet. I put my best foot forward, working some nights until 1am and still found the energy to complete my schoolwork. I was on the Dean's list every year in college. I made no excuses. I did whatever was necessary to succeed no matter how tired I was. I was determined to not go backwards, only forward. One thing I can tell you is this, it is worth the effort, and it is worth the work. It feels great to be on the other end of things. The only way to fail is to fail to try.

When I got on that bus, that was me trying to have a better life and believing I could have a better life. Could I see it at that moment? No, but that did not stop me from having faith that things would get better. Imagine if I would have declined the offer from my best friend. I would not be here today to confess my truths and hopefully inspire others. It is not easy, and I would not pretend it is. It feels great to have control over my life for the first time.

Prior to this, I felt like my life was spinning out of control and I had no way to stop it. I had all the power all along, and just needed to recognize it. The power lives within us. Your life is yours to live the way you see fit.

As I said before, this is a lifestyle, and I am just getting started. The pieces of my broken crayon will color many more pages. Every single day is another day to do more and be more. Every single day is a new chance to grow to new heights because growth is a never-ending journey. When we are given the underrated blessing of opening our eyes each day it is just another chance to be who we are destined to be. Cherish each day and understand your mess is the message someone else may need to keep moving or get moving. Remember, you can come back from ANYTHING, do not ever count yourself out.

This Broken Crayon Still Colors

About Ricardo

Ricardo was born in Chicago, Il., but was raised in northwest Indiana. Ricardo studied network and communications management at DeVry University in Illinois where he put himself through college. Due to the adversities of his life Ricardo has always been able to uplift and motivate those around him turning any negative into a positive. Ricardo is an upcoming entrepreneur and app developer. He considers his faith and family to be most important to him. Ricardo currently works as a broker for United Healthcare. When Ricardo is not working, he is reading a book or playing his PS4. He loves tacos almost as much as he loves helping others.

Chapter 35

Black Shadow

BY TIA GRAY

Black, black, black, oh how my soul feels so black.
We have all done a lot of things that we cannot take back.
When I was a child, I wanted things.
my parents could not give me back.
If we can be anything we want to be,
why do we live in shadows
of things that are so off track?
For the world may see you one way, but you long to just
be seen for your own truth.
Or are you hiding from you and the world truly does notice
you?
We have been many shades but our own.
Living in places we know we do not belong.
Breaking our own crayon, applying too much pressure.
When if only we just let it flow, let it go.
We would recognize ourselves as our biggest treasure.

All my life I feel I have always walked in everyone's shadow casting a black silhouette. Sometimes seeming grand, sometimes miniature. Little do we know; we are not done coloring yet. The thing I like the most about being black is that a combination of multiple colors used together creates the color black. Black appears one way, but inside it is full of so much creativity, color, and wonder. If you are not careful the world will tell you, you are dull and remind you of all the things you lack. I never understood the way of life as a kid because my parents kept a lot of things hidden. Now, let us not start pointing fingers, for when you point one, three point back at you. And when you start to heal you will cast away the negative things. Since it was done to me, I vow not to do it to you too.

As a small-town girl growing up in rural Tennessee, I never realized that so many of us were enslaved, still in modern day. I watched my parents, aunts, uncles, cousins, and grandparents hustle hard even into their elder years, running in hay fields, parking cars on a midday in July, for a bunch of confederate flag flying, big truck, big tires, loud pipes, good ole boys, their southern belle wives, and devilish, sneaky children. It took my own spiritual journey to discover who I was, following the saying, "You do not know where you are going, if you do not know where you have been." Well, I took that a step further than myself, digging into my family history, observing traits within my family and community. I never knew why I was not black enough for my cousins on one side of the family. Then on the other side, I was too much for TV. Landing in white spaces, that I could never really be a part of, finding my safe space in sports. This was the beginning of living in the shadows. In a family like mine, everything is about sports. That is where I found a breakthrough in my family lineage. If we had nothing else, we had sports, family, and a mean work ethic. When you spend a lot of time in towns like Adams, Tennessee, you are what I like to call," living somewhat outside of the matrix of the world." There are just things that you will not grow up having access to. Then to add to that, your family is one of the slim to none, black families in the town that once enslaved our ancestors.

As a child I loved every bit of the freedom I had to create something out of nothing. A childhood of creating new paths in uncharted territory, running from three legged dogs, to bicycling backroads, and learning to stick together in the event a white person tried to provoke us, blurting out racial slurs at us as we rode by. Oh--and most importantly making it home before the streetlights came on! What I grew to realize was that I was blind to the disadvantages we had, because of the protectiveness of my family. I never understood why my mother kept me so heavily involved in white spaces. That's not to say I am not grateful for all of my many white friends. I genuinely love them all. Though, as an adult, things are not quite the same. I recall so many people doing and saying things that should have never been accepted.

All of the countless factors that contributed to dulling down the vibrant colors roaming so freely inside of me. All hidden by my blackness. Whether skin shade, or the now vision you only see when you want to daydream.

Black is a shade that absorbs light, embracing many colors. For me, this was the foundation for my shaping into everything everybody wanted me to be, later being called an Oreo. You know when you're black on the outside, but other people consider you white on the inside. How wrong were they. My blackness makes me one and won. As the old saying goes, "what is done in the dark, will always come to the light." My broken crayon still colors. Combining all the many colors of my soul, my writing will be on the walls, whenever we cross paths. No matter how many times I have been broke down, drug through the mud, I still color even when they smear my name!

The best part of this journey is unboxing the colors within, and remaining true to me, and who I am. The unboxing is not always pretty; when we judge those around us, we learn things about ourselves. It is so easy to place blame all around us, like the shade of black; the things that trigger us the most are just trapped colors all scrabbled together. We must unlearn the labels that we once wore as badges of honor. Giving all that we have to everyone else, neglecting ourselves, or chasing things that do not align with where we are going are all products of living in other people's shadows.

My father would always quote Forrest Gump, "Stupid is what stupid does." While for me, I preferred, "Life is like a box of chocolates, you never know what you are going to get." Although I must say, his words ring in my ears, after having made a mistake; that had to be unboxed, as well. Sometimes such simple things can cause so much pain. The questions I had to ask myself were, "Is this true about you?" "Are you stupid?" "Why does it bother you?" "What can I do differently next time?" "What part of this do you take responsibility for?" "Do you not own your space to be who you say you can be? "

And then, the colors danced all around the black silhouette, as if the water dancers and fire dancers had merged together to create such a vibrant, strong, masterpiece of life, that rebirths continuously. Black is known to represent darkness, but its hue holds so much beauty. Feeling majestic, as demanding as light, shades of black make everything feel like a magical unity. The fire will rage, and water may rise, no longer will it be out of control, because you hold the power this time. Black.

Black, black velvet like smooth shea butter.
Radiates a glow, shines like no other.
M-hm BLACK, you always had my back.

Until I started to dance again, my body just passed as a black shadow, with no real direction and running full speed ahead at life. Roaming in places that brought out the rage inside of me that I never knew I had. Mad at the world, only to realize I was mad at myself. Mad at myself for not standing my ground. Not speaking up for myself. Not choosing me the first time. The fire blazes in my eyes, heart, and soul. Almost feeling like it is locked inside.

Black, Black, Black! Bring that sweet child back. That inner child has been trapped inside screaming to color on the walls with no guidance. Stepping back to look at what has been created up until this point, will there be sadness, depression, or inspiration? We have been going through life fighting internally to be free to color the chapter it was designed to color. As adults, we start coloring outside of our own lanes because of labels we accepted from the outside world. When we notice what our inner child has done, we run back to the shadows of others, never embracing our true beauty.

Black is you; black is me, black is anything I want it to be. Whether the color of skin, or the color of this pin. Black is everything I want it to be, Black is free. Black is ME.

Then you wake up and realize you have never been trapped; you were always able to live free. Holding yourself back from choosing who you wanted to be. Until the water rises, and the fire begins to shape. You learn to control the fire and flow like water.

Dancing semi-professionally for MCM Dance Team of Nashville, Tennessee, I learned how the energy in the body can cause imbalance in dance when trapped. I learned everything my body needs, so does life. When learning to embrace myself and my own beauty, I thought of my two daughters, who will need the tools to embrace their own beauty. Dance with their rage and flow like water. Though being a mother is not always easy, and at times I just want to quit, I find a way to dance as the fire and the water dance in sync and all is well. The darkness does not have to be scary; it is just the unknown. While also being in a place of peace and stillness, what would star gazing be without a black sky. As a black woman, we have been conditioned to live in the shadow of white women, suppressing all the majestic creativity that we possess. Though no matter how far into the shadow you may go, your glow is always demanding, always creating spaces of unity in common spaces, because no matter where you go, we always find a community. Though things will change, as they always do, we know how to better control our fires, because we know where it takes us when it controls us. We will flow like water, shaping and controlling the rage that wants to rise. Dance in the rain and release the energy inside of you. Whether a nibble, half of a crayon, or melted back together, your crayon is still capable of coloring. The power is in your hands.

About Tia

Latia Gray was born and raised in a small town outside of Nashville, where her ancestors were enslaved at what was once the largest tobacco plantation. Springfield Tennessee, has been her home for the majority of her life outside of the three years spent in Memphis TN. During her few years between Holly Springs, Mississippi and Memphis, Tennessee she had her first gift and beautiful daughter, Tramiya Scott and four years later, birthing her second creative and loving daughter, Ziri Gray.

Raised to work hard and never quit! As a child, her first paid job was parking cars which taught her endurance and how to stand up for herself. Latia's mission in life is to constantly evolve and embrace the changes that life brings, learn as much as she can, and vow to always act as her highest self.

Coming from the environment of a small town, Tia knew there was more to life and strives to continuously grow and create safe spaces, that she may be the change she wished to see. She understands that no matter the person's race or age, every living thing serves a purpose; and as they cross her path, they come to serve a purpose in her life, as she is to theirs. Her mission is to not only see people in the physical but spiritual and/or energetic realm. She also vowed that no matter how bad things may seem to be, always lead with love, and be love.

Chapter 36

Life After

You are more beautiful because you have been broken.

Trauma is a thief, and it loves to steal your joy, your sense of worth, your sense of safety, and your ability to trust. Trauma involving death or the threat of death, abuse, neglect, serious injury, or sexual violence are some of the causes of PTSD. I have been through all these and anxiety, panic, and depression still show up in the most overwhelming, distressing, and debilitating way, getting in the way of how I function. I have experienced night terrors, fatigue, hopelessness, helplessness, and fear.

There were times the impact of trauma made me feel like broken was my normal. I have been shattered, damaged, smashed, and split open both literally and figuratively and, many times, I wanted to declare myself healed. I wanted to ignore and dismiss my triggers because they caused me shame. It was easier to hide under a mask of empowerment, to call myself a survivor because I did not want the stigma of being a victim, to bask in the glory of having risen above and overcome those tragedies.

We are often deceived thinking that being beautiful means being perfectly put together: flawless. Heartbreak, betrayal, abuse, lack, disappointment, tragedy, trials, and trauma can be unavoidable, and there is no shame in feeling the pain, but as we learn to embrace our brokenness, we can allow ourselves to be healed, mended, and blessed. And we find that we are still able to color. I don't know about you, but I am done hiding my scratches, lines, chips, and cracks. I want to embrace my brokenness and believe that I am more beautiful for having been broken.

What broke me does not define me… but if I am honest, it did change me. If there is one thing I've learned from every experience is that brokenness can lead to breakthrough if we let it.

Scientific evidence now suggests that trauma can improve all areas of your life. Researchers and experts have found positive psychological changes that happen as a result of distressing, scarring, disturbing events and call it by the name of post-traumatic growth.

We are all fragile and we all go through struggles that tear, damage, and crush us. No matter the cause of our drop, sometimes we feel the damage is irreparable, that we are beyond repair, and therefore, worthless, and what is worse, just like a broken crayon, useless.

True life begins when the crayon breaks.

Brokenness is not beautiful in itself, the beauty lies in knowing that when we are hurt and shattered, we can choose to stay broken, to hide our suffering, or to allow ourselves to go through a painful, difficult, lengthy rebuilding process that is guaranteed to give purpose to our history.

I look at my scars, my stretch marks, and my triggers and they are definitely not as beautiful as golden seams, but there are indeed lessons I've learned that are far more precious than any metal or stone. Embracing my brokenness is accepting my humanity, acknowledging that though there are pieces of me I'll never recover, I am better for having let go of them, and it means appreciating my ability to truly connect with those who may have just been knocked down or are a few steps behind in the recovery process. But being grateful for my progress on the path to wholeness doesn't mean that I've mastered the art of being broken. I often wonder about what my life would be like without the painful drops.

I also sometimes question whether "that one piece" was salvageable and I was wrong for letting it go, and, at times, I have to recognize I rebuilt myself with some pieces that didn't belong and now have to go. And most of the time, I don't feel much of a masterpiece. I focus on being useful and end up being used – and feel like I'm then tossed to the side like the broken crayon that I feel I am, flawed, imperfect, and not good enough.

So now I speak in present tense and I am truly vulnerable. I am still broken. I am in progress – under construction – and I am at peace with that. And I am coloring vibrantly.

Like me, many of you have experienced rejection, abandonment, betrayal, failure, fear, limiting beliefs, self-sabotage, heartbreak, shame, guilt, regret, and disappointment, and you are more beautiful because you have been broken, even when all you see is brokenness and ugliness.

If you sometimes feel inferior, insignificant, unlovable, awkward, inadequate, unworthy, hopeless, deficient, defective, disgraceful, discarded, deserted, disowned, or lost, you are not alone. If you love others in your brokenness, yes, even those who shattered you to pieces, you have found true wisdom, beauty, and purpose. Hurt people can hurt people, but healed people can heal people, even when there's more healing to do.

I know it's hard and I know it hurts, but you're still here, and that's a miracle in itself.

I promise you no matter what broke you, you can still color. Broken Crayons Still Color.